SALAFISM AND TRADITIONALISM

One of the most contentious topics in modern Islam is whether one should adhere to an Islamic legal school or follow scripture directly. For centuries, Sunni Muslims have practiced Islam through the framework of the four legal schools. The twentieth century, however, witnessed the rise of individuals who denounced the legal schools, highlighting cases where they contradict texts from the Qur'ān or Sunna. These differences are exemplified in the heated debates between the Salafi ḥadīth scholar Muḥammad Nāṣir al-Dīn al-Albānī and his Traditionalist critics. This book examines the tensions between Salafis and Traditionalists concerning scholarly authority in Islam. Emad Hamdeh offers an insider's view of the debates between Salafis and Traditionalists and their differences regarding the correct method of interpreting Islam. He provides a detailed analysis of the rise of Salafism, the impact of the printing press, the role of scholars in textual interpretation, and the divergent approaches to Islamic law.

A scholar of Islamic law and intellectual history, EMAD HAMDEH is an Assistant Professor at Embry-Riddle University.

Salafism and Traditionalism

Scholarly Authority in Modern Islam

EMAD HAMDEH
Embry-Riddle University

CAMBRIDGE
UNIVERSITY PRESS

CAMBRIDGE
UNIVERSITY PRESS

University Printing House, Cambridge CB2 8BS, United Kingdom

One Liberty Plaza, 20th Floor, New York, NY 10006, USA

477 Williamstown Road, Port Melbourne, VIC 3207, Australia

314–321, 3rd Floor, Plot 3, Splendor Forum, Jasola District Centre, New Delhi – 110025, India

79 Anson Road, #06–04/06, Singapore 079906

Cambridge University Press is part of the University of Cambridge.

It furthers the University's mission by disseminating knowledge in the pursuit of education, learning, and research at the highest international levels of excellence.

www.cambridge.org
Information on this title: www.cambridge.org/9781108485357
DOI: 10.1017/9781108756594

First published 2021

A catalogue record for this publication is available from the British Library.

ISBN 978-1-108-48535-7 Hardback

Dedicated to my parents Mohammad
and Etidal, my wife Sana, and my
daughters Zayna, Safiya, and Maryam.

أحِبُّ الصالِحينَ وَلَستُ مِنهُم
لَعَلّي أَن أَنالَ بِهِم شَفاعَه
وَأَكرَهُ مَن تِجارَتُهُ المَعاصي
وَلَو كُنّا سَواءً في البضاعة

- الإمام الشافعي

Contents

Acknowledgments

This book, as with any major project, is the result of years of work. There are many who have helped me along the way. I would like to thank Yahya Michot and Robert Gleave for providing essential feedback during the initial stages of this book. Their guidance and insight played an important role in the early part of my academic career. I am especially grateful to Michot for being generous with his time. I particularly enjoyed his attention to detail and sense of humor.

There are many others who also supported me along the way. My dear friend and brother Osamah Salhia read several drafts of the book and provided feedback, shared resources, and moral support. Our conversations have been very valuable, and I thank him for that. I must also extend my sincere gratitude to Emin Poljarevic for reading through the entire book and offering constructive and detailed feedback. I would like to thank Yasir Qadhi whom I troubled countless times and he always generously shared his insights. I would also like to thank Jonathan Brown for providing valuable suggestions on several occasions.

Qutaiba Al-Bluwi also read several chapters of this book. I remain inspired by his mannerisms as well as his extensive knowledge of Islamic law. I am grateful for his friendship and feedback on several parts of the book. Iftikhar Zaman, an extraordinary ḥadīth scholar, helped provide direction and resources on several occasions.

I owe an enormous debt of gratitude to those who gave me detailed feedback or helped with their constructive discussions and insights including: Joas Wagemakers, Aaron Rock-Singer, Tesneem Alkiek, Bernard Haykel, Henri Lauziere, Ovamir Anjum, Kecia Ali, Jawad Qureshi, Edward Ryan Moad, Abdul Rahman Mustafa, and Massoud Vahedi. I would also like to thank the anonymous reviewers for their helpful suggestions. Any mistakes or shortcomings in this book are my own.

While I worked on this book, those who sacrificed the most were my wife Sana Khan, and three daughters Zayna, Safiya, and Maryam. I apologize for all the time I took away from you to write this book. You all bring so much joy and happiness to my life and I love you more than anything in the world. My wife has been my main pillar of support. I am blessed and honored to have her as my partner through the ups and downs of life. Your encouragement, love, and companionship when times get challenging are what keep me sane and hopeful. I thank and love you from the depth of my heart.

Those who I thank the most are my parents, Mohammad and Etidal Hamdeh. Your love, encouragement, support, prayers, and many other ways you helped me can never be repaid. To you I owe everything, and this book is a result of your efforts and support. I pray that you have a long life full of happiness and good health. Finally, and most importantly, I thank God, for without Him none of this would have been possible.

Introduction

How does one understand scripture? What role do scholars play in understanding religious texts? What should lay Muslims do when they encounter scripture that conflicts with a scholarly opinion? These questions are often at the center of religious disputes among Muslims in the modern world and have sparked debates among scholars and nonscholars alike. The fierce intellectual debates between Salafis and Traditionalists have been a prominent feature of Islamic intellectual history in the twentieth century. Although they both draw from the same sources, each of these groups considers itself to be the authentic version of Islam. Traditionalism is an institutional understanding of Islam that developed over centuries of scholarship. Traditionalists advocate a deference to precedent (*taqlīd*) of the *madhhab*s as a means for Muslims to understand Islam.[1] On the other hand, purist Salafis view themselves as a group that is purifying the syncretic practices that crept into the faith over many centuries. Salafis consider the uncritical following of the *madhhab*s to be the root cause of the Muslim world's political, economic, and social decline. They advocate for a return to the Qur'ān and Sunna as they were understood by the earliest Muslim generations.

Throughout Islamic history, the *ʿulamāʾ* played a leading role in developing Islamic law and dogma. Prior to the advent of modernity, states were not robust enough to define religion across vast geographical regions. It was the *ʿulamāʾ* who spoke for Islam and had a monopoly over religious education

[1] *Taqlīd* has been translated as "blind imitation," "uncritical following," and "slavish imitation." Sherman Jackson's translation of *taqlīd* as deference to precedent is more accurate because it represents the utilization and capacity of *taqlīd* in Islamic law. See Sherman Jackson, "*Ijtihād* and *taqlīd*: Between the Islamic Legal Tradition and Autonomous Western Reason," in *Routledge Handbook of Islamic Law*, ed. Khaled Abou El Fadl, Ahmad Atif Ahmad, and Said Fares Hassan (New York: Routledge 2019), 261.

and authority. Since the mid-nineteenth century, both state and lay intellectuals have emerged as other voices. These lay intellectuals were usually not trained in Islamic sciences, but their voices were often in accordance with western thought or appealed to modern sensibilities. Muḥammad Nāṣir al-Dīn al-Albānī (d. 1999) is one of the twentieth century's most successful Salafi leaders who attracted millions of followers throughout the Muslim world. His teachings challenged the religious authority of traditionally trained *ʿulamāʾ*. His call to follow the Qurʾān, Sunna, and the *salaf* sparked debates about the authority of the *ʿulamāʾ* in interpreting religious texts. These debates were not limited to scholarly circles, but they occurred in mosques, coffee shops, online, and in social gatherings. The points of contention between Albānī and his critics impacted the religious understanding of millions of Muslims. At the crux of the issue is defining what the Sunna is, who best represents it, and how it is properly understood.

Other individuals or movements who attempted to start a ḥadīth-focused movement did not have the same impact as Albānī. For instance, the Ahl al-Ḥadīth movement was limited to a particular Muslim context like India but had little influence outside the South Asian context. Albānī's ideas spread internationally because he was a recognizable intellectual power across the Muslim world. Of all Salafi thinkers from the 1960s until today, he is the most recognizable. Albānī is the Salafi that most non-Salafis know because he proselytized his Salafi thought to them in a way that others did not. His fame and reputation were not only due to his dissemination of Salafi thought, but also his encyclopedic knowledge of ḥadīth. He was a self-taught populist who rebelled against the scholarly class in an attempt to purify Islam from unauthenticated scholarly traditions. His teachings appealed to ordinary people who were dissatisfied with Traditionalist *ʿulamāʾ*. He rejected the idea of following any school or methodology except the pristine texts. As such he only referred to himself as a Salafi because he wished to follow an untainted version of Islam. Albānī is often referred to as the greatest ḥadīth scholar of modern times and his supporters gave him the title of a *mujaddid*. He was not only admired for his knowledge, but for his commitment and keenness to purging Islam from foreign elements.[2]

The post-Ottoman political and religious context facilitated the contestation of traditional *ʿulamāʾ* and the issue of religious authority took center stage. Colonization, modernization, and globalization all contributed to

[2] See J. Wagemakers, "Salafism's Historical Continuity: The Reception of 'Modernist' Salafis by 'Purist' Salafis in Jordan," *Journal of Islamic Studies*, 30, no. 2 (2019), 213. Also see Jacob Olidort, *The Politics of "Quietist" Salafism* (Washington, DC: The Brookings Institution, 2015), 15–19.

creating a plethora of religious movements all claiming authenticity and contesting the authority of traditional *'ulamā'*. Although Muslim feminists, progressives, secularists, and Salafis are all different, they share an anticlericalist approach to Islamic studies. They view the *'ulamā'* as backward and as a barrier that prevents the masses from identifying the "true" teachings of Islam. While this book focuses on the tensions between purist Salafis and Traditionalists, it has broader implications for the status of the *'ulamā'* as the gatekeepers of Islamic knowledge. The purpose of this book is to analyze the assumptions, implications, and impact of Salafis and Traditionalists on modern Islamic thought. We cannot properly understand either Salafis or Traditionalists without analyzing how they interacted with each other.

Experts in Near Eastern studies suggest that Salafism is symptomatic of the modern political turmoil in the Muslim world. Religious studies scholars have highlighted Salafi disagreements with traditional *'ulamā'*; but they tend to operate under the assumption that modern Salafism is a transcription of purist movements of the past replicated or cloned into modernity. Only recently have academics begun turning their attention to Salafism, but most works focus on the political aspect of the movement. Failure to account for the compelling nature of the religious message of Salafism will result in the mischaracterizing of the movement as politically, rather than religiously, driven. Overemphasizing the political aspects of Salafism is problematic because Salafism is not a political movement but rather a method of understanding Islam. Political stances do not define what makes one a Salafi, instead they are identified by their religious beliefs and practices. To remedy this gap, I focus on the religious message of Salafism and how it created a version of Islam that stands in stark contrast to Traditionalism.

I do not attempt to speak of Salafism at large, rather I focus on Albānī's brand of purist Salafism. The decision to focus on Albānī is due to his distinction among Salafis. Unlike other leading Salafis, he was intensely engaged in scripturally charged and heated debates with Traditionalists throughout the Muslim world. These disputes were not limited to scholarly circles, but large numbers of students and religious activists served as audiences.

Searching the term "Salafism" on any academic database results in dozens of articles almost all of which mention Albānī. He was a towering and compelling individual in Salafi circles and the most aggressive disseminator of Salafi thought in modern times. Many Salafis see this influential figure as *the* representative of an authentic and scripture-based Islam. They consider his legal, political, and religious stances to be based on authentic scriptural proof-texts. To many Salafis, Albānī was a reformer who sought to help Muslims return to the authentic teachings of Islam, mainly the path of the Muslim forefathers. Others, however, perceive him to be a thinker who has gone astray due to his bypassing of Muslim legal institutions.

Albānī's life and works are important because he played a major role in establishing and propagating modern Salafism. Traditionalists were threatened by his anticlerical message because they believed that it collapsed any division between the scholarly class and those with no religious training. In other words, they feared that if everyone approached the Qur'ān and Sunna directly, then the *'ulamā'* would no longer be the gatekeepers to "authentic" Islamic knowledge. As a result, Traditionalists throughout the Muslim world felt the need to refute and respond to Albānī and his followers. These debates and discussions resulted in dozens of books and treatises between Albānī and Traditionalist scholars.

This should not give the impression that this book is only about Albānī because it equally focuses on Traditionalism. Purist Salafis and Traditionalists are best understood in light of the dialogues and debates they had with each other. Neither group was formed in a vacuum, but their stances on religious issues were almost always developed as a response to each other. Both groups typify a particular religious phenomenon in contemporary Islam. The larger methodological problems of textual interpretation in modern Islam are exemplified by their differences in a particularly pertinent way. The convergence between purist Salafis and Traditionalists over the contested role of the *madhhab*s is key for understanding how Islamic scriptures are understood and interpreted in the modern Muslim world.

Leading anti-*madhhab* Salafis inspired a new group of young intellectuals in the Muslim world to begin redefining Islam by taking its interpretation out of the iron grip of the Traditionalist *'ulamā'* and seizing for themselves the power to interpret Islam. Through a detailed reconstruction of the dynamically heated debates between the two groups, I analyze the context of the scripturally charged rhetoric against and in defense of particular hermeneutical methods.

Among the arguments I make is that the primary difference between purist Salafis and Traditionalists is not necessarily the content of what it means to be a practicing Muslim, but rather their attitude toward scholarly tradition. While Traditionalists view scholarly tradition as an essential component for the proper understanding of Islam, purist Salafis do not consider it a necessary precondition to Islamic scholarship. I illustrate how their conflicting approaches impact how both groups approach Islamic education, law, and ḥadīth.

This book is divided into three sections. The first is historical, contextualizing Traditionalism and purist Salafism in the twentieth century. The second focuses on their differences in Islamic law and the third on ḥadīth. Chapter 1 introduces the main religious movements that will be discussed in the book, namely Salafis and Traditionalists, and how they relate to Islamic Modernists. Chapter 2 provides a biography of Albānī and contextualizes the origins of his critique of Traditionalism.

In Chapter 3, I analyze how religious authority is produced in traditional Islamic circles. I explain how their educational methods, and how the degeneration of these methods, as well as the rise of print and technology, mass literacy, modernity, and secularism, resulted in the emergence of self-taught reformers.

In the second part of the book my focus shifts to Islamic law. In Chapter 4, I analyze the differences between purist Salafis and Traditionalists concerning legal pluralism, consensus, and certainty in Islamic law. Chapter 5 expounds on the role of scholars in interpreting scripture. In particular, I shed light on the differences between purist Salafis and Traditionalists on *taqlīd*, *ijtihād*, and adhering to the *madhhab*s.

Along with his efforts to purge Islamic law, Albānī tried to purify the Sunna and make it more accessible to common Muslims. In this final part of the book, I analyze their differences concerning ḥadīth studies. Chapter 6 focuses on the use and value of weak ḥadīth and Albānī's controversial project of removing all weak narrations from the canonical ḥadīth collections. Chapter 7 examines the impact Albānī had on the field of ḥadīth studies and his ḥadīth methodology.

Part I

History

1

Traditionalism and Salafism

With the fall of the Ottoman Empire, scholars and activists in the Muslim world struggled to revive the life of a fallen caliphate. The social, economic, and political turmoil faced by the Muslim world in the nineteenth and twentieth centuries motivated Muslim scholars and reformers to seek a practical model for the restoration of a Muslim society. Beginning in the mid-nineteenth and early twentieth centuries, several groups emerged with the aim of reforming Islam. These reformers viewed Islam as the main unifying idiom of their society prior to the colonial encounter. The solution they proposed was that returning to a pure version of Islam would unify Muslims in political and social resistance. They wanted Muslims to chart their own destiny and have parity with the west. Three main groups can be distinguished: Islamic Modernists, Traditionalists, and Salafis. These three groups will be discussed in this chapter in order to locate their place in modern Islamic thought. It is essential to understand the religious context in which Salafis and Traditionalists engaged with each other.

Each of these groups shares a belief in God and in Muhammad as God's final messenger. Given this acceptance and veneration of Muhammad, his life exemplifies God's commandments par excellence. In Sunni Islam, the Prophet and the earliest Muslim generations were considered to be the best people of all time and Muslims seek to relive, even partially, that time period. All of these movements seek to revive the way of the early Muslim generations, and those who led these movements were individuals who symbolized the expectations of their community. Many of these reformers believed that the revival of the Muslim world depended on the morality and spiritual state of individuals, and all three of these groups considered Islamic knowledge and practice to be the key to political, social, and economic success.

However, these individuals were not infallible, and their authority could be challenged. There is no priesthood in Islam. Sunni Muslims do not grant anyone special authority based on family or lineage. Those with religious knowledge, piety, wisdom, and insight are recognized by the community and this recognition is what gives them authority. These modern reformers attempted to act as representatives of the Prophet in the twentieth century and, despite their similarities, they competed for religious authority. They shared an understanding that Muslims had gone astray from the true teachings of Islam; what they differed on is what those true teachings were. They agreed that Muslims were alienated from and out of touch with the original teachings of Islam: thus, an important question was whether Muslims should understand Islam by going back to the Qurʾān and teachings of Muhammad, or if they should follow traditions established by previous scholarly generations?

Much of this debate revolves around the question of who speaks for Islam. The historical answer to this question for 1,300 years was that it was the *ʿulamāʾ*, traditional scholars who developed Islamic law and dogma. As states, prior to the advent of modernity, were not robust enough to define religion across vast geographical regions, it was the voices of Muslim scholars that mattered. However, since the mid-nineteenth century, both state and lay intellectuals have emerged as other voices. These lay intellectuals were not always trained in Islamic sciences, but their teachings resonated with Muslims seeking authenticity.

ISLAMIC MODERNISM

Islamic Modernists are sometimes referred to as Salafiyya or Salafis however, it is historically inaccurate to apply these terms to them. The most famous Islamic Modernists of the nineteenth century include individuals such as Jamāl al-Dīn al-Afghānī (d. 1897), Muḥammad ʿAbduh (d. 1905), and Rashīd Riḍā (d. 1935). These individuals attempted to reform Islam so that it became compatible with the political, economic, social, scientific, and educational advancements of their time. They considered themselves to be moderate Muslims who followed a balanced form of Islam identical to that of the Prophet and his Companions. Instead of resisting the accomplishments of the west, Islamic Modernists embraced them as part of Islam. They regarded scientific advancements, women's rights, and modern political institutions to be in conformity with the true teachings of Islam.

Islamic Modernists accepted new ideas about reason, progress, science, and technology, and incorporated them into a vision of Islam that held out to Muslims the promise of remaining true and authentic to their Muslim identity while also adopting knowledge from the west. They were concerned with making Islam relevant and meaningful to the present, and, as a result, placed a strong emphasis on the use of reason. The movement targeted the educated and intellectual class in hopes of freeing Muslims from what they perceived to be stagnant tradition. Modernists highlighted the intelligence and versatility of the earliest Muslim generations in order to encourage Muslims to break free from tradition, which was mainly excessive Sufism and strict adherence to the *madhhab*s, and open themselves to western advancements.

Islamic Modernists directly interpreted the principal Islamic texts, understood reason, and sought *ijtihād* through the prism of modernity, which was perceived as the internalized powerful influence against which the project of Islamic reconstruction and revival was envisioned.[1] Therefore, Islamic Modernism arose mostly as a response to the western colonization of the Muslim world, and only partly from within the Islamic tradition itself. The movement emerged from the reservations of Muslims concerning the west's advancements over the apparently regressive Muslim world. For Islamic Modernists, it was essential to reform Islamic teachings in light of modern advancements in order to make Islam relevant and meaningful to the present.

They considered their reform comprehensive because it sought to influence law, society, politics, as well as intellectual and moral issues. What made the movement so significant was its scholarly élan and the specifically intellectual and spiritual issues that it addressed. This awakening struck a new and powerful chord in the minds of many Muslims because they believed that intellectual issues had remained under self-imposed stagnation and dormancy at the insistence of a conservative orthodoxy for centuries.[2] One of the most important figures of the Islamic Modernist movement was Muḥammad ʿAbduh, an intellectual Egyptian theologian whose legal and political theory attracted many followers in the Muslim world. Among ʿAbduh's most important goals was to challenge uncritical acceptance of opinions and "rigid" ways of interpreting religious texts. He placed great

[1] Basheer Nafi, "The Rise of Islamic Reformist Thought and Its Challenge to Traditional Islam," in *Islamic Thought in the Twentieth Century*, ed. Suha Farouki and Basheer Nafi (London: I. B. Tauris, 2004), 40.

[2] Fazlur Rahman, "Islamic Modernism: Its Scope, Method and Alternatives," *International Journal of Middle East Studies*, 1, no. 4 (1970), 317.

emphasis on the principle of public welfare (*maṣlaha*) and social needs of the time.

Rashīd Riḍā, ʿAbduh's main student, is usually viewed in a more positive light among conservative Muslims compared to his teacher, because Riḍā was not considered to be a staunch modernist like ʿAbduh. As a leading Muslim scholar, Riḍā's ideas would later influence a variety of Muslim thinkers in the twentieth century. Riḍā focused on the weaknesses of Muslim societies compared to dominant western nations and called on Muslims to return to the authentic teachings of the religion. Riḍā's criticism of excessive Sufism and *taqlīd* would later inspire Salafis, like Muḥammad Nāṣir al-Dīn al-Albānī, to the study of ḥadīth in an effort to "purify" Islam.[3] At the same time, Riḍā's student Maḥmūd Abū Rayya (d. 1970) doubted and rejected most of the ḥadīth corpus. Abū Rayya only accepted *mutawātir* ḥadīth,[4] undermined Abū Huraira's credibility, and asserted that most ḥadīth collections were simply fabrications.[5] Abū Rayya furthered the arguments of Islamic Modernism by arguing that "true Islam" was in accordance with the main sensibilities of the omnipresent west. In order to return Islam to its modernistic essence, it was essential to do away with medieval scholarship that was the work of fallible humans.[6]

Islamic Modernists attempted to reform Islam from within Islamic tradition, and this reform stemmed from a sense of inferiority to the west. In order for Muslims to advance, they had to lead western lifestyles. They responded to western technology and imperialism by rejecting many aspects of Islam that were not in conformity with the west. For instance, ʿAbduh would only accept traditions that dealt with dogma such as paradise, hell, and judgment. Although ʿAbduh was not a secularist, his methodology opened the door to secularism in the Muslim world. For instance, he held the perspective that if the Prophet is fallible, then what he did as a leader of a community, as a person, and a legislator is not part of the religion. If the Prophet's message was only spiritual in nature, then everything else he said or did becomes irrelevant.[7]

[3] Daniel Brown, *Rethinking Tradition in Modern Islamic Thought* (Cambridge: Cambridge University Press, 1996), 64–66.

[4] *Mutawātir* ḥadīth are sayings of the Prophet that have been narrated by such a large number of people in every generation that it is impossible for all of them to have gathered upon a lie, therefore making *mutawātir* representative of the highest level of authenticity.

[5] Maḥmūd Abū Rayya, *Aḍwāʾ ʿalā al-Sunna al-Muḥammadiyya* (Cairo: Dār al-Maʿārif, 1980).

[6] Jonathan Brown, *Misquoting Muhammad: The Challenge and Choices of Interpreting the Prophet's Legacy* (London: Oneworld, 2014), 79.

[7] D. Brown, *Rethinking Tradition*, 64–66.

Conversely, Salafis and Traditionalists consider all of the Prophet's words and actions to be divinely inspired and consequently cannot be dismissed. Both Salafis and Traditionalists do not pay much attention to Islamic Modernists and dismiss them as imitators of Orientalists. Jonathan Brown correctly points out that "for both groups, Westernization and any Muslim contaminated by it are evils beyond the scope of dialogue."[8] Associating with the west or being influenced by it was considered evil not only by Traditionalists and Salafis, but by the general Muslim population. As a result, Islamic Modernists were not very successful in their efforts to reform Islam, although they did certainly lay the foundation for the emergence of modern Salafism.

The eighteenth and nineteenth centuries witnessed an increasing rise of scholars in the Muslim world who were calling for reform. Some of these well-known reformers were: Shah Walī Allāh al-Dahlawī (d. 1762), ʿAbd al-ʿAzīz al-Dihlawī (d. 1824), Sayyid Aḥmad Khān (d. 1898), and Ṣiddīq Ḥasan Khān (d. 1888) in India; Muḥammad b. ʿAbd al-Wahhāb (d. 1792) in the Arabian Peninsula; Muḥammad al-Shawkānī (d. 1834) in Yemen; Muḥammad b. ʿAlī al-Sanūsī (d. 1859) in Libya; Jamāl al-Dīn al-Qāsimī (d. 1914) and Ṭāhir al-Jazāʾirī (d. 1920) in Damascus; and Muḥammad al-Zābidī (d. 1791), Muḥammad ʿAbduh, and Rashīd Riḍā in Cairo. Each of these individuals was distinct; however, each played a role in laying the ground for the emergence of Albānī and his brand of Salafism. For instance, Islamic Modernists' critique of *taqlīd* and traditional *ʿulamāʾ* paved the way for anti-*madhhab* Salafis. What Salafis have most in common with Islamic Modernists is their criticism of *taqlīd* and their call to return to the ways of the earliest Muslim generations.

During the nineteenth century, when the Ottoman Empire was in decline, Ottoman rulers adopted measures that removed religious personnel and principles from their customary roles in administrative, legal, and educational institutions. This step toward secularism transformed the upper class of Arab cities such as Damascus. For centuries, this group mostly consisted of Traditionalist scholars, but within a few decades they were almost totally displaced from their powerful positions. The responses to this secularism were varied. Some *ʿulamāʾ* responded by either holding closely to legal tradition or turning to a scripturally literalist methodology. While some Muslims adopted and embraced secularism, Islamic Modernists such as ʿAbduh remained convinced that Islam and western teachings, although

[8] Jonathan Brown, *The Canonization of al-Bukhārī and Muslim* (Leiden: Brill, 2007), 307.

different, do not contradict each other. For Islamic Modernists, the inadequacy of the Muslim world in relation to the west only made sense if one believed that Muslims had strayed from "true" Islam, hence the necessity of returning to scripture.[9] ʿAbduh believed in a modernity that was different from the west, which, as he was a Muslim, incorporated a view of modernism that was not secular. Unlike western secularism, it incorporated religion, the individual, community, and state; but, in his view, it was no less modern.[10]

Additionally, Islamic Modernists understood that the west presented a military threat to the Muslim world and countering this required that Muslims unite by overlooking their differences. Islamic Modernists and Salafis considered these differences to have stemmed from excessive Sufism and preferring *fiqh* over authentic proof-text. They also believed that Muslims could only overcome their differences by returning to scripture and the spirit of Islam, and it was in Damascus, among other cities, where this anti-traditional movement was growing. The anti-*madhhab* attitude found in Salafism did not arise out of a vacuum, but existed among earlier Modernists such as Jamāl al-Dīn al-Qāsimī who, although he had a different methodology, shared an anti-Traditionalist attitude with the Salafis.[11] While ʿAbduh and Riḍā shared a preference for certain concepts with Salafis, such as an emphasis on *tawḥīd* and a rejection of *taqlīd*, ultimately theirs was a thoroughly modernist discourse, as opposed to the purist approach of Salafis.[12]

The origins and significance of the Islamic Modernist trend in late Ottoman Damascus represented their response to secularist tendencies in Ottoman educational and legal institutions on the one hand, and the projection of European power in the Middle East on the other. The Islamic Modernists' vision of remaining true to Islam while simultaneously adopting knowledge from the west clashed with the vision of many *ʿulamāʾ*, who believed that the best way to preserve Islam was by holding on to its remaining bastions such as the religious court, school, and mosque.[13] Itzchak Weismann argues that reform movements in late Ottoman Syria

[9] David Commins, *Islamic Reform Politics and Social Change in Late Ottoman Syria* (New York: Oxford University Press, 1990), 3.

[10] Samira Haj, *Reconfiguring Islamic Tradition: Reform, Rationality, and Modernity* (Stanford, CA: Stanford University Press, 2009), 28.

[11] D. Commins, *Islamic Reform*, 4.

[12] Joas Wagemakers, *A Quietist Jihadi: The Ideology and Influence of Abu Muhammad al-Maqdisi* (Cambridge: Cambridge University Press, 2012), 7.

[13] D. Commins, *Islamic Reform*, 5.

have their origins in the efforts of religious men of learning and mysticism. They sought to carve a middle path that avoided the rigidity of legal scholars who ignored mystic thought, and popular Sufis who neglected religious learning. The combination of *ʿilm* and *taṣawwuf* gave the Modernist reformists a claim to orthodoxy they might not have had otherwise.[14] Weismann notes that the reformist members of the Akbariyya turned from the teachings of Ibn ʿArabī (d. 638/1240) to the more scripture-based teachings of Ibn Taymiyya (d. 728/1328), which formed the early beginnings of Islamic Modernism and Salafism.[15] Their organization was mostly a response to the popular *ʿulamāʾ* and Sufi shaykhs whose preeminence seemed to stem more from their connection with the government than through their piety or knowledge. As a result, early Islamic Modernists focused their attention on the local masses of Damascus.[16]

Islamic Modernists primarily attracted recent graduates of the Ottoman high school in Damascus. They appealed to Syrian youth who were state educated by formulating Islam in a manner that harmonized their Muslim identity with their desire to adopt western advancements. Islamic Modernists and high school graduates were united by their intellectual elitism, an ethic of professionalism, and frustrated ambitions in religious and political reform.[17] Many Islamic Modernists in Damascus such as al-Qāsimī belonged to rural or small urban families, not to the entrenched *ʿulamāʾ* aristocracy of the urban notables. In this sense, Damascene reformers had no particular interest in maintaining the status quo, which had heavy social implications for the Traditionalist establishment.[18]

This struggle between the Islamic Modernists and Traditionalist scholars who held high positions began to divide the two classes of scholars in Damascus. Many Muslims found themselves joining one side or the other, and the Islamic arena in Damascus became indefinitely divided. Damascene reformers like al-Qāsimī and al-Jazāʾirī were calling for *ijtihād* as an Islamic way of celebrating rationality and reason, while simultaneously portraying Traditionalists as blind followers.[19] They criticized *taqlīd* of the *madhhab*s and rejected religious innovations and often implicitly criticized Traditionalists who dominated religious establishments in Damascus. Traditionalists were trying to maintain the religious, political, and social

[14] Itzchak Weismann, *A Taste of Modernity: Sufism, Salafiyya, and Arabism in Late Ottoman Damascus* (Leiden: E. J. Brill, 2009), 310–315.

[15] I. Weismann, *Modernity*, 149–156.

[16] I. Weismann, *Modernity*, 274.

[17] D. Commins, *Islamic Reform*, 5.

[18] D. Commins, *Islamic Reform*, 38–48; B. Nafi, "Reformist Thought," 40.

[19] B. Nafi, "Reformist Thought," 34–39.

status quo. Religious careers and establishments in late Ottoman Syria were in steep decline. Administration, education, and law were once careers that were exclusive to trained scholars, but they became the realm of those who were trained in western and modern educational models.[20] The seed of anti-Traditionalism in Damascus was planted, and Traditionalism was viewed as a weed in the soil from which authentic Islam was to grow.

CONTEMPORARY MODERNISTS

Muḥammad al-Ghazālī (d. 1996) and Yūsuf al-Qaraḍāwī are contemporary Islamic Modernists who were influenced by Riḍā. Ghazālī is one of Qaraḍāwī's most influential teachers. Despite their similarities, they have had a very different impact on the Muslim world, and Qaraḍāwī is usually viewed as an independent school. What distinguishes Qaraḍāwī is his emphasis on *wasaṭiyya* or taking the middle ground. Their efforts for reform are different from those of ʿAbduh and Riḍā because they lived in different eras. Nevertheless, Islamic Modernists like Riḍā, Ghazālī, and Qaraḍāwī agree with Salafis on the importance and status of ḥadīth in Islam, but they differ in their method of interpretation. Similar to Traditionalists, Qaraḍāwī and Ghazālī make ḥadīth subservient to Islamic legal theory and the overarching teachings of the Qurʾān. However, Qaraḍāwī and Ghazālī do not limit themselves to a specific legal school when interpreting Islam. Ghazālī takes a more unstructured interpretive approach, which sometimes means dismissing ḥadīth he disagrees with or going against consensus. Qaraḍāwī on the other hand often came to similar conclusions as Ghazālī, but did so through a much more systematic method, while maintaining the authoritative place of consensus in Islamic law. Nevertheless, several Salafis such as Albānī, ʿAbd al-ʿAzīz Ibn Bāz (d. 1999), and Ṣāliḥ al-Fawzān were critical of Qaraḍāwī's method, especially the perceived liberalism in his work *The Lawful and Prohibited in Islam.*[21]

Both Qaraḍāwī and Ghazālī have similar inclinations, but their style of argumentation is vastly different. David Warren argues that Qaraḍāwī's cautiousness and structure were often a response to Salafi critiques. Qaraḍāwī tried to preserve unity or reconcile between the unstructured

[20] D. Commins, *Islamic Reform*, 39–64.

[21] David Warren, "Debating the Renewal of Islamic Jurisprudence (Tajdīd al-Fiqh): Yusuf al-Qaradawi, His Interlocutors, and the Articulation, Transmission and Reconstruction of the Fiqh Tradition in the Qatar-Context" (Ph.D. Dissertation, The University of Manchester, 2015), 66. Also see Muḥammad Nāṣir al-Dīn al-Albānī, *Ghāyat al-Marām fī Takhrīj Aḥādīth al-Ḥalāl wa l-Ḥarām* (Beirut: al-Maktab al-Islāmī, 1980).

approach of Ghazālī and the punctilious approach of Albānī and other Salafis.[22] They both aim to define the role of the Sunna not merely in isolation, but in the broader context of Islamic law. Qaraḍāwī, for instance, outlines three general characteristics of Islam as it is reflected in the Sunna: universality, balance, and simplicity. If the Sunna represents all these things, then any ḥadīth that contradicts them does not represent the true Sunna. In other words, the Sunna can only be known within this broader framework of Islamic legal principles. However, Qaraḍāwī is more cautious than Ghazālī in the application of this method and he affirms that the Sunna rules over the Qurʾān.[23] The approach of Qaraḍāwī and Ghazālī can be traced back to Riḍā, who argued that any ḥadīth that contradicts the Qurʾān should be rejected regardless of its chain of narration.[24] Although they approached this issue in different ways, both thinkers were open to reform in Islamic law and were willing to go against the apparent meanings of an authentic ḥadīth, whereas Salafis held closer to the direct and apparent meaning. Albānī accuses both Ghazālī and Qaraḍāwī of whimsically interpreting Islam according to their modernist tendencies. Albānī states:

> The point is that they have the same methodology (*manhaj*) which contradicts the Sunna. When Ghazālī declares a ḥadīth to be weak you will find that Qaraḍāwī agrees with him and vice versa . . . Qaraḍāwī wants to tailor Islam to modernity. He wants Islam to be modified to conform with the desires of modernists in these times, he often does this and there appears to be a hidden motive behind it all.[25]

He reproaches them for following their whims because they appear to give more attention to the *matn* of the ḥadīth while disregarding its *isnād.* They do not only strengthen weak ḥadīth, but also weaken authentic ḥadīth depending on the message it contains and not the *isnād.* Ghazālī was more liberal in his approach to ḥadīth than Qaraḍāwī. Qaraḍāwī acknowledges the problematic nature of using only the *matn* to determine a ḥadīth authenticity, because of the inherent subjectivity in a scholar's interpretation. Qaraḍāwī insists that the *isnād* must be used as a means to measure the potential authenticity of a text. However, it does not necessarily follow that

[22] D. Warren, "Islamic Jurisprudence," 90–91.

[23] D. Brown, *Rethinking Tradition*, 119. Also see Yūsuf al-Qaraḍāwī, *Approaching the Sunnah: Comprehension and Controversy* (London; Washington, DC: The International Institute of Islamic Thought, 2006).

[24] D. Brown, *Rethinking Tradition*, 120.

[25] Muḥammad Nāṣir al-Dīn al-Albānī, "Refutation of Yusuf al Qaradawi," lecture from www.youtube.com/watch?v=Lg4RYBCdfI, last accessed November 1, 2018.

simply because a ḥadīth is authentic it is applicable. The context, language, and the intent of the Prophet must be taken into consideration. If a ḥadīth appears to contradict another ḥadīth or the Qur'ān, there must be an attempt to reconcile them before disregarding it.[26] Nevertheless, there were not many fierce debates between Islamic Modernists and Albānī because the former did not pose a great threat to the scholarly authority of Salafis.

Some Islamic Modernists were Salafi in creed but not in their political inclinations or legal methodology. Although Salafis regularly criticized the political activism of Islamic Modernists, many of the latter were primarily concerned with maintaining unity and therefore did not engage Salafis in religious debate. On the other hand, Salafis were suspicious of the *madhhab*s and regularly criticized those who abided by them. This caused sharp debate with Traditionalists and the stakes were crucial for both sides.

TRADITIONALISM

With the acknowledgment that this group is not uniform, my usage of the term "Traditionalists" refers to Muslim scholars who consider adherence to a *madhhab*, speculative theology, and Sufi orders to be representative of the true embodiment of Islam.[27] Tradition is often used to refer to practices of a particular group that stands in contrast to modernity or accepting change.[28] However, in Islamic history, religious knowledge was primarily validated by a connection to past individuals and institutions, such as an *isnād* leading back to the Prophet, an *ijāza* tracing back to a teacher, or a disciple connecting himself back to a Sufi master.[29] William Graham argues that "Traditionalism" is not a rejection of change and challenge, but that it

[26] D. Warren, "Islamic Jurisprudence," 73–74.

[27] Several other scholars have similarly defined this group. See J. Brown, *Misquoting Muhammad*. Suheil Laher correctly notes that Traditionalism is composed of a "three-fold knot": adherence to a *madhhab*, theology, and Sufism. See Suheil Laher, "Re-forming the Knot: ʿAbdullāh al-Ghumārī's Iconoclastic Sunnī Neo-Traditionalism," *Journal of College of Sharia and Islamic Studies*, 1 (2018), 202.

[28] On modernity, see Emin Poljarevic, "Islamic Tradition and Meanings of Modernity," *International Journal for History, Culture, and Modernity*, 3, no. 1 (2015), 27–59.

[29] William Graham, "Traditionalism in Islam: As Essay in Interpretation," *Journal of Interdisciplinary History*, 23, no. 3 (1993), 522. On tradition, rather than traditionalism, see Muhammad Q. Zaman, "The ʿUlamāʾ: Scholarly Tradition and New Public Commentary," in *The New Cambridge History of Islam, Vol. 6*, ed. Robert W. Hefner (Cambridge: Cambridge University Press, 2010), 335–354; Talal Asad, *The Idea of an Anthropology of Islam* (Washington, DC: Centre for Contemporary Arab Studies, Georgetown University, 1986); Kasper Mathiesen, "Anglo-American 'Traditional Islam' and Its Discourse of Orthodoxy," *Journal of Arabic and Islamic Studies*, 13 (2013), 191–195.

consists of a belief that connection with a model past and persons is the only sound way of reforming society. In other words, Traditionalism is based on the past but is fluid and not stuck in it. It could be likened to science, where present works build on and cite past experiments which are deemed "credible." Traditionalism is primarily a commentary tradition where it is essential to cite and take into consideration previous scholarship. Traditionalism is not a mere inheritance from the past, but rather, as Muhammad Qasim Zaman notes, "is a tradition that has had to be constantly imagined, reconstructed, argued over, defended, and modified."[30] When Traditionalists refer to the past, they are no different than American jurists who seek to understand what the forefathers intended in the Constitution or Bill of Rights.[31]

Alasdair MacIntyre explains that tradition is an argument extended through time in which certain fundamental agreements are defined and redefined in terms of two kinds of conflict. The first is with critics external to the tradition who reject all, or essential, elements that are fundamental to it. The second conflict is internal debates through which the meaning and rationale of fundamental agreements come to be expressed and by whose progress a tradition is constituted.[32] Therefore, tradition is better understood as discourses extended through time. It is a method of inquiry rather than a set of unchanging doctrines or mandates. Tradition is therefore not simply the repetition of the past, but a continuous effort to understand the present by referring to a set of texts, methodologies, arguments, and practices. It is from within this tradition that claims are accepted or rejected as being Islamic.[33] In one sense, Traditionalists view "tradition" as simply being the Sunna. In another, it is an affective bond between scholars and students linking books with humans. It is through this form of tradition that the Sunna is constantly revived.[34]

[30] M. Zaman, "The ʿUlamāʾ," 10. In this sense, Traditional scholarship always consisted of a rethinking, adaption, and expansion of legal tradition. This is contrary to modern scholarship which often portrays premodern Islamic scholarship as rigid and stagnant. Recent works on the history of premodern Islamic law have demonstrated that the door to *ijtihād* was never closed, but the schools of law were continuously evolving. See M. Zaman, "The ʿUlamāʾ," 18–21; Sherman Jackson, *Islamic Law and the State: The Constitutional Jurisprudence of Shihāb al-Din al-Qarāfī* (Leiden: E. J. Brill, 1996); Wael Hallaq, "Was the Gate of Ijtihad Closed?," *International Journal of Middle East Studies*, 16 (1984), 3–41.

[31] S. Haj, *Reconfiguring Islamic Tradition*, 5.

[32] Alasdair MacIntyre, *Whose Justice? Which Rationality?* (Notre Dame, IN: University of Notre Dame Press, 1989), 12.

[33] S. Haj, *Reconfiguring Islamic Tradition*, 4–5.

[34] Brannon Ingram, *Revival from Below: The Deoband Movement and Global Islam* (Oakland: University of California Press, 2018), 5.

What distinguishes Traditionalists from others is not necessarily the content of what it means to be an observant Muslim, but that they are primarily concerned with the proper modes by which religious knowledge is acquired. For Traditionalists, it is not sufficient for one to hold the correct beliefs and practice the rituals of Islam. One must also acquire knowledge of Islam through the *ijāza* system. This meant learning from a teacher who is well grounded in the tradition through an established chain of teachers going all the way back to the Prophet.[35] Mohammad Fadel explains:

> Mastery of religious values emerges through a process of acculturation that enables novices to embody those values. This process of acculturation is distinct from, and transcends, intellectual cognition (*ʿilm*) of religious truth. While religious truth may be a proper subject of instruction (*taʿlīm*), mere instruction, without reliable teachers who properly embody Islamic teachings, cannot produce properly acculturated religious subjects.[36]

Therefore, Traditionalists believe that individuals cannot achieve virtue on their own and need assistance from a teacher or mentor to lead a virtuous life. Accordingly, Traditionalists do not view themselves as a reform movement, but as individuals who are connected to the Prophet through a scholarly chain of authorities.[37] The teachers in this chain make up tradition. The crux of traditional learning is a pedagogical process of "handing down" knowledge and the attitude of valuation and attachment to the maintenance of tradition (i.e., the content or ideas). However, as Sherman Jackson correctly explains, "tradition is not [only] the result of the simple act of transmission or handing down, but of a process of evaluation, amplification, suppression, refinement, and assessing the polarity between would-be tradition and contemporary, indigenous innovations or nonindigenous ideas and practices."[38] ʿAbd al-Fattāḥ Abū Ghudda (d. 1997), a leading Traditionalist, notes that traditional knowledge is valued because it has been examined, reviewed, and refined thousands of times.[39]

35 Mohammad Fadel, "Islamic Law and Constitution-Making: The Authoritarian Temptation and the Arab Spring," *Osgoode Hall Law Journal*, 53, no. 2 (2016), 474–475.

36 M. Fadel, "Islamic Law," 474–475.

37 The term Traditional Islam or Traditionalism incorporates the essential antithesis to many manifestations and versions of reformist, modernist, and even revivalist Islam in the modern period in its very name. See K. Mathiesen, "Anglo-American," 193–194.

38 Sherman Jackson, *Islam and the Problem of Black Suffering* (Oxford: Oxford University Press, 2009), 42.

39 Abū Ghudda, Lecture in Turkey, lecture from www.youtube.com/watch?v=dobft16fNe8, last accessed December 20, 2016.

Traditionalist scholarly discourse is primarily done through explaining, commenting on, and editing classical works. Traditionalist scholarship is primarily a commentary tradition and it is uncommon to write independent works.[40] For instance, approximately fifty-five of Abū Ghudda's seventy-three publications are commentaries on the works of previous scholars. What is most important about this conversation across the generations is not the ingenuity of the commentaries that result from it, but the fact that new generations are trained in how to carry it on.[41] Furthermore, Traditionalists do not view themselves as a reform movement, but as an uninterrupted continuation of *fiqh* scholars.

Traditionalism is best defined as a current within Islam that adheres to what is considered authentically rooted in revelation, has crystallized under the banners of scholarly consensus (*ijmāʿ*), and been passed on as Islamic knowledge (*ʿilm naqlī*) in chains of scholarly authority (*isnād*). It is a current that is didactic and instructional, which stands in opposition to autodidactic "do it yourself" Islam.[42] Zaman explains that "it is a combination of their intellectual formation, their vocation, and, crucially, their orientation, viz. a certain sense of continuity with the Islamic tradition, that defines the ʿulama as ʿulama."[43] Traditionalism allows for gradual change over time, ideally taking place during times of stability, not under duress during and from periods of social upheaval.

It is the sense of continuity that distinguishes Traditionalist *ʿulamāʾ* from other autodidactic, reformist, or modernist versions of Islam. Put simply, my use of the term "Traditionalist" broadly refers to the *ʿulamāʾ*, who view themselves as guardians, transmitters, and interpreters of Islamic legal tradition. They are the *ʿulamāʾ* who insist that one must follow a *madhhab* and not break from scholarly consensus. They require that Islam be understood through the schools of law. For Traditionalists, Islam can only be properly understood under the tutelage of a teacher. This must not be misunderstood as a complete rejection of books, but a rejection of them as the only means of learning and obtaining religious authority. Additionally, the terms "Traditional Islam" or "Traditionalism" incorporate the essential antithesis to many manifestations and versions of reformist, modernist, and even revivalist Islam in the modern period in its very name.[44]

[40] See Muḥammad Āl Rashīd, *Imdād al-Fattāḥ bi-Asānīd wa-Marwīyāt al-Shaykh ʿAbd al-Fattāḥ: wa-huwa Thabat al-ʿAllāma al-Muḥaddith al-Faqīh al-Uṣūlī al-Adīb al-Musnid Faḍīlat al-Shaykh ʿAbd al-Fattāḥ Abū Ghudda* (Riyadh: Maktabat al-Imām al-Shāfiʿī, 1999), 180–215.

[41] M. Zaman, "The ʿUlamāʾ," 338.

[42] K. Mathiesen, "Anglo-American," 193–194.

[43] M. Zaman, "The ʿUlamāʾ," 10.

[44] K. Mathiesen, "Anglo-American," 193–194.

By the end of the thirteenth century, Traditionalism had reached its mature, institutional form. At the core of Traditionalism were the four *madhhab*s which provided systematic interpretations of Islamic law and to which Muslim scholars and their educational systems held guild-like loyalty. These reproduced themselves in the madrasa, the center of legal study and broader education led by scholars supported by endowments that were usually gifted by wealthy members of the ruling class. Political rulers and Traditionalist scholars had a mutualistic relationship, with the scholars supporting the political status quo in return for authority in their social and religious institutions.[45]

The fall of the Ottoman Empire and the rise of secular governmental institutions in the Muslim world resulted in the reduction of the traditional pedagogical methods necessary to hold positions of religious leadership. The caliphate served as an embodiment of Muslim unity, not only politically, but also in terms of scholarship. Those who were employed by the state were traditionally trained scholars and they held important positions in government and education. In the Ottoman Empire the role of the scholars expanded as the respective bureaucracies expanded.[46]

It was the scholars who were responsible for the education of the nobility, who staffed various levels of judiciary, and who oversaw the charitable establishment of the Empire. Leading members of the scholarly class ranged from those who led the prayers in small towns to the most prestigious courtiers.[47] Through their control of important positions such as judges and muftis, the *ʿulamāʾ* eventually became the spokesmen for Islam. They held the recognized authority to interpret scripture and define the religious outlook of society.[48] In the nineteenth and twentieth centuries, strong divisions arose among Traditionalists in their following of the *madhhab*s. Mosques often had separate prayers for different *madhhab*s and this later caused Salafis and Islamic Modernists to consider the *madhhab*s as a source of division in the Muslim community.

45 Jonathan Brown, "The Salafi Transformation from Quietism to Parliamentary Giant: Salafism in Egypt and the Nour Party of Alexandria," an unpublished paper based on a talk delivered at a conference, Islam in the New Middle East, March 29–30, 2012, University of Michigan-Ann Arbor, 2–3.

46 See Noah Feldman, *The Fall and Rise of the Islamic State* (Princeton, NJ: Princeton University Press, 2012).

47 Barbara Metcalf, *Islamic Revival in British India: Deoband, 1860–1900* (New Delhi: Oxford University Press, 2002), 18–20.

48 Suha Farouki and Basheer Nafi, *Islamic Thought in the Twentieth Century* (London: I. B. Tauris, 2004), 6.

Because Traditionalists believe that religion cannot be understood without transmission, it was necessary for Muslims to follow the *madhhab*s and not deviate from their teachings. They consider the principles that were established by the *madhhab*s to be based on proof-texts, and it is only by following these principles that one can come to authentic Islamic rulings. A common misconception is that Traditionalists follow the eponym of a legal school. Rather, they follow *madhhab*s because they consider them to be a continuation of scholarly discourse over many centuries, which in turn formed a scholarly tradition. A *madhhab* literally means a "way," and it is primarily an interpretive methodology that binds a group of scholars. The *madhhab*s are named after their founders, but scholars of the *madhhab* may express opinions that are not held, or contradict, that of the founder. All of the opinions within a particular *madhhab* remain part of that *madhhab* as long as they adhere to the methodology laid down by the founder of the school.

Traditionalism stems from a lack of trust in the individual and trust in the scholarly community. Traditionalists maintain that the Qur'ān and the Sunna are what need to be followed, but the Qur'ān and the Sunna always have an interpreter. That interpreter can be the individual or it could be a collective council of scholars. They would consider those who bypass the *madhhab*s and go directly to the Qur'ān and Sunna as committing a "Protestant error."[49]

However, Salafis rightly point out that there is often a tendency among Traditionalists to shield tradition from the process of review rather than actually undertake it. For instance, if a historical ruling contradicts the apparent meaning of a text, or is not based on any text, and it is to be accepted that the scholar who made that ruling had a valid rationale for it, then it is entirely valid to require that the rationale be made clear and available for examination. The Traditionalists claim of "who are we to do such an examination" is often a means of resisting this very method of continuous examination, which Traditionalists claim makes the tradition valid. Even when Traditionalists provide the rationale for a ruling, they nevertheless advocate limiting discussion of the rationale only to the scholarly elite. They might even describe asking for such a rationale as a violation of *adab*, influenced by modernity or Salafism. Accordingly, Salafism often finds its appeal in promising to provide Muslims with the

49 Abdul Hakim Murad, "The Salafi Fallacy," lecture from www.youtube.com/ watch?v=1MRXs5fqlXQ, last accessed May 7, 2013.

authentic or true meaning of scripture, free from any obscurities or biases toward a particular scholar or legal school.

SALAFISM

The definition of the term "Salafism" has resulted in some debate among scholars.[50] To date, most works have focused on the political aspect of Salafism. By doing so, they miss its legal and hermeneutical underpinnings.[51] For instance, Wiktorowicz divides Salafis according to their involvement, or lack thereof, in politics. One must ask why they should be divided as such and not according to, for instance, their interpretive methodology.[52] Overemphasizing the political aspect of Salafism is problematic because Salafism is not a political movement, but rather a method of understanding Islam. Failure to account for the compelling nature of the religious message of Salafism will result in mischaracterizing the movement as politically, rather than religiously, driven.

Using the term "Salafism" can lead to confusion because in essence every Muslim would consider themselves a Salafi in the sense that they are trying to emulate the Prophet and the early Muslim community (the *salaf*). Salafis label themselves as such since they aspire to follow the *salaf* because they were closest to the era of the Prophet and are understood to best embody pristine and pure Islam. Those who describe themselves as Salafi do so in order to highlight the authenticity of their particular understanding of Islam. The use of the term "Salafi" could be understood as a tactic some modern Muslims use to increase their authority, influence, and power. However,

[50] Frank Griffel, "What Do We Mean by 'Salafi'? Connecting Muḥammad ʿAbduh with Egypt's Nūr Party in Islam's Contemporary Intellectual History," *Die Welt des Islams*, 55 (2015), 186–220; Henri Lauzière, "The Construction of Salafiyya: Reconsidering Salafism from Perspective of Conceptual History," *International Journal of Middle East Studies*, 42, no. 3 (2010); idem, *The Making of Salafism: Islamic Reform in the Twentieth Century* (New York: Columbia University Press, 2015); idem, "What We Mean versus What They Mean by 'Salafi': A Reply to Frank Griffel," *Die Welt des Islams*, 56, no. 1 (2016), 89–96; Bernard Haykel, "On the Nature of Salafi Thought and Action," in *Global Salafism*, ed. Roel Meijer (New York: Columbia University Press, 2009), 33–57; J. Brown, "Salafi Transformation," 3; Ovamir Anjum, "Salafis and Democracy: Doctrine and Context," *The Muslim World*, 106, no. 3 (2016), 448–473.

[51] Thomas Hegghammer, "Jihadi-Salafis or Revolutionaries?," in *Global Salafism*, ed. Roel Meijer (New York: Columbia University Press, 2009), 244–266; Quintan Wiktorowicz, "Anatomy of the Salafi Movement," *Studies in Conflict & Terrorism*, 29 (2006), 207–239; Christopher M. Blanchard, *The Islamic Traditions of Wahhabism and Salafiyya* (Washington, DC: Congressional Research Service, Library of Congress, 2007).

[52] Q. Wiktorowicz, "Anatomy."

Salafis are not monolithic and, unlike the individual *madhhabs*, Salafis do not have one shared legal methodology.

One should note that definitions of such abstract terms can shift and change over time. This has also been the case with the term "Salafism." The term "Salafi" has been applied to a variety of people, such as Albānī, Rashīd Riḍā, Yūsuf al-Qaraḍāwī, Ibn Taymiyya, Ibn Qayyim (d. 751/1350), and even Osama b. Laden (d. 2011). Obviously, each of these individuals is distinct, and in many cases radically different in methodology despite sharing the label of "Salafi." Nevertheless, though controversial, the terms "Salafi" and "Salafism" are unavoidable. Henri Lauzière traces the history of the term *salafiyya* and argues that the term "Salafism" being used to refer to a particular group is a modern phenomenon. He argues that "Salafism" and "Salafi" are used anachronistically, omitting scholars and movements from the fourteenth century to the present day with great inaccuracy. An actual coherent, self-identifying Salafi movement did not emerge until the twentieth century. In other words, Salafism as a label for a movement is of recent origin.[53]

The relationship between Islamic Modernism and the modern Salafi movement, and the use of the term "Salafi," has been subject to confusion among academics. The two movements are not directly linked. In the early twentieth century, during Riḍā's lifetime, being a Salafi and a modernist at the same time posed no conceptual problem because "Salafi" was primarily a theological label: unlike today, the two were not mutually exclusive. So, just as an Ashʿarī could be a modernist, so could a Salafi. Riḍā was an Islamic Modernist, which meant that he stood against certain traditional patterns in the Muslim world which he considered to be deviant from the original Islamic model of the Prophet and early Muslim generations. Modernists believed that these practices were responsible for the stagnation and rigidity of Islam and consequently prevented Muslims from joining the modern world. They were critical of practices like *taqlīd* which they understood to be the uncritical following in the footsteps of the last generation of scholars within one school of law and performing acts of worship that were not sanctioned by the Qurʾān and Sunna.

From their point of view, the dynamism and spirit of modernity were always part of the original teachings of Islam, but Muslims lost this spirit due to certain historical developments and became rigidly traditional in their thinking. While the Muslim world was stagnant, the west picked this spirit

53 H. Lauzière, "Construction."

up and modernized further. Therefore, ʿAbduh and Riḍā were primarily modernists, rather than Salafis. Riḍā on occasion did refer to himself as Salafi, but his usage of the label did not have the same meaning as it would today. This is primarily because the term "Salafism" is not an accurate term to describe the modernist movement, nor did it represent a clear trend.[54]

There were scholars before Riḍā who identified their views with the "righteous predecessors" (*al-salaf al-ṣāliḥ*) to underline their Islamic authenticity, in contrast to the views of those they deemed to be deviant. Because much of the Islamic Modernist movement's works were published by the Salafi publishing house, the movement came to be known as the Salafi one. It interpreted Islam in such a way that it was largely compatible with modern reason and with many of the accomplishments of modern western civilization.

In the eighteenth century, Muḥammad b. ʿAbd al-Wahhāb introduced his own purist version of Islam in the Arabian Peninsula. Like Islamic Modernists who appeared a century after him, ʿAbd al-Wahhāb rejected what he considered innovative acts such as saint worship or worship of natural beings like trees. Unlike Islamic Modernists, ʿAbd al-Wahhāb did not seek to revolutionize Islamic law; rather, he primarily followed the Ḥanbalī school. The Salafiyya publishing house established a branch in the Arabian Peninsula and started to publish works from Wahhabi scholars. After some time, the term "Salafism" came to be identified with a more purist version of Islam. The movement of ʿAbduh and Riḍā did try to move in the direction of the *salaf* but with a different objective than Albānī's understanding of Salafism. Wagemakers correctly states: "Although these reformists shared a preference for certain concepts with their present-day namesakes, such as an emphasis on *tawḥīd* and a rejection of *taqlīd*, in the end theirs was a thoroughly modernist discourse, as opposed to the purifying tone of contemporary Salafis."[55]

This anti-*taqlīd* modernist movement may have prepared the Islamic arena for the emergence of modern Salafism, but the two movements are quite different. At most, what could be said is that Salafis were inspired by this anti-*taqlīd* movement. Riḍā developed the classical jurisprudential principles of *maṣlaḥa* (public interest) and *ḍarūra* (necessity) into expansive tools through which one could adapt the Sharia to the exigencies of modern life, thus sidestepping many of the substantive rulings of medieval jurisprudence without confronting them head on. However, the central concern

[54] H. Lauzière, "Construction"; J. Wagemakers, *Quietist*, 6. [55] J. Wagemakers, *Quietist*, 7.

driving this reform was a modernist one. The concerns of Salafis were different and more indigenous to the Islamic tradition. Their methodology is vastly different from that of Islamic Modernists. Salafis believe that Islam provided a single solution to every question. As a result of their ḥadīth-based methodology, Salafis did not only differ with the reformists and modernist movement of Riḍā, but often arrived at completely opposite conclusions.[56]

Despite the fact that Salafism did not exist as a label for a movement prior to the twentieth century, modern Salafis draw on a history of iconoclastic scholars such as Ibn Taymiyya, Ibn Qayyim, and Muḥammad al-Shawkānī. While it is true that modern Salafism is not a transcription of purist movements of the past, simply replicated into modernity, it does have similar tendencies to historical movements. Although the usage of the term "Salafi" to describe premodern scholars may be useful, one must keep in mind that religious movements are organic and ever-changing because they are composed of individuals who affect and are affected by their circumstances.

The ultimate question is what makes one a Salafi? Is it their rejection of *taqlīd* and emphasis on *tawḥīd*? Or is it their labeling themselves as Salafi? Those who describe themselves as Salafi do so in order to highlight their own purity, and the impurity of other movements. Salafis do not have one shared legal methodology like the adherents of a *madhhab*. Moreover, portraying the *salaf*, or early Muslim generations, as being homogeneous further complicates the issue. When one labels themselves a follower of the early generation, which individual or group among them are they referring to? The Prophet's Companions and early Muslims, like Muslims today, disagreed in their understanding and interpretation of Islam.

The generic nature of the term "Salafism" is complicated by the fact that dozens of groups identify themselves as Salafi and each of them claims to exclusively represent "true Salafism."[57] Many groups call themselves Salafis, or do not object to being called Salafi, yet differ with each other on several issues, such as the necessity of following a *madhhab*, level of allegiance toward an Islamic ruler, and theological positions on what constitutes faith.[58]

However, there are some general characteristics that pertain to all Salafis without exception, such as the fact that they consider themselves as correctly

[56] Daniel Lav, *Radical Islam and the Revival of Medieval Theology* (New York: Cambridge University Press, 2012), 110.

[57] Yasir Qadhi, "On Salafi Islam," http://muslimmatters.org/2014/04/22/on-salafi-islam-dr-yasir-qadhi, last accessed June 26, 2014.

[58] J. Wagemakers, *Quietist*, 10.

espousing the teachings and beliefs of the *salaf* and the creed that was transmitted from them. Yet, even on the issue of creed they differ when it comes to the theological position on faith and whether actions constitute a requisite part of faith or are subsidiary to it.[59] All Salafis reject any possibility of metaphoric or symbolic interpretation of God's divine names and attributes (*tawḥīd al-asmāʾ wa-l-ṣifāt*). Additionally, they affirm God's exclusive right to be worshipped (*tawḥīd al-ulūhiyya*) and reject anything that may directly or indirectly compromise it. Hence, certain Sufi practices such as saint veneration and intercession of the dead are strongly condemned.

Salafis also reject religious innovation (*bidʿa*) and disassociate themselves from those who ascribe to it. Salafis tend to respect and take recourse to the legal and theological opinions of Ibn Taymiyya; however, it is important to note that Ibn Taymiyya cannot be considered a progenitor for the modern Salafi movement, as Salafis view themselves as having no one single founder after the Prophet Muhammad.[60]

Nonetheless, as discussed above, there are many diverse trends within Salafism. Saudi Salafism, sometimes referred to as Wahhabism, is made up of major Saudi religious figures and they often adhere to the Ḥanbalī *madhhab*.[61] They tend to be quietist and Salafi in creed but not law. Another group is the *Ṣaḥwa* Salafi movement which is primarily made up of Saudi scholars who call for political and social activism, but they do not go so far as to call for the overthrow of Muslim rulers who do not rule by Islamic law. The term *Ṣaḥwa* conveys political activism and social involvement. This movement is led by individuals such as Safar al-Ḥawālī and Salmān al-ʿAwda, who is one of the Saudi kingdom's most prominent religious figures.[62]

Madkhalism is a strain of Salafism based on the teachings of Rabīʿ al-Madkhalī. Madkhalism is particularly supportive of Arab regimes and was primarily a reaction to the *Ṣaḥwa* movement. Madkhalīs refer to *Ṣaḥwa* Salafis as Quṭbīs because of their connection with the political thoughts of Syed Quṭb (d. 1966). Rabīʿ al-Madkhalī derived many of his teachings from

59 J. Wagemakers, *Quietest*, 10; Y. Qadhi, "Salafi Islam."

60 J. Wagemakers, *Quietest*, 3–4; Y. Qadhi, "Salafi Islam."

61 The term "Wahhabi" is primarily used by the critics of this group. The members of this group reject the term because they do not consider themselves to be followers of Muḥammad b. ʿAbd al-Wahhāb. On Wahhabism see David Commins, *The Wahhabi Mission and Saudi Arabia* (London: I. B. Tauris, 2006); Natana DeLong-Bas, *Wahhabi Islam From Revival and Reform to Global Jihad* (New York: Oxford University Press, 2004); Madawi Al-Rasheed, *Contesting the Saudi State: Islamic Voices from a New Generation* (Cambridge: Cambridge University Press, 2006).

62 Y. Qadhi, "Salafi Islam."

Albānī and they share a purist ideology and intolerance toward their opponents. However, Madkhalīs are far more intolerant and are consistently debating among themselves about who is on the correct path (*manhaj*). Unlike Albānī's followers, Madkhalīs are a shrinking community, which may be because most Salafis do not consider religious fatwas of Madhkhalīs to be academically sound due to their support for secular governments in the Muslim world.

There are also jihadi Salafis who believe that violence is necessary to produce political change. There are several Salafi jihadi groups, although some only write about the importance of jihad while not actually participating in it, such as Abū Muḥammad al-Maqdisī and Abū Muṣʿab al-Sūrī. Although groups such as al-Qaeda and ISIS have some theological points in common with other Salafis, they are usually condemned by most Salafis for their acts of violence. Some scholars and policy makers have argued that ISIS is a direct result of Salafi methodology. This is inaccurate not only because it ignores the political causes of the rise of ISIS, but because most Salafis and Wahhabis routinely condemn ISIS as misinterpreting and distorting the teachings of Salafism and Wahhabism. Furthermore, very few Salafis succumb to ISIS and are quite capable of seeing how it contradicts the teachings of mainstream Islam.

Ḥātim al-ʿAwnī, a renowned Saudi cleric who at an earlier stage of his life was well respected and admired by mainstream Wahhabis, has gained fame and notoriety by championing the claim that these jihadist movements are in fact representative of true classical Wahhabi thought. He claims that the architects and justifiers of such jihadist movements rely heavily on *Al-Durar al-Saniyya*, the primary collection of Wahhabi writings dating from the eighteenth century. ʿAwnī uses ISIS's inspiration from Salafism to invite mainstream Salafis to review and reform their methodology.[63] Although there may be a link between ISIS and Salafism, any interpretive tradition may give rise to certain kinds of apocalyptical theologies that are perversions of that tradition's dominant ideals. The link between the two is similar to the association between Reformation Anabaptists and Protestants. The essential point is that these are perversions, just as mob rule is a perversion of democracy, even if it is, in an important way, enabled by the latter.

Salafis in Egypt were popular prior to the Arab spring, but have lost much of their credibility since. This group was primarily apolitical and criticized all

[63] Yasir Qadhi, "Reformation or Reconstruction: Dr. Ḥatim al-ʿAwnī's Critiques of Modern Wahhabī Thought," presentation of an unpublished paper at the American Academy of Religion, November 21, 2016.

political involvement until the overthrow of Hosni Mubarak (d. 2020) in the Arab spring, at which point they shifted their stance as they had an opportunity at governing Egypt. Currently, they have conflicting views on political involvement within the movement: some of them are critical of the Egyptian government, others remain apolitical, while the Noor party is particularly supportive of the current ruler Abdel Fattah el-Sisi.[64] They are purists with regard to their legal methodology and do not follow the *madhhabs*.[65]

Each of these groups aspires to live according to "the way of the *salaf*." In acknowledging that the early Muslim generations represent an ideal, they recognize that the past is gone and that they can only try to relive it, though it will not come alive today as it was then. The way modern Muslims interact with their tradition has fundamentally changed. In addition, the meaning of a term like "Salafism" and the ideal Muslims attempt to embody is not fixed, changes over time, and is contingent on the way individuals define it. The previously mentioned types of Salafis demonstrate the diversity found within Salafism, and also illustrate how using the term "Salafi" to simultaneously describe all these groups can be confusing and problematic.

PURIST SALAFISM

This book focuses on the version of Salafism practiced by Albānī and his students, and I refer to them as purist Salafis. This brand of Salafism quickly spread throughout the Muslim world in the late twentieth century. Albānī was staunchly opposed to the *madhhabs* and advocated a textualist-based jurisprudence. His strand of Salafism also tends to be the most literalist in *fiqh* and strict in its application of the concept of *bidʿa* to practices that most other Salafis would view as innocuous.[66]

A strong anti-*madhhab* campaign lies at the heart of purist Salafism. Although purist Salafi anti-*madhhab*ism may have been inspired by the likes of Ibn Taymiyya, Ibn Qayyim, and Muḥammad b. ʿAbd al-Wahhāb, their attitude toward the *madhhabs* is distinct. Although these three scholars were anti-*taqlīd* to varying degrees, they were not anti-*madhhab*. Indeed, many scholars who are identified with Salafism, such as Ibn Taymiyya and Ibn

64 On the Salafi Nour Party see J. Brown, "Salafi Transformation"; Khalil al-Anani and Malik Maszlee, "Pious Way to Politics: The Rise of Political Salafism in Post-Mubarak Egypt," *Digest of Middle East Studies*, 22, no. 1 (2013), 57–73.

65 On purist Salafis in Egypt, see Richard Gauvain, *Salafi Ritual Purity: In the Presence of God* (London: Routledge, 2013).

66 Y. Qadhi, "On Salafi Islam."

Kathīr (d. 774/1373), were themselves members of a *madhhab*.[67] Ibn Taymiyya did not prohibit *taqlīd* for laypeople. Even regular scholars could perform *taqlīd*, with the exception of matters where the evidence is clear that their *madhhab*'s position contradicts the Qur'ān and Sunna, or that another *madhhab* has stronger evidence. Besides these instances, Ibn Taymiyya advised people to stick to their *madhhabs*. By contrast, Albānī and purist Salafis refuse to be affiliated with any scholar or *madhhab*.[68]

This refusal distinguishes him from Saudi Salafi scholars like ʿAbd al-ʿAzīz Ibn Bāz and Muḥammad b. Ṣāliḥ al-ʿUthaymīn (d. 2001), and other Saudi clerics who follow the Ḥanbalī *madhhab*. Although they acknowledged that a stronger proof-text would trump the school's teachings, this concession was largely rhetorical. Whereas Albānī was a systematic and principled anti-*madhhab*ist in both rhetoric and practice, these Saudi clerics were not concerned with persuading other Muslims to abandon the *madhhabs*. In this regard, Albānī has more in common with anti-*madhhab* Islamic Modernists than he does with Saudi scholars who adhered to the Ḥanbalī school. The large number of heated book-length responses between Albānī and Traditionalists throughout the Muslim world indicates how much they felt threatened by each other.[69]

67 Ismāʿīl Ibn Kathīr, *Ṭabaqāt al-Shāfiʿiyya* (Beirut: Dār al-Madār al-Islāmī, 2002), 6.

68 Emad Hamdeh, "Qur'ān and Sunna or the Madhhabs?: A Salafi Polemic against Islamic Legal Tradition," *Islamic Law and Society*, 24, no. 3 (June 2017), 1–43.

69 For Traditionalist responses to Salafism see ʿAbd al-Fattāḥ Abū Ghudda, *Kalimāt fī Kashf Abāṭīl wa Iftirāʿāt* (Aleppo: Maktabat al-Maṭbūʿāt al-Islāmiyya, 1990); Ismāʿīl al-Anṣārī, *Ibāḥat al-Taḥallī bi l-Dhahab al-Muḥallaq wa l-Radd ʿalā al-Albānī fī Taḥrīmi-hi* (Riyadh: Maktabat al-Imam al-Shāfiʿī, 1988); idem, *Taṣḥīḥ Ṣalāt al-Tarāwīḥ ʿIshrīn Rakʿa wa l-Radd ʿalā al-Albānī fī Taḍʿīfi-hi* (Riyadh: Maktabat al-Imam al-Shāfiʿī, 1988); Muḥammad ʿAwwāma, *Adab al-Ikhtilāf fī Masāʾil al-ʿilm wa l-Dīn* (Beirut: Dār al-Bashāʾir al-Islāmiyya, 1997); idem, *Athar al-Ḥadīth al-Sharīf fī Ikhitlāf al-Aʾimma al-Fuqahāʾ Raḍī Allāhu ʿan-hum* (Beirut: Dār al-Bashāʾir al-Islāmiyya, 1997); Ḥabīb al-Raḥmān al-Aʿẓamī (d. 1992), *Al-Albānī: Shudhūdhu-hu wa Akhṭāʾu-hu* (Kuwait: Maktabat Dār al-ʿUrūbah, 1984); Muḥammad Ramaḍān al-Būṭī, *Al-Lā Madhhabiyya Akhṭar Bidʿa Tuhaddid al-Sharīʿa al-Islāmiyya* (Damascus: Dār al-Farābī, 2005); ʿAbd Allāh al-Ghumārī (d. 1993), *Al-Radd ʿalā al-Albānī* (Beirut: Dār al-Janān, 1991); Gabriel F. Haddad, *Al-Albani: A Concise Guide to the Chief Innovator of Our Time*, http://sunnah.org/history/Innovators/al_albani.htm, last accessed June 17, 2020; idem, *Albani & His Friends: A Concise Guide to the Salafi Movement* (Birmingham, UK: AQSA Publications, 2004); Maḥmūd Mamdūḥ, *Al-Taʿrīf bi-Awhām man Qassama al-Sunan ilā Ṣaḥīḥ wa Ḍaʿīf* (Dubai: Dār al-Buḥūth li'l-Dirāsāt al-Islāmiyya wa Iḥyāʾ al-Turāth, 2000); idem, *Tanbīh al-Muslim ilā Taʿaddī al-Albānī ʿalā Ṣaḥīḥ Muslim* (Cairo: Maktabat al-Mujallad al-ʿArabī, 2011); idem, *Wuṣūl al-Tahānī bi Ithbāt Sunniyyat al-Subḥa wa l-Radd ʿalā al-Albānī* (Cairo: Dār al-Imām al-Tirmidhī, 1994); Muḥammad al-Nuʿmānī (d. 1999), *Makānat al-Imām Abī Ḥanīfa fī l-Ḥadīth*, ed. ʿAbd al-Fattāḥ Abū Ghudda (Beirut: Maktabat al-Maṭbūʿāt al-Islāmiyya, 2007); Ḥasan Saqqāf, *Iḥtijāj al-Khāʾib bi-ʿIbārat man Iddaʿā al-Ijmāʿ*

The Salafi imagination reconstructs the early Muslims' religious, cultural, and ethical habits, and insists on emulating them in ethics and theology. The attraction of Salafism lies mainly in the form of authority it promotes, and reproduces, as well as the particular hermeneutics it advocates. A typical Salafi argument is that, unlike other Muslims, their views are based only on proof-texts. Hence, Salafis view themselves as pure and others as in need of purification.[70] Albānī considered the legal confusion, illicit innovation in religion, and all other problems facing Islam and Muslims were a result of not properly adhering to the science of ḥadīth.

For Albānī, the application of the apparent meaning of scripture took precedence overall. He applied ḥadīth in a direct and confrontational manner which furthered his iconoclastic reputation. His unconventional views and character attracted much confrontation, not only with Traditionalists, but also with other Salafis in Saudi Arabia and Jordan. Scholars from throughout the Muslim world felt the need to refute and debate Albānī. These debates may appear to revolve around trivial issues compared to the larger problems facing the Muslim world at the time. However, what consumed both sides in the debate was an attempt to defend their particular method of interpreting scripture and "authentic" Islam.

Albānī and purist Salafis cannot be understood outside of the context of the many confrontations they had with Traditionalists. Salafism is purist in nature and is often compared to Protestantism because it strips interpretive authority from religious institutions and empowers individual interpretation of Islamic scripture. On the other hand, Traditionalism can be compared to Catholicism in the sense that it is an institutional understanding of Islam that developed over centuries of scholarship. The Salafi movement has been characterized as the Protestant reformation of Sunni Islam because Salafis view themselves as purifying the syncretic practices that crept into the faith over the many centuries in the exact same manner that Martin Luther viewed himself as purifying a culturally corrupted Christianity.[71]

Fahuwa Kādhib (Amman: Maktabat al-Imām al-Nawawī, 1990); idem, *Qāmūs Shatā'im al-Albānī* (Amman: Dār al-Imām al-Nawawī, 1993).

70 B. Haykel, "Salafi Thought," 34–36.

71 Interview with Asma Afsaruddin and Jonathan Brown, "How Islamic Is Isis, Really?," Here & Now, Boston NPR News Station (Boston, MA: WBUR, November 19, 2015). See J. Brown, *Misquoting Muhammad*, 161–175. Yasir Qadhi explains that "Salafis are the Protestant reformation of Sunni Islam. There is no question about it that Salafis view themselves as the Protestant reformation. They are purifying the syncretic practices that crept into the faith over the many centuries in the exact same manner that Martin Luther viewed himself as purifying a cultural corrupted Christianity." Interview with Yasir Qadhi, "Salafi Muslims: Following the Ancestors of Islam," *Interfaith Voices* (February 21, 2013).

Purist Salafis are suspicious of scholars who belonged to Traditionalist institutions. Consequently, they were critical of the *madhhab*s and circumvented them in order to interpret the scripture anew. In other words, purist Salafis hold that scripture is clear and "speaks for itself." Hence Albānī often argues that laypeople should follow the texts rather than scholarly institutions that interpret them. He used the availability of information through print to deconstruct Traditionalist textual hermeneutics and construct his own means for interpreting the jurisprudential requirements of sacred scripture.

For Traditionalists, scholarly tradition is indispensable to the acquisition of religious knowledge and virtues because the mastery and embodiment of religious values by novices emerges through a process of acculturation. This process of acculturation is distinct from and transcends intellectual cognition of religious truth. While religious truth may be a proper subject of instruction, without reliable teachers who properly embody Islamic teachings, mere instruction cannot produce properly acculturated religious subjects.[72] For this reason, Traditionalism continues to place great emphasis on Sufi tradition because of the belief that the institutions and practices that Sufism cultivates, including the hierarchical relationship between teacher and student, are indispensable in the production of a properly embodied practice of Islam. Under the Traditionalist scheme, then, individuals lack the independent capacity to achieve virtue and need assistance from others in order to enable them to live virtuous lives.[73]

Albānī does not reject the distinction Traditionalists make between intellectually understanding the truth of Islam and the actual embodiment of its teachings. However, he rejects the necessity of tradition as a precondition for embodying Islamic teachings. He maintains that any properly motivated individual who has sufficient intellectual skills may study the basic sources of Islam independently and obtain an adequate degree of religious knowledge and virtue. Despite his critics, he considers himself to have reverence for the scholarly teachings found in the *madhhab*s, but his loyalty and allegiance is ultimately to the truth. He has no problem with being unsympathetic or antagonistic toward the *madhhab*s if they contradict authentic proof-texts. In contrast, Traditionalists believed that texts could only be properly understood in light of scholarly tradition, legal or otherwise. They often subjugate

[72] For a study of this acculturation in contemporary learning circles see Rudolph T. Ware, *The Walking Quran: Islamic Education, Embodied Knowledge, and History in West Africa* (Chapel Hill: University of North Carolina Press, 2014).

[73] Mohammad Fadel, "Islamic Law," 2–3.

scripture to legal principles whereas purist Salafis maintain that texts override all non-textual sources. Traditionalists oppose not only the unconventional opinions held by purist Salafis, but their legal, exegetical, and pedagogical methodology as well because it threatens their scholarly authority and institutions.

ALBĀNĪ AND MODERNISTS

As previously noted, many reform movements of the twentieth century were not producing change in the Muslim world. Purist Salafis were discontented with most Islamic reform movements, despite being inspired by some of their members or some slight similarities between them. Like Modernists, Albānī challenged the traditional manner of interpreting Islamic texts; but, unlike them, he emphasized their authenticity and was not concerned whether a ruling served contemporary social welfare needs or was relevant to modern advancements. Albānī followed a more literalist understanding of Islam based only on scripture and the precedent of the early Muslim community. He focused on purifying religious beliefs and actions and therefore rejected much of what is considered traditional Islam. Albānī's early interest in ḥadīth studies, which constitutes a turning point in challenging tradition, began when he encountered an article in the *al-Manār* journal written by Rashīd Riḍā.[74]

Riḍā criticized Abū Ḥamid al-Ghazālī's (d. 505/1111) *Iḥyāʾ ʿulūm al-dīn* (*Revival of the Religious Sciences*) for its use of weak ḥadīth and its Sufism. Ghazālī and his works are celebrated by many in the Muslim world, particularly his work the *Iḥyāʾ*. Many Muslims take their religious knowledge and practices from this book and have great reverence for Ghazālī who is viewed as a religious reformer.[75] Riḍā's criticism of the *Iḥyāʾ* played a significant role in inspiring Albānī to criticize everything he considered to be extra-textual to the religion.

Albānī was influenced by Riḍā's willingness to challenge tradition; not only did he challenge a celebrated and revered scholar like Ghazālī, but he also encouraged Muslims to question the works of classical scholars.

[74] Muḥammad Nāṣir al-Dīn al-Albānī, "Tarjamat al-Shaykh al-Albānī: Nashʾat al-Shaykh fī Dimashq," lecture from www.islamway.com, last accessed May 30, 2011.

[75] There are many Muslims and scholars who strongly condemned the *Iḥyāʾ* for its use of fabricated ḥadīth and fictitious stories. In 503/1109, the scholars of Andalusia gathered to burn the *Iḥyāʾ* in the courtyard of the city's mosque. See Kenneth Garden, "Al-Ghazālī's Contested Revival: Iḥyāʾ ʿUlūm al-Dīn and Its Critics in Khorasan and the Maghrib" (Ph.D. Dissertation, University of Chicago, 2005), 152–153.

Riḍā's article led Albānī to read a book by Zayn al-Dīn al-ʿIrāqī (d. 806/1404) which detailed the weak ḥadīth found in Ghazālī's *Iḥyāʾ*, which caused Albānī to be suspicious of Sufism and weak ḥadīth, both of which were means for foreign teachings to enter Islam. This motivated Albānī to study ḥadīth in an effort to purge Islam and its sciences from its impurities. Hence, Albānī's endeavor to purify the religion was inspired by Riḍā, but Riḍā's influence on Albānī was limited to that spark of interest in the field of ḥadīth.[76]

At the time, the *al-Manār* journal was the major vehicle for spreading Muslim reformist thought. Although he was influenced by Riḍā, Albānī's methodology was different in several ways. Riḍā allowed reason to play a central role in understanding religious texts, but Albānī believed that the use of reason must be removed from the legal process. In Albānī's view, reason is limited to understanding the direct meaning of scripture. Additionally, despite the fact that Riḍā had called for the reexamination of *āḥād*[77] ḥadīth, he was reluctant to question the authenticity of *mutawātir* ḥadīth. Albānī , on the other hand, called for a reexamination of the entire corpus of ḥadīth, including the *mutawātir*.[78]

What Riḍā and Albānī have in common is their rejection of *taqlīd* and challenging what they believed to be false practices of their time. However, Riḍā differs from Albānī in his modernism and rationalization. Albānī noted that Riḍā's works often departed from the Sunna.[79] Riḍā was primarily interested in reforming Islam in a modernist way. Unlike Albānī, purging all Islamic literature of weak ḥadīth was not Riḍā's primary focus.[80] Albānī did not give much attention to Islamic Modernists like ʿAbduh and Riḍā because he did not view them as a serious threat to his scholarly authority. In fact, he considered many Islamic Modernists to be whimsical when it came to interpreting Islam. As previously noted, Albānī accused both Muḥammad al-Ghazālī and Qaraḍāwī of interpreting religious texts based on their whims.[81]

Qaraḍāwī and Ghazālī sympathized with Albānī's reformist tendencies, and there was never much debate between them. Because they were both part of the Muslim Brotherhood, they emphasized unity of Muslims and

[76] Emad Hamdeh, "The Formative Years of an Iconoclastic Salafi Scholar," *The Muslim World*, 106, no. 3 (2016), 411–432.
[77] *Aḥād ḥadīth* is best defined as a ḥadīth that does not meet the conditions of *mutawātir*.
[78] D. Brown, *Rethinking Tradition*, 41.
[79] Muḥammad Nāṣir al-Dīn al-Albānī, "Masāʾil wa Ajwibatuhā," *Al-Aṣāla* (1994), 39.
[80] See J. Wagemakers, "Salafism's Historical Continuity," 214–215.
[81] N. al-Albānī, "Refutation of Yusuf al Qaradawi."

hence remained respectful toward Albānī despite his numerous attacks on them. Unity among Muslims is one of Qaraḍāwī's main concerns and he therefore sought to seek a middle ground between Ghazālī and Albānī.[82] On the other hand, Traditionalists were in a constant struggle over interpretive authority with Albānī, and hence much of his criticisms were directed toward them. Albānī viewed them as unwavering, blind followers of the four legal schools. Albānī also criticized Sufism and viewed it as completely foreign to Islam. This resulted in debates concerning topics such as *tawassul*, the use of prayer beads, and whether the dead can hear.

However, these debates almost always developed into arguments about the authenticity of particular ḥadīth. Due to Salafi criticisms of Traditionalists' interpretive methodology, Traditionalists throughout the Muslim world attacked Salafis as being simplistic literalists. Islamic Modernists and Salafis both criticized *taqlīd* and Traditionalists, but for different reasons. Islamic Modernists blamed Traditionalists for the fall of the Islamic caliphate because they were "backward" and out of touch with the modern world. Salafis placed blame on Traditionalists because they held on to a tradition that was full of "incorrect" opinions that went against the Sunna. At a time when Traditionalists were facing all of the challenges of modernity and the fall of the caliphate, Albānī emerged and furthered the spread of purist Salafism.

ALBĀNĪ AND THE SPREAD OF SALAFISM

Albānī played an important role in promoting Salafism as not only a creed, but a methodology that encompassed legal, political, and social elements. Some scholars have credited Albānī with empowering common Muslims and students to challenge scholars by asking them for proof-texts.[83] Albānī's books became very famous in the Muslim world and his students recorded and spread most of his lectures. He has proven to be very influential in Salafi circles. For instance, if one reads the fascinating account of how Bilal Philips was thrown off "the *manhaj*" by his peers, then one would notice an interesting phenomenon. To prove his worth and authenticity as a true Salafi he continually invoked his relationship with Albānī and his service to his works. He talked about how he used to sit at his feet, and how he has a library full of his unreleased lectures. The

[82] See D. Warren, "Islamic Jurisprudence."

[83] See Stéphane Lacroix, *Awakening Islam: The Politics of Religious Dissent in Contemporary Saudi Arabia* (Cambridge, MA: Harvard University Press, 2011), 85.

fact that he never once invoked anyone else speaks volumes on Albānī's position among contemporary Salafis.[84]

Albānī's understanding of Islam has similarities to important authorities such as Ibn Taymiyya, Ibn Qayyim, and Muḥạmmad al-Shawkānī. Despite the fact that he was different to these individuals, he was inspired by their attempts to purify particular aspects of the religion, such as creed, and took it a step further by trying to purify the entire religion. This brand of Salafism was also different than Wahhabism because the latter followed the Ḥanbalī *madhhab*, while Albānī and his followers did not. Although Wahhabis were strict with regards to differing in issues of creed, they were tolerant concerning differences in law and legal theory.

Purist Salafis project themselves into history: they retell the history of their historical forefathers and attempt to make themselves in their image. This sometimes leads to confusion in terminology. Essentially, every Muslim would claim that they are following the Prophet and the early Muslims; but Albānī used the term "Salafi" to describe his own, particular, and perhaps unprecedented understanding of Islam. Albānī had tremendous influence and his views and methodology shaped Muslims' understanding of Salafism. He made Islamic scripture, especially ḥadīth, accessible to a large group of people, whereas before it was primarily limited to the scholarly class.

He understood what arguments appealed to laypeople and employed them in a religious context. For instance, a Shāfiʿī scholar's authority is validated and supported by the school he belongs to and the teachers he studied with. Albānī did not have the reinforcement of a *madhhab* organization or a teacher, yet he managed to create this powerful reform movement which he called Salafism. Albānī had the ability to put together a very straightforward methodology and extend it to every area of *fiqh* and ḥadīth even if it resulted in unpopular decisions.

LITERALISM

Purist Salafis are often referred to as literalists, and although they had literalist tendencies, they were not literalists like the Ẓāhirī school or Ibn Ḥazm (d. 456/1064). Some Salafis encouraged their followers to follow the literal meaning of texts in acts of worship. For example, Muqbil al-Wādiʿī (d. 2001), a leading Salafi in Yemen, rejected *qiyās* as a source of law based on the fact that the Prophet would often wait for revelation when asked a

[84] See Bilal Philips "Reply to Critics," article from www.bilalphilips.com, last accessed August 28, 2012.

question. He permitted scholars to use *qiyās* but rejected it as a source of law. In his view, *qiyās* is a human endeavor and its results cannot be attributed to God. The sources of Islam are only the Qur'ān and Sunna.[85] When asked about Ibn Ḥazm's Ẓāhirism, al-Wādi'ī said "We advise every Muslim to be a Ẓāhirī."[86] His understanding of Ẓāhirism was a direct following of texts and rejected performing the *taqlīd* of Ibn Ḥazm or any other scholar. By holding closely to the literal meanings of Islamic scripture, Wadi'ī, like Albānī, established an understanding of Islam that he believed to be correct, unlike all others.

Albānī focused on reviving the Sunna as it is compiled in ḥadīth collections. The *madhhab*s, Sufism, and involvement in speculative theology were barriers between Muslims and the words of God and the Prophet. The departure from the texts of the Qur'ān and Sunna have led Muslims to engage in unorthodox rituals that threatened Islam's core teachings. Consequently, Albānī considered it necessary to purge Islam of all foreign elements. In this process many scholars attacked him, accusing him of discarding scholarly tradition.

Albānī's iconoclastic views resulted in disputations with many of those around him. He differed with the Wahhabis in Saudi Arabia, the Muslim Brotherhood in Jordan, and Traditionalists throughout the Muslim world. Naturally, his students and followers also clashed with members of these movements. Hence, the movement he established was one that carried the reputation of being intolerant and confrontational.

Although they thought that it is only by applying their understanding of Islam that the Muslim world will be saved, Albānī and his students often failed to realistically describe how following the *salaf* can be manifested in the modern world. With technological advancements, the world has rapidly changed since the premodern period. Albānī calls for a "returning to the Salaf" but does not usually explain what this will look like in practice. The political situation in the Muslim world likely frustrated Albānī as well as his critics, and many resorted to a focus on ḥadīth, law, and rituals rather than politics, jihad, and social justice. As Albānī was a quietist, for whom political involvement in any shape or form is prohibited, many questioned the effectiveness of his brand of Salafism.

[85] See Muqbil al-Wādi'ī, Response to question on his leaning toward Ibn Ḥazm's teachings, www.muqbel.net/fatwa.php?fatwa_id=4463, last accessed May 1, 2020.

[86] Muqbil Al-Wādi'ī, *Ijābat al-Sā'il 'alā Aham al-Māsā'il* (Cairo: Dār al-Ḥaramayn, 1999), 562.

2

A Controversial Salafi

FROM A YOUNG AGE, ALBĀNĪ REJECTED ANY KIND OF institutionalization of Islam. He broke with his father and the Albanian community in Syria by refusing to follow the Ḥanafī *madhhab.* The assumed logical progression is that Albānī, as part of an ethnic minority in Syria, would have adhered to the societal norms and expectations of his family. However, his clash with his father and the Ḥanafīs in Syria was so serious that it resulted in his father asking him to either conform to the community's religious norms or leave their home, and Albānī chose the latter. Although Albānī and his father quarreled over the *madhhab*s, there are likely other factors that contributed to their bitter relationship.

One might have imagined that Albānī would have found himself fitting into relatively conservative Saudi Arabia, but even there he rejected the Wahhabism, Ḥanbalism, and the religious culture of the region. In Jordan, he took issue with the Muslim Brotherhood because they were what he called a political party (*ḥizb*). He was a nonconformist who wanted to follow a version of Islam that was not loyal to individuals or institutions but only to God and the Messenger. Albānī built his popularity outside of formal institutions and structures and by suggesting that other versions of Islam were corrupted.

His religious convictions, even when they were unconventional, were so strong that he was not afraid to challenge his family, the Albanian community, or the consensus of Muslim scholars. He questioned what others considered long-standing and established teachings of Islam. It was both his conviction and questioning of tradition that determined individuals' responses to him. This made him an appealing and charismatic leader, while his questioning of tradition caused his opponents to view him as a pretentious scholar.

ALBĀNĪ'S FORMATIVE YEARS

Albānī was born in the city of Shkoder, Albania in 1914. Two years prior to his birth, Albania became independent from Ottoman rule. In 1925, Ahmet Zogu (d. 1961) became the country's ruler and sought to make Albania a secular nation.[1] Albānī's father refused to live in a country that had secular values and chose to leave Albania. He moved with his family to Damascus, Syria. By 1920 Syria was under a French mandate and Albānī grew up in a country that was impacted by colonization. After Albānī completed his elementary education in a private school run by the Charitable Relief Organization (*jamʿīyat al-isʿāf al-khayrī*), his father did not enroll him in the public-school system because he disliked their poor religious education. Albānī started studying Ḥanafī jurisprudence with his father and joined the family business of repairing watches.

In post-Ottoman Syria, Muslims manifested a strong loyalty to the *madhhab*s, particularly to the Ḥanafī school. Several scholars observed this, some of whom were themselves Ḥanafīs. For example, the Ottoman judge and legal scholar ʿAlī Ḥaydar (d. 1935) states that in the latter part of the Ottoman period, Ḥanafī scholars were unwilling to include opinions of anyone other than the Ḥanafīs while compiling the *Majalla*, a systematic codification of Islamic law.[2] Muḥammad ʿAbd al-Ḥayy al-Laknāwī (d. 1304/1886) also complained that many followers of the Ḥanafī *madhhab* were becoming too rigid in their adherence to the school.[3] Albānī grew up in a religious atmosphere that had a strict adherence to the Ḥanafī school.[4] His father was regarded among the Albanians in Syria as among the most knowledgeable Ḥanafī scholars. Albānī spent his free time reading books in his father's shop. When the two were in the shop, they would have tense discussions on whether one should follow the Ḥanafī *madhhab* or ḥadīth. When he was asked by his

[1] Ahmet Zogu was the president of Albania from 1925 to 1928. In 1928, he declared himself king of Albania, he also abandoned his Turkic name Ahmet and the 'u' from Zogu. He crowned himself as Zog I, King of the Albanians and remained in power until 1939. See Miranda Vickers, *The Albanians: A Modern History* (London: I. B. Tauris, 1995), 117–125; William Miller, *The Ottoman Empire and Its Successors, 1801–1927* (New York: Frank Cass, 1966), 561.

[2] See ʿAlī Ḥaydar, *Durrar al-Ḥukkām Sharḥ Majallat al-Aḥkām* (Riyadh: Dār ʿĀlam al-Kutub, 2003), 9–15. On the Ḥanafization of Sharia courts in the nineteenth and twentieth centuries, see Kenneth M. Cuno, *Modernizing Marriage: Family, Ideology, and Law in Nineteenth- and Early Twentieth-Century Egypt* (Syracuse, NY: Syracuse University Press, 2015), 123–128.

[3] Muḥammad ʿAbd al-Ḥayy al-Laknāwī, *Al-Fawāʾid al-Bahīyya fī Tarājum al-Ḥanafiyya* (Beirut: Dār al-Maʿrifa, 1975), 1–10.

[4] See E. Hamdeh, "Formative Years."

student Abū Isḥāq al-Ḥuwaynī if this was considered a form of disobedience, Albānī responded: "I do not think any practicing Muslim would consider this disobedience; if that were the case, Abraham, peace be upon him, would have also been considered disobedient. You could say that concerns disbelief (*kufr*) and the Oneness of God (*tawḥīd*). I would reply: Yes, but here it is Sunna and *taqlīd*."[5]

Although *taqlīd* and *shirk* are very distinct from one another, Albānī did not want to compromise on what he thought was true. He may have chosen to learn on his own because he was dissatisfied and turned off by the rigid Ḥanafism and Sufi practices in Syria at the time. This prompted him to search for an unadulterated version of Islam, one that was uncontaminated, free from superstitions, cultural practices, and nonproof-text legal opinions. Albānī compensated for his lack of a formal Islamic schooling by studying on his own, mainly in the Ẓāhiriyya library in Damascus, to which he was ultimately offered his own key. In his capacity as a scholar and a religious leader Albānī tried to purge Islamic tradition both at the scholarly level and as well as among the general Muslim masses. A prolific scholar, he authored 217 books on various topics such as ḥadīth, *fiqh*, and creed.

His interest in Islamic studies started when he encountered Rashīd Riḍā's article in the *Manār* journal in which he mentioned one of Zayn al-Dīn al-ʿIrāqī's books where he attempted to purge Abū Ḥāmid al-Ghazālī's *Iḥyāʾ ʿUlūm al-Dīn* of its weak ḥadīth. Albānī was inspired by Riḍā's willingness to challenge tradition, particularly the work of a well-known scholar like Ghazālī. ʿIrāqī's book prompted Albānī to suspect that foreign teachings had entered Islam through weak ḥadīth and Sufism. He devoted himself to the study of ḥadīth in an attempt to purge Islam and its sciences of all impurities. His opposition to the *madhhab*s emerged when he was a teenager and it created tension with his father and with the predominantly Ḥanafī Albanian community in Syria. He criticized the rigid and uncritical adherence to the Ḥanafī school. Ultimately, his father told him to move out of their home because he could not tolerate his son's nonconformity with the Ḥanafī *madhhab*. Other major Salafi figures view Albānī's conflict with his father in a positive light. In spite of all odds, they admire his commitment to Salafism. Muqbil al-Wādiʿī was proud of the opposition he faced from his family and local Zaydi community. While Albānī compared himself to Abraham or might have seen himself as an Ibn Taymiyya or Aḥmad

[5] Muḥammad Nāṣir al-Dīn al-Albānī, "Sīrat al-Imām al-Albānī 1," lecture from www.alalbany.net/?p=4654, last accessed May 28, 2018. Also see E. Hamdeh, "Formative Years."

b. Ḥanbal (d. 241/855) type, al-Wādiʿī compared himself to Albānī who defied his father.[6]

As a poor Albanian immigrant residing in Syria, Albānī was of low social status, and in terms of power or wealth he had little chance of advancing. This may have played a part in his selecting the route of religious reformer. When he began delivering weekly lessons throughout Syria in the 1950s, his reputation as a scholar and reformer began. Albānī was not only attempting to reform Islam among scholars, but he was also an activist. He did not limit himself to writing books, but also traveled all over Syria to deliver lectures and sermons in an attempt to call people back to the Qurʾān and Sunna. He traveled from city to city, condemning what he considered heresies and innovations. Since Syria's Muslim population was predominantly Ḥanafī, Albānī made it a point to summon the Syrian Ḥanafī scholars to reexamine the rulings of their school which were not based on authentic ḥadīth.[7] Although he distanced himself from politics, Albānī's popularity began to worry the Syrian government and he was placed under surveillance.[8]

His works and his scholarly activism caused his popularity to swiftly grow as one of the world's foremost Salafi leaders and reformers. His friend Zuhayr Shāwīsh (d. 2013), a Damascene Salafi, began publishing Albānī's books with al-Maktab al-Islāmī and they quickly became very popular. Albānī was invited to teach at the Islamic University of Medina and he accepted the invitation as a means to escape his troubles with the Syrian government. His name was suggested by his good friend ʿAbd al-ʿAzīz b. Bāz,[9] a blind scholar who was then the vice president of the university. Ibn Bāz had close personal and intellectual ties to Albānī and shared his interest in the reexamination of ḥadīth. Upon arriving at the university, Albānī's views quickly stirred controversy and his career lasted for a short period of three years, from 1961 to 1963, after which he was expelled from Saudi Arabia. Albānī had tremendous love and respect for the University of

[6] Muqbil al-Wādiʿī, *Tarjamat Abī ʿAbd al-Raḥmān Muqbil b. Hādī al-Wādiʿī* (Sanaʿa: Maktabat al-Athariyya, 1999), 12. Also see Laurent Bonnefoy, *Salafism in Yemen: Transnationalism and Religious Identity* (New York: Columbia University Press, 2011), 55.

[7] On Abū Ḥanīfa's use of ḥadīth as a source of law, see Sahiron Syamsuddin, "Abū Ḥanīfah's Use of the Solitary Ḥadīth as a Source of Islamic Law," *Islamic Studies*, 40, no. 2 (2001), 257–272. Syamsuddin explains that the notion that Abū Ḥanīfa paid little attention to solitary ḥadīth is incorrect. Rather, he rejected many ḥadīth on the grounds that they did not meet his criteria of authenticity.

[8] ʿAwda ʿAṭiyya, *Ṣafaḥāt Bayḍāʾ min Ḥayāt al-Imām Muḥammad Nāṣir al-Dīn al-Albānī* (Al-Sanaʿa: Maktaba al-Islāmiyya, 2001), 37–38.

[9] Ibn Bāz was a renowned Saudi Arabian scholar; he was the Grand Mufti of Saudi Arabia from 1993 until his death in 1999.

Medina; when he died, he chose to donate his personal library to the University of Medina and not to any of his students.[10]

After leaving the University of Medina and returning to Syria, Albānī's popularity began to worry the Syrian government and he was arrested in 1967. Among the summary of accusations with which he was charged was promoting a Wahhabi ideology that distorted Islam and confused Muslims.[11] After his release, he was invited to head the graduate division of the faculty of Sharia in Mecca by Ibn Bāz, but the move failed due to opposition from Saudi authorities, which indicates that he was still a controversial figure in Saudi Arabia. Albānī was imprisoned again a few years later in Syria for eight months and then moved to Jordan in 1979.[12]

After the Jordanian regime allowed him to reside permanently in Jordan in the early 1980s, Albānī's outlook and vision of Salafism finally matured into a consistent form. Many young men began flocking around Albānī calling themselves students of Islamic sciences (*ṭalabat al-ʿilm al-sharʿī*).[13] Albānī's arrival in Jordan precipitated an explosion in Salafi activism. Because Albānī was one of only a handful of well-known Muslim scholars in Jordan at the time, he became a natural focal point for young students and the number of Salafis increased dramatically.[14] The most notable representatives of this group amongst Albānī's students included Muḥammad Ibrāhīm Shaqra, ʿAlī al-Ḥalabī (d. 2020), Salīm al-Hilālī, and Muḥammad Mūsā Nāṣir. They then established the Imām Al-Albānī Center in Amman, Jordan. Later, Albānī would spend most of his time writing from the publication house of his then friend, Zuhayr al-Shāwīsh, before their relationship soured.[15]

He was able to write a significant number of books while he worked for the publishing house.[16] Albānī lived in Amman for nearly two decades. During that time, he worked on writing books mostly linked to his two

[10] On the Islamic University of Medina see Michael Farquhar, *Circuits of Faith: Migration, Education, and the Wahhabi Mission* (Stanford, CA: Stanford University Press, 2016).

[11] Mohammad Abu Rumman and Hassan Abu Hanieh, *Conservative Salafism: A Strategy for the "Islamization of Society" and an Ambiguous Relationship with the State* (Amman: Friedrich-Ebert-Stiftung, 2010), 43.

[12] S. Lacroix, *Awakening*, 85. [13] M. Abu Rumman and H. Abu Hanieh, *Conservative*, 45.

[14] Quintan Wiktorowicz, *The Management of Islamic Activism: Salafis, the Muslim Brotherhood, and the State Power in Jordan* (Albany, NY: SUNY Press, 2000), 121.

[15] The relationship between Albānī and Shawīsh soured when Albānī discovered that Shawīsh was stealing and tampering with some of his books. See Albānī's long discussion on Shāwīsh in Taqī al-Dīn Ibn Taymiyya, *Al-Kalim al-Ṭayyib ed. Muḥammad Nāṣir al-Dīn al-Albānī* (Riyadh: Maktabat al-Maʿārif, 2001), 4–42.

[16] M. Abu Rumman and H. Abu Hanieh, *Conservative*, 45–46.

initiatives of *al-Taṣfiya wa l-tarbiya* (Purity and Education) and *Taqrīb al-Sunna bayna yaday al-umma* (Bringing the Sunna Nearer to the Community). While in Jordan, Albānī gave lessons from his home because he was not allowed to teach in mosques or publicly. Despite the ban on where he could teach the number of his followers and students gradually and consistently increased.[17]

In 1999 the Salafi world mourned the deaths of two leading Salafi scholars, Ibn Bāz and Albānī. That same year the King Faisal Prize for Islamic Studies was awarded to Albānī. He received this award despite being kicked out of Saudi Arabia more than thirty years earlier. This might be due to the fact that in his formative years, it was unclear who Albānī would become. He was very controversial, iconoclastic, and callous with those he disagreed with. But his contributions to the field of Islamic studies became evident during the latter portion of his life. At many levels, he became far more influential than other reformers because he reached average, ordinary, everyday people, giving himself a much more comprehensive audience.

Albānī became very sick during the last three years of his life. He died on October 2, 1999, at approximately 4:30 p.m. He was buried in a small private family graveyard near his home. He advised that he be buried as soon as possible and his friends and relatives who were far away should not be informed until after he was buried in order that they did not delay his burial since the Sunna instructs the deceased to be buried as soon as possible. According to ʿAwda, there were approximately 5,000 people at his funeral.[18] Throughout his life, Albānī married four times and left behind thirteen children, seven males and six females. Albānī states: "And from God's guidance upon me is that He inspired me to name all of my sons as servants to Him[19] . . . then I was blessed with a son in 1383/1963 when I was in Medina and I named him Muḥammad in remembrance of [the Prophet's] city."[20]

17 Wiktorowicz notes that in his first lesson in Jordan, Albānī delivered an unadvertised lecture on the roof of a house that attracted approximately 500 people who filled the surrounding streets. See Q. Wiktorowicz, *Management*, 121.

18 A. ʿAwda, *Ṣafaḥāt*, 97–101.

19 Their names from oldest to youngest, from his first wife: ʿAbd al-Raḥmān, ʿAbd al-Laṭīf, ʿAbd al-Razzāq. From his second wife: Anīsa, ʿAbd al-Maṣūr, Āsīya, Salāma, ʿAbd al-Aʿlā, Muḥammad, ʿAbd al-Muhaymin, Ḥassāna, Sakīna. From his third wife he had one daughter named Hibat Allāh. He had no offspring from his fourth wife. See A. ʿAwda, *Ṣafaḥāt*, 46–47.

20 A. ʿAwda, *Ṣafaḥāt*, 46–47.

CLASHING WITH SAUDI SALAFIS AT THE UNIVERSITY OF MEDINA

The controversies in Albānī's life were not restricted to his father or Ḥanafī scholars in Syria. He took his iconoclasm with him everywhere he went even to relatively conservative countries like Saudi Arabia. Because of his experiences in Medina, his relationship with Saudi Traditional Salafis who followed the Ḥanbalī *madhhab* changed. He was dissatisfied with Traditionalism right from the outset and refused to join the Saudi Traditional Salafi hierarchy because he was committed to the truth rather than the Salafiyya, *madhhab*s, or any particular individual. Upon arrival at the University of Medina, it soon became apparent that Albānī was not a traditional Wahhabi. Albānī denounced Wahhabis' connection to the existing Ḥanbalī school and condemned them for restricting themselves to a *madhhab*'s interpretive methodology. Albānī made several statements about Muḥammad Ibn ʿAbd al-Wahhāb that stirred controversy. These include accusing Abd al-Wahhāb of being a Salafi in creed but not in law, and of not being well versed in the science of ḥadīth because one of his books contains several notoriously weak ḥadīth. Although Albānī was critical of Wahhabism, he found the Saudi religious context to be much more open to embracing purist Salafism, particularly at the University of Medina.[21]

At that time, the University of Medina was still under the leadership of Ḥanbalī scholars, led by mufti Muḥammad b. Ibrāhīm Āl al-Shaykh (d. 1969). Several Saudi scholars responded to Albānī, the most critical of them being Ismāʿīl al-Anṣārī (d. 1997) the student of Abū Ghudda. When Albānī was at the University of Medina, the institution's scholars were offended by his religious verdicts. The mufti, Muḥammad b. Ibrāhīm, refusing to lower himself to a person he still considered a second-tier scholar, delegated the task of refuting Albānī to Ismāʿīl al-Anṣārī who was one of his chief assistants.[22] Anṣārī wrote several book-length responses to Albānī in defense of Muḥammad ʿAbd al-Wahhāb, the permissibility of circular gold for women, and the number of units in the *tarāwīḥ* prayers.[23]

Along with his remarks on Ibn ʿAbd al-Wahhāb, Albānī's fatwas angered Saudi scholars on several fronts, such as his ban on females wearing gold and

[21] E. Hamdeh, "Formative Years," 429.

[22] Stéphane Lacroix, "Between Revolution and Apoliticism: Nasir al-Din al-Albani and His Impact on the Shaping of Contemporary Salafism," in *Global Salafism*, ed. Roel Meijer (New York: Columbia University Press, 2009), 66.

[23] See I. al-Anṣārī, *Ibāḥat*; idem, *Al-Intiṣār*; idem, *Taṣḥīḥ*.

his opinion that the face veil was not compulsory.[24] His call to *ijtihād* outside the framework of the established schools of law compromised the authority of the Wahhabi scholars in the university. Lacroix notes:

> But these ulema were in an awkward position because Wahhabism had been characterized from its inception by an ambivalence between the theoretical aspiration to fulfill the duty of *ijtihad* – an inspiration that al-Albani did not hesitate to take advantage of – and juridical practice that represented a continuation of the Hanbali school. Moreover, al-Albani's religious authority was difficult to challenge because his conception of the creed was impeccably Wahhabi.[25]

The use of the word *ijtihād* by Lacroix is centered on the understanding that *ijtihād* can only occur when fully independent of a *madhhab* (*mujtahid muṭlaq*). The notion that there is ambivalence between the aspiration to fulfill the duty of *ijtihād* and legal practice that represented the continuation of the *madhhab* is not accurate. There is no conflict between the two because it is possible to perform *ijtihād* while simultaneously adhering to a *madhhab.* Furthermore, it is not possible to ascertain that Wahhabism promoted *ijtihād* outside of the framework of *madhhab*, especially keeping in mind that Ibn ʿAbd al-Wahhāb himself was a Ḥanbalī.[26] Rather, purist Salafis like Albānī, and not Wahhabis, were the primary group that encouraged bypassing the *madhhab*s by going directly to the Qurʾān and Sunna.

Albānī was becoming very popular and the scholars of Saudi Arabia were forced to wait for him to make a serious mistake before they could get rid of him. Albānī was finally dismissed from his teaching responsibilities after producing a controversial fatwa arguing that women were not required to wear face veils, something which was unacceptable in all Saudi religious circles.[27] Biographies of Albānī written by his admirers do not present these controversial aspects of Albānī's time in the University of Medina and collectively highlight the envy of fellow professors as the cause of Albānī's dismissal from the university. According to his biographers, Albānī had such a great relationship with the students that it caused other professors to be envious of him.[28] His popularity among students might have caused envy

[24] S. Lacroix, "Between Revolution," 67. [25] S. Lacroix, *Awakening*, 84.

[26] N. DeLong-Bas, *Wahhabi Islam*, 110. Although Ibn ʿAbd al-Wahhāb never directly claimed to be a Ḥanbalī, his legal methodology is consistent with the Ḥanbalī school.

[27] S. Lacroix, "Between Revolution," 65–66.

[28] See A. ʿAwda, *Ṣafaḥāt*, 40–42. Also see Muḥammad al-Shaybānī, *Ḥayāt al-Albānī wa-Āthāru-hu wa Thanāʾ al-ʿUlamāʾ ʿalay-hi* (Cairo: Maktabat al-Sarrāwī, 1986), 60.

and led to his dismissal, but it is more likely that it was due to his iconoclasm and controversial opinions.

Suhaib Hasan was one of eighteen Pakistani students who joined the university in 1962 and spent two years studying with Albānī. He explained that Albānī's Salafi movement was gaining popularity in the Arab world and it was in constant conflict with Traditionalists, who were usually very strict Ḥanafīs or Shāfiʿīs and therefore spoke ill of Albānī. They disliked hearing his name not only because of his skill in ḥadīth, but also because of his disparaging their scholarship. Hasan notes that Albānī gained fame because of his sharp criticism of those who performed *taqlīd* of one imam or *madhhab*, which at the time was the case with most Saudi Arabia scholars. Since they were all Salafi it was not an issue of creed, but a question of his attitude toward *fiqh*.[29]

IMPACT ON THE SAUDI RELIGIOUS LANDSCAPE

Although Albānī spent only a short amount of time at the University of Medina, he left a strong impact on the Saudi religious landscape. On one hand, most Saudi religious scholars dismissed Albānī, with the exception of Ibn Bāz – who ultimately outranked all of them. Yet he had a profound impact on the Saudi religious scene at the popular level and with students who would go on to lead many religious establishments. His ideas revived great interest in the reexamination of ḥadīth which in turn influenced all other fields of religious knowledge. Yūsuf al-Daynī, a former student of Albānī, explains:

> It had become a quasi-dictatorship of hadith. When a sheikh quoted a hadith in a sermon or a lecture, he could be interrupted any time by one of his students asking him: "Has this hadith been authenticated? Has al-Albani verified it?" That could not help but strengthen the antipathy the ulema of the religious establishment felt toward al-Albani.[30]

This depicts a social situation in which the harshness and rudeness of differences of opinion (*ikhtilāf*) are evident. In the social context, Albānī and his students had particular practices that distinguished them from others. Most of these practices were based on the fatwas of Albānī that were contrary to the Wahhabi-Ḥanbalī consensus.[31] For example, they followed

[29] Suhaib Hasan, Interview by author. Phone interview. London, August 26, 2013. Hereafter "Interview by author."

[30] S. Lacroix, *Awakening*, 85.

[31] S. Lacroix, *Awakening*, 85.

the rulings in a book about prayer published by Albānī, titled *Ṣifat Ṣalāt al-Nabī* (*The Characteristics of the Prophet's Prayer*). In this work, Albānī allowed Muslims to wear shoes while praying inside mosques and pointed that the correct position of the hands in prayer was different from what had been suggested by Ḥanbalī jurisprudence for centuries. Albānī's promotion of different positions for the hands in prayer became a serious concern for Saudi scholars. This is illustrated by the mind-numbing volume of fatwas by Saudi scholars on this topic. Albānī's followers also considered the *miḥrāb*[32] to be a reprehensible innovation and eventually built their own mosques that did not contain them. Due to the conspicuousness of these ritual distinctions, Albānī's students provoked controversy and disputes in the mosques in Medina and throughout Saudi Arabia.

Some of Albānī's zealous students started to destroy posters or portraits of human beings because Albānī considered them to be against Islamic law. This led to clashes with the locals of Medina. In 1965, after an attack on a shop displaying woman mannequins, the police cracked down on these students. This incident gave those who were contemplating to initiate an organization a decisive reasoning, and thus created a group called *al-Jamā'at al-Salafiyyat al-Muḥtasiba.*[33]

In the mid-1960s *Al-Jamā'a al-Salafiyyat al-Muḥtasiba* was formed and from it emerged the Juhaymān movement which was led by Juhaymān b. 'Utaybī (d. 1980). On November 20, 1979, the Juhaymān group stormed and seized control of the great mosque in Mecca, the most sacred place in Islam.[34] The goal of the Juhaymān group was to have one of its members, Muhammad al-Qaḥṭānī (d. 1979) consecrated as the Mahdi between the black stone corner of the *Ka'ba* (*al-rukn al-aswad*) and Ibrahim's station of prayer (*al-maqām*) as the ḥadīth on the Mahdi require.[35] The militants barricaded themselves in the compound, taking thousands of worshippers hostage and awaiting the approach of a hostile army from the north, as promised by the eschatological traditions.[36]

32 A *miḥrāb* is a niche in the wall of a mosque that indicates the direction of the *qibla.*

33 S. Lacroix, *Awakening*, 89–90.

34 For a thorough study on the takeover of the Grand Mosque and the Juhaymān movement, see Thomas Hegghammer and Stéphane Lacroix, "Rejectionist Islamism in Saudi Arabia: The Story of Juhayman al-'Utaybi Revisited," *International Journal of Middle East Studies*, 39, no. 1 (2007), 103–122. Also see Thomas Hegghammer and Stéphane Lacroix, *The Meccan Rebellion: The Story of Juhayman al-'Utaybi Revisited* (Bristol: Amal Press, 2011).

35 See Sulaymān b. al-Ash'ath Abū Dāwūd (d. 275/889), *Sunan Abī Dāwūd* (Damascus: Dār al-Risāla al-'Ālamīya, 2009), *Sunan, Mahdī* v. 6, no. 4286.

36 See Abū Dāwūd, *Sunan, Mahdī* v. 6, no. 4286.

To his misfortune, authorities in Saudi Arabia accused Albānī of being the primary mastermind behind the Juhaymān movement and he was subsequently denied entry into Saudi Arabia thereafter.[37] However, owing to his good friend Ibn Bāz's petition, this ban was quickly removed.[38] The ban was also lifted because of the inaccuracy of the accusation. The charge against Albānī as being the mastermind behind the group is really a stretch especially keeping in mind that Juhaymān went into hiding for almost two years before the incident, with little communication with the outside world.[39] Furthermore, Albānī left Medina around 1963, Juhaymān stormed the Meccan sanctuary in 1979, and never directly studied under Albānī. Juhaymān may have attended some of Albānī's, Ibn Bāz's, and other major Salafi scholars' lessons, and this definitely influenced some of his opinions on creed, *fiqh*, and ḥadīth as it did for many Salafis. Nevertheless, it is incorrect to say that Albānī was the mastermind or the primary influence behind Juhaymān's takeover, particularly considering that Albānī was a quietist.

THE MUSLIM BROTHERHOOD

There was a powerful presence of the Muslim Brotherhood in both Syria and Jordan. Albānī was regularly interacting with members of the movement. Due to their overparticipation in politics, Albānī had a particular problem with the Muslim Brotherhood. The Muslim Brotherhood started to settle itself in Syria in the 1930s. Albānī had close relations with the Muslim Brotherhood's Salafis in his early career, but he participated in debates with a number of Muslim Brotherhood leaders in Syria, such as the Ḥanafī Abd al-Fattāḥ Abū Ghudda in Aleppo.[40] He also published in *al-Tamaddun al-Islāmī* with members of the Muslim Brotherhood.

In the 1980s, Albānī moved to Jordan where there was a large presence among the Muslim Brotherhood, and he remained critical of their

37 M. Abu Rumman and H. Abu Hanieh, *Conservative*, 44.

38 The influence and authority that Ibn Bāz and other leading Salafi scholars held is quite interesting. This may be due to the fact that officially recognized scholars in Saudi Arabia preached a strong obedience to the ruler. Hence, when Ibn Bāz took a stance, it was in the interest of the Saudi regime to comply with his religious verdicts and requests. Furthermore, although Salafis preach against *taqlīd*, one finds that Salafi authorities such as Ibn Bāz, Albānī, and Ibn ʿUthaymīn are rarely questioned or challenged. Indeed, the Salafi movement has great respect for its authorities, and the opinions of Albānī, Ibn Bāz, and Ibn ʿUthaymīn are taken very seriously.

39 T. Hegghammer and S. Lacroix, "Rejectionist," 110.

40 M. Abu Rumman and H. Abu Hanieh, *Conservative*, 43.

participation in politics. His quietist position, which is also the position of officially recognized scholars of Saudi Arabia, maintains that all types of political organization, let alone violence, are banned because they can lead to internal conflicts among Muslims. Obedience to Muslim rulers, even the unjust among them, is a religious obligation.[41] Albānī was therefore also a powerful opponent of the Muslim Brotherhood because he thought they were more involved in politics than in religious knowledge. Albānī insisted that his priorities were different and stated that part of politics is to stay out of politics (*min al-siyāsa tark al-siyāsa*).[42] This is ironically similar to some Sufis who explain that one must change one's heart then everything else will change. He fails to explain how implementing rituals at the individual level will lead to societal change. Focusing on religion and legislation by Albānī led his detractors to question how he wants to bring about true change. He believes that everything else will come into place after certain theological beliefs and practices have been prioritized. He makes an implicit reference to the Muslim Brotherhood in a speech he gave in Medina in 1977 and notes: "All Muslims acknowledge that an Islamic state needs to be established, but they vary on the technique to achieve that objective. I think that the source of their disagreements can only be removed by adhering to *tawḥīd*, so that they can march towards their goal in unified ranks."[43] This view does not take into account how a systematically corrupt political environment undermines the possibility of moral excellence among individual citizens. Purist Salafis as well as quietest Traditionalists are often criticized for being obsessed with aspects of ritual purity, like menstruation, while missing the more important matters such as political oppression.[44] Emin Poljarevic notes:

> The manhaj of "the saved" is centered on the *knowledge* of the "true" faith and the authentic practice of everyday rituals, which, in the case of pietists, lead to political seclusion and the avoidance of what is perceived as "public disorder." Nonetheless, the risks for those who choose pietism are still there and are often seen in the extent of the subsequent public and/or family ridicule/isolation.[45]

For purist Salafis, reform is achieved by teaching Muslims how to return to the Qurʾān and Sunna as embodied by the *salaf*. It is important to note that although purist Salafis are apolitical, they are not pacifist; they are

[41] B. Haykel, "Salafi Thought," 48–49. [42] S. Lacroix, "Between Revolution," 69.
[43] S. Lacroix, *Awakening*, 86–87. [44] B. Haykel, "Salafi Thought," 49.
[45] Emin Poljarevic, "The Power of Elective Affinities in Contemporary Salafism," *The Muslim World*, 106, no. 3 (2016), 496.

obedient-minded people who are willing to take up arms if ordered to do so by the leader.[46] The purist Salafi position emphasizes that any political action will lead to corruption unless and until religious theology and practice is purified.

Albānī's relationship with the Muslim Brotherhood soured in the mid-1960s and early 1970s. In 1966, Sayyid Quṭb was executed on Gamal Abdel Nasser's (d. 1970) orders. When Muslim leaders from all different tendencies, as well as Salafi leaders like Ibn Bāz, were paying homage to Quṭb's martyrdom, Albānī was one of the few who used this opportunity to openly criticize Quṭb. He attacked Quṭb for what Albānī perceived to be signs of the doctrine of oneness of being (*waḥdat al-wujūd*). Albānī also criticized the founder of the Muslim Brotherhood, Ḥasan al-Bannā (d. 1949), stating that his religious teachings contradicted the Sunna. Albānī's students took his positions and formed them into much more systematic attacks against the Muslim Brotherhood.[47] As a result, in the 1970s leaders of the Muslim Brotherhood warned their followers off from reading Albānī's works or attending his lectures and called for a boycott of everything associated with him.

By the 1980s, Albānī's stance was no longer tenable; he tried to temper his positions and make himself appear more moderate. He said, for example, that while it was essential to refute Quṭb, it must be done without demonstrating hostility toward him or disregarding his virtues. After all, Albānī says, Quṭb was murdered for calling to Islam, while those who killed him are the enemies of God. When pressed by a questioner about Sayyid Quṭb's "heretical" beliefs, Albānī attempted to end the discussion. He limited himself to saying that Quṭb was not a scholar; rather, he was a writer who wrote about Islam according to his own understanding. The inquirer kept pressing Albānī with questions about certain phrases Quṭb wrote that might be blasphemous. Albānī angrily responded by saying: "Our opinion is that he was a man who was not a scholar and the matter is over! What more do you want?! If you are hoping that I excommunicate him, then I am not from those who excommunicate."[48] Interestingly, although Albānī was living among students who were very hostile toward those who they disagreed with, Albānī refused to excommunicate Quṭb and other Muslims. Like the questioner above, Albānī was pressured by many of his students to excommunicate others, but he refused. After Albānī criticized Quṭb he

[46] B. Haykel, "Salafi Thought," 49. [47] S. Lacroix, *Awakening*, 86–87.

[48] Muḥammad Nāṣir al-Dīn al-Albānī, "Kalimat ḥaq wa Inṣāf fī Muʾalifāt Sayyid Quṭb Raḥimahu Allāh," lecture from www.islamway.com, last accessed December 25, 2011.

realized how powerful and influential his statements were and he became more cautious. In 1982, the Muslim Brotherhood in Jordan pushed the government to exile Albānī. One of Albānī's students had close relations with some policy makers and was able to reverse the decision. Albānī was permitted to remain in Jordan on the condition that he would no longer teach in public.[49]

TRADITIONALIST DETRACTORS OF SALAFISM

Traditionalists across the Muslim world found the need to respond to Albānī's anti-*madhhab* rhetoric, not only because of his unconventional positions, but because the manner in which he conveyed them. It is important to keep this in mind when discussing the relationship among Albānī and Traditionalists. The dispute between them was not a debate between scholars in ivory towers, but they had an audience of religious Muslims closely following their disputations. Either Albānī or his opponents would clarify on several occasions that the other party is not worth reacting to, but that they only do it so that the untrained readers are not deceived into believing them. Traditionalists believe that the classical institutions of the schools of law, theology, and Sufi guilds offer the only correct path for understanding Islam.[50] They recoiled at Albānī's influential and barbed criticisms of the *madhhabs*, broad rejection of Sufism, and controversial legal rulings.[51]

Traditionalists throughout the Muslim world responded to the critiques made by Albānī and other purist Salafis. The Syrian scholar Abd al-Fattāḥ Abū Ghudda was one of the greatest critics of Albānī. Similar to Albānī, Abū Ghudda was regarded as one of the twentieth century's greatest ḥadīth scholars.[52] Abū Ghudda was the student of many influential Traditionalists such as Muṣṭafā Ṣabrī (d. 1954), who was the last Shaykh al-Islam of the Ottoman Empire.[53] He was most renowned as the most devoted student of Muhammad Zāhid al-Kawtharī (d. 1951), who served as an adjunct to Muṣṭafā Ṣabrī. Therefore, Abū Ghudda experienced first-hand the frustration of decline of the authority of traditional *'ulamā'*. Kawtharī was a

[49] M. Abu Rumman and H. Abu Hanieh, *Conservative*, 56.

[50] J. Brown, *Canonization*, 305.

[51] J. Brown, *Canonization*, 324–325.

[52] A few of Abū Ghudda's students have written biographies of him. Muḥammad Hāshimī, *Al-Shaykh 'Abd al-Fattāḥ Abū Ghudda Kamā 'Araftuh* (Beirut: Dār al-Bashaī'r al-Islāmīya, 2004); Maḥmūd Mamdūḥ, *Al-Shadhā al-Fawwā Min Akhbār al-Shaykh 'Abd al-Fattāḥ Abū Ghudda, 1337–1418 H* (Cairo: Dār al-Baṣā'ir, 2009); M. Āl Rashīd, *Imdād*, 141–177.

[53] On Muṣṭafā Ṣabrī see Mona Hassan, *Longing for the Lost Caliphate: A Transregional History* (Princeton, NJ: Princeton University Press, 2017), 236–243.

strong advocate of the Ashʿarī and Ḥanafī schools, and was often regarded by Albānī and others as being a blind adherent to the Ḥanafī school.[54] While studying at al-Azhar, Abū Ghudda met Ḥasan al-Bannā, the founder of the Muslim Brotherhood.[55] Abū Ghudda left Syria after the Baʿth 1963 revolution for a lengthy exile in Saudi Arabia. He ultimately returned to Syria and reluctantly served as the Inspector General (*murāqib ʿām*) of the Muslim Brotherhood between 1976 and 1982. Abū Ghudda then returned to Saudi Arabia where he taught at King ʿAbd al-Azīz University in Jedda where he died and was buried in the city of Medina.[56]

The problems between Albānī and Abū Ghudda began when Abū Ghudda confronted Albānī for inserting the word "authentic" when citing ḥadīth from the *Ṣaḥīḥ*s of Bukhārī and Muslim. Inserting the term "authentic" implies that some of the ḥadīth in these two books are inauthentic. This resulted in a heated discussion between them in the presence of other scholars and their relationship fell apart.[57] While Abū Ghudda worked as a professor in Muḥammad b. Saʿūd University the administration asked his opinion about a version of the book *ʿAqīda al-Ṭaḥāwiyya* edited by Albānī. Abū Ghudda recommended an earlier edition that did not contain Albānī's comments. Abū Ghudda explains that after Albānī and his students discovered this, they insistently attacked him with many accusations. Abū Ghudda says that Albānī and his students knew his views on this for several years, but it was only when he did not suggest the book to the administration that they became hostile toward him.[58] Albānī says that Abū Ghudda never discussed the book with him and that on numerous occasions he tried to discuss this with Abū Ghudda, but the latter always refused.[59]

Albānī would then use the introductions of future editions of *Sharḥ al-ʿAqīda al-Ṭaḥāwiyya* to attack Abū Ghudda. It then spiraled into more accusations, with Albānī accusing Abū Ghudda of being a Kawtharite, anti-Ibn Taymiyya, and anti-Wahhabi only concealing his true beliefs in order to keep his position at the university. Abū Ghudda was invited to teach at the university by Muḥammad b. Ibrāhīm, the same man who had

[54] M. Āl Rashīd, *Imdād*, 154.

[55] M. Āl Rashīd, *Imdād*, 155. Abū Ghudda studied in al-Azhar from 1944 to 1950.

[56] For more on Abū Ghudda's conflicts with the Syrian regime, see Eyal Zisser, "Syria, the Baʿth Regime and the Islamic Movement: Stepping on a New Path?" *The Muslim World*, 95, no. 1 (2005), 52–53.

[57] A. Abū Ghudda, *Kalimāt*, 3.

[58] A. Abū Ghudda, *Kalimāt*, 1–3.

[59] Muḥammad Nāṣir al-Dīn al-Albānī, *Kashf al-Niqāb ʿAmmā fī Kalimāt Abī Ghudda min al-Abāṭīl wa l-Iftirāʾāt* (Damascus: n.p., 1978), 13–14.

discharged Albānī from his teaching position from the University of Medina. Abū Ghudda notes that although he was a student and admirer of Kawtharī, he did not agree with all of his views. Abū Ghudda also points out that while he was in prison in Syria, he wrote to a Ḥanafī scholar in India defending Ibn Taymiyya's status. He also published several works by Ibn Taymiyya and Ibn Qayyim, often referring to the former as Shaykh al-Islām.[60] Interestingly, Abū Ghudda was obliged to prove his "correct" beliefs by showing his loyalty and respect to figures whom Salafis hold in high esteem. It might be that Albānī was trying to get Abū Ghudda removed from the university by accusing him of hiding views that did not correspond to the predominant Wahhabi community at the time.[61]

In 1975 Albānī wrote a book titled *Kashf al-Niqāb ʿAmmā fī Kalimāt Abī Ghudda min al-Abāṭīl wa l-Iftirāʾāt* (*Removing the Veil from the Falsehood and Fabrications in Abū Ghudda's Words*), attacking Abū Ghudda for criticizing him and Salafis, yet refusing to have a discussion in person. Albānī's book is an excellent example of the emotionally charged debates that took place between Albānī and Traditionalists. Albānī attacked Abū Ghudda, calling him ignorant, an intentional liar, transgressor, and fabricator, an enemy of Ibn Taymiyya, Ibn Qayyim, Muḥammad b. ʿAbd al-Wahhāb, and even implied that Abū Ghudda was a spy. Albānī's attacks on Abū Ghudda were very personal. For instance, he despised Abū Ghudda to the extent that he made the supplication: *Ashal Allāhu yadaka wa qaṭaʿa lisānaka* ("May God paralyze your hand and cut off your tongue!").[62] Albānī also said to a group of his students: "In my view, the students of knowledge like yourselves know very well that Abū Ghudda is in relation to knowledge like the gland of a camel (*ghudda ka ghuddat al-baʿīr*). Do you know the gland? You know that he does not have a sound creed, neither does he have knowledge of the Qur'ān and Sunna."[63]

Abū Ghudda, who rarely mentioned Albānī by name, protested against Albānī for beginning a book about religious creed with insults. He also objected to how Albānī constantly refers to him as a Ḥanafī in a derogatory manner, "as though being a follower of Abū Ḥanīfa is something to be

[60] A. Abū Ghudda, *Kalimāt*, 11–12.

[61] Muḥammad Nāṣir al-Dīn al-Albānī, *Sharḥ al-ʿAqīda al-Ṭaḥāwiyya* (Beirut: Al-Maktab al-Islāmī, 1984), 45–56.

[62] N. Albānī, *Kashf*, 103.

[63] Audio clip of Muḥammad Nāṣir al-Dīn al-Albani, "Ṭāmāt wa Munkirāt al-Jahūl al-Albānī al-Wahhābī Muddaʿī al-Salafiyya Raḥima-hu Allāh," www.youtube.com/watch?v=yRpKoWWUECU&feature=player_embedded#, last accessed December 12, 2011.

ashamed of."[64] Despite Albānī's open criticism, Abū Ghudda did not immediately respond by publishing a work directly attacking Albānī. He states that he was compelled to publicize a book explicitly mentioning Albānī by name because he was accusing him of many different things. Abū Ghudda published a work titled *Kalimāt fī Kashf Abāṭīl wa Iftirāʿāt* (*Words About Uncovering Falsehood and Fabrications*).

This work was written in 1974 and did not mention Albānī or anyone else by name due to what Abū Ghudda referred to as "the etiquette in refutation."[65] The idiosyncrasies of scholarly character were important to Abū Ghudda, which is why he did not want to explicitly mention Albānī by name.[66] Initially, Abū Ghudda only gave this book to individuals who requested it in order to share his side of the story. However, when Abū Ghudda published the second edition in 1991 he did mention Albānī and Zuhayr al-Shawīsh by name.

Abū Ghudda also edited a refutation of Albānī by Muḥammad al-Nuʿmānī (d. 1999) titled *Makānat al-imām Abī Ḥanīfa fī l-ḥadīth* (*The Status of Imam Abū Ḥanīfa in ḥadīth*). This book was written in response to Albānī's opinion that Abū Ḥanīfa was not a great ḥadīth scholar. Nuʿmānī criticizes Albānī in this work, and perhaps Abū Ghudda chose to edit this book to refute the accusation against Abū Ḥanīfa. Many of Abū Ghudda's students also entered the debate and critiqued Albānī and purist Salafism.[67]

Because many of Albānī's critiques were against the Ḥanafī school, scholars from the Indian subcontinent felt the need to respond to him.[68] The Darul Uloom, sometimes referred to as the al-Azhar of the Indian subcontinent, is a Traditionalist institution that emphasizes the *madhhab*s and Sufism. Many scholars and students of Darul Uloom have heated

64 A. Abū Ghudda, *Kalimāt*, 11, 39.

65 ʿAbd al-Fattāḥ Abū Ghudda, *Jawāb al-Ḥāfiẓ Abī Muḥammad ʿAbd al-ʿAẓīm al-Mundhirī al-Miṣrī ʿAn Asʾilah fī l-Jarḥ wa l-Taʿdīl: wa-Yalīh Umarāʾ al-Muʾminīn fī al-Ḥadīth wa-Kalimāt fī Kashf Abāṭīl wa Iftirāʿāt* (Aleppo: Maktab al-Maṭbūʿāt al-Islāmīyah, 1990), 13.

66 Abū Ghudda did eventually write a few books where he directly mentions Albānī by name such as *Khuṭbat al-Ḥāja Laysat Sunna fī Mustahal al-Kutub wa l-Muʾallafāt* (Beirut: Dār al-Bashāʾir al-Islāmiyya, 2008). This work was written in response to Albānī's book titled *Khuṭbat al-Ḥāja* (*The Sermon of Need*) in which he had argued that all books should begin with the sermon of need, which is usually recited in the beginning of a sermon or lecture. See Muḥammad Nāṣir al-Dīn al-Albānī, *Khuṭbat al-Ḥāja* (Beirut: Al-Maktab al-Islāmī, 1979).

67 Muḥammad ʿAwwāma was one of Abū Ghudda's most dedicated students. He wrote two books that are highly circulated and valued in Traditionalists circles; see M. ʿAwwāma, *Adab*; idem, *Athar*.

68 On Abū Ghudda's relationship and role in introducing the works of Indian scholars to the Arab world see M. Āl Rashīd, *Imdād*, 155–158.

debates with the scholars from the *Ahl al-Ḥadīth* movement in the region, who are very similar to purist Salafis.[69] One such critic of Albānī was Ḥabīb al-Raḥmān al-Aʿẓamī (d. 1992), a famous Indian ḥadīth scholar.[70]

Albānī once praised Aʿẓamī, but similar to Abū Ghudda, after Aʿẓamī criticized Albānī their relationship became bitter. Aʿẓamī only has one book directly attacking Albānī, titled *al-Albānī Shudhūdhu-hu wa Akhṭāʾu-hu* (*Albānī's Anomalies and Errors*).[71] He first published this in 1984 under the pseudonym Arshad Salafi. Later Aʿẓamī published it under his own name after being convinced that it would give more credibility to the book. Prior to publishing the book under his actual name, Aʿẓamī visited Damascus and spent a few nights in Albānī's home. Albānī invited some of his students over in the hope that they would probe Aʿẓamī to discover if he was the author of the work. During a car ride from Damascus to Aleppo, Albānī's students questioned Aʿẓamī in an attempt to initiate a discussion. Aʿẓamī did not answer their questions and referred them to Albānī. After several attempts to end the discussion Aʿẓamī told them "I did not come here for research and debate."[72] At the time Aʿẓamī was old and sick and Albānī asked his students to refrain after he saw it was discomforting Aʿẓamī.[73]

On another occasion, Aʿẓamī stayed near the home of Zuhayr Shāwīsh. Albānī and some of his students visited al-Shāwīsh while Aʿẓamī was present. They started discussing a range of subjects, including *fiqh* issues in which the Ḥanafī *madhhab* contradicted the Sunna. A discussion developed on these issues between Albānī and Aʿẓamī; while Aʿẓamī was championing the Ḥanafī *madhhab*, Albānī was citing ḥadīth. A student disrupted and put an end to the discussion by saying: "We want nothing but the Sunna or what is equal to it. May God have mercy on the imams for saying: If the ḥadīth is authentic, then it is my *madhhab*."[74] Albānī later described Aʿẓamī: "One of the enemies of the Sunna, *Ahl al-Ḥadīth*, and the known callers to *tawḥīd* is no other than shaykh Ḥabīb al-Raḥmān

69 For an excellent work on the Deoband School and its rival Ahl al-Ḥadīth, see B. Metcalf, *Islamic Revival*.

70 Abū Ghudda obtained an *ijāza* from Aʿẓamī. He also gave an *ijāza* to a number of students in a school that was run by Aʿẓamī. See M. Āl Rashīd, *Imdād*, 217, 266.

71 This work generated a response from two of Albānī's students. See Salīm al-Hilalī and Ḥasan ʿAbd al-Ḥamīd, *Al-Radd al-ʿIlmī ʿAlā Ḥabīb al-Raḥmān al-Aʿẓamī al-Muddaʿī bi Ana-hu Arshad Salafī fī Raddi-hi ʿalā al-Albānī wa Bayān Iftirāʾu-hu ʿalya-hi* (Amman: Al-Maktaba al-Islāmiyya, 1983).

72 S. Hilalī and H. ʿAbd al-Ḥamīd, *Radd*, 1: 11.

73 S. Hilalī and H. ʿAbd al-Ḥamīd, *Radd*, 1: 11.

74 S. Hilalī and H. ʿAbd al-Ḥamīd, *Radd*, 1: 12–13.

al-Aʿẓamī who hid behind the name "Arshad Salafī" due to his cowardliness and lack of academic courage and manners."[75]

Many other scholars also attempted to refute Albānī. Two of Albānī's most persistent critics are Ḥasan b. ʿAlī al-Saqqāf and Maḥmūd Saʿīd Mamdūḥ, both of whom are followers of the Shāfiʿī legal school. Both were students of well-known ḥadīth experts and critics of Albānī such as the Moroccan brothers Aḥmad al-Ghumārī (d. 1961) and ʿAbd Allāh al-Ghumārī (d. 1993) and Abū Ghudda.[76] Aḥmad al-Ghumārī had a heated debate with Albānī and this later continued between his younger brother and Albānī. The debate became bitter and involved many character attacks.

Mamdūḥ wrote several books against Albānī, the most famous being his six-volume refutation of Albānī's ḥadīth methodology *Al-Taʿrīf bi-Awhām Man Qassama al-Sunan ilā Ṣaḥīḥ wa Ḍaʿīf* (*Making Known the Mistakes of the One Who Divided the Sunan into Authentic and Weak*).[77] Similarly, Saqqāf and Albānī had many heated debates. Albānī described him as "a liar, fabricator, *khalafī*,[78] Ashʿarī, Sufi. Every affliction can be found in him." The relationship between Saqqāf and Albānī was one full of insults and character attacks. Saqqāf's hatred for Albānī is so strong that whenever he mentions Albānī's name in some of his books, Albānī's name is always in smaller font compared to the rest of the text. This was intended to belittle and insult Albānī. Saqqāf compiled an entire book *Qāmūs Shatāʾim al-Albānī* (*Dictionary of Albānī's Slandering*) that highlights each instance in which Albānī spoke ill of other scholars.[79] He continually accused Albānī of trying to make himself appear as the greatest scholar of all time who outdid classical scholars. After pointing out some alleged contradictions in Albānī's works, Saqqāf states:

> We say and emphasize that anyone who claims this level of infallibility should not have more mistakes, errors, and contradictions than classical and contemporary scholars. In fact, he has hundreds of mistakes, actually he has even more than that . . . It is not allowed to depend on his editing, or

[75] Muḥammad Nāṣir al-Dīn al-Albānī, *Ādāb al-Zafāf fī l-Sunna al-Muṭahhara* (Amman: Al-Maktaba al-Islāmiyya, 1988), 8.

[76] M. Āl Rashīd, *Imdād*, 222.

[77] See M. Mamdūḥ, *Taʿrīf*; idem, *Tanbīh*; idem, *Wuṣūl*. For a Salafi response to Mamdūḥ's work see Ṭāriq ʿAwaḍ Allāh, *Radʿu al-Jānī al-Muʿtadī ʿalā al-Albānī* (Abū Dhabi: Maktabat al-Tarbiyaa al-Islāmiyya, 2009).

[78] *Khalafī* is one who follows later scholars, not the early Muslims. It is used as an accusation that the person is not on a proper and authentic understanding of Islam.

[79] H. Saqqāf, *Qāmūs*.

to be deceived by his authentication or weakening of ḥadīth. He blames scholars for things and then falls in it himself.[80]

Saqqāf's books against Albānī were clearly full of enmity and bias. In fact, most of the suggested contradictions are actually untrue. A more measured response against Albānī came from Muḥammad Ramaḍān al-Būṭī (d. 2013).[81] Būṭī was a Syrian Traditionalist and a staunch proponent of the four schools of laws, some Sufi practices, and Ashʿarī theology. He argued that *Salafiiyya* is not a school, but rather a time period. The *salaf* were not monolithic and never shared a single methodology. Rather, different methodologies existed such as that of *ahl al-ḥadīth* and *ahl al-raʾy*.[82]

It is important to keep in mind that when Albānī and Traditionalists adopted a specific position, wrote a book, or delivered a public speech, they usually did so with each other in mind. Therefore, a proper understanding of these two groups requires that one take into consideration the many battles they were fighting with each other. These disputes reveal much more than personal attacks and differences. They demonstrate a struggle for authority between Salafis and Traditionalists. Each group considers itself the authentic version of Islam and the other to be misguided and a threat to "authentic" Islam. What all of Albānī's detractors have in common is an allegiance to the *madhhab*s and a rejection of his approach to Islamic legal tradition. They consider his method of understanding of Islam to be a threat to their authority. However, purist Salafism was an attractive alternative to what many perceived as outdated Traditionalism.

80 Hasan Saqqāf, *Tanāqaḍāt al-Albānī al-Wāḍiḥāt* (n.p., 2007), 1: 6–7. Also see Ḥasan Saqqāf, *Iḥtijāj*; idem, *Majmūʿ Rasāʾil al-Saqqāf* (Amman: Dār al-Rāzī, 2000).

81 On the life of Būṭī, see Andreas Christmann, "Islamic Scholar and Religious Leader: A Portrait of Shaykh Muḥammad Saʿīd Ramaḍān al-Būti," *Islam and Christian–Muslim Relations*, 9, no. 2 (1998), 149–169.

82 See Muḥammad Ramaḍān al-Būṭī, *Al-Salafiyya Marḥala Zamaniyya Mubāraka lā Madhhab Islāmī* (Damascus: Dār al-Fikr, 1988); idem, *Al-Lā Madhhabiyya.*

3

Gatekeepers of Knowledge

Self-Learning and Islamic Expertise

THE LAST 100 YEARS HAVE WITNESSED AN UNPRECEDENTED RISE in the accessibility of information through books, media, and the internet.[1] Print and media put experts and laypeople in direct contact after centuries of having clearly distinct roles. This certainly changed the way lay Muslims interact with scripture and scholarship.[2] One of the primary critiques Traditionalists make against Salafis is that they are often self-learned. This chapter will explain why Traditionalists consider their educational methods to be necessary to what they conceive as the proper framework for understanding Islam. I analyze the nature of Traditionalist education and explain how it lost its monopoly over Islamic education. I illustrate that several factors facilitated the emergence of self-educated scholars such as Albānī. Among them are the Ottoman Empire's collapse, mass education, and increase in new media. These elements created a democratization of knowledge that led to the decline of Traditionalist education and opened a space for autodidacts to emerge as religious authorities.

[1] This chapter is a slightly modified version of my article "Shaykh Google as Ḥāfiẓ al-ʿAṣr: The Internet, Traditional ʿUlamāʾ, and Self Learning," published in the *American Journal of Islam and Society*. Reproduced with written permission by the publisher and copyrights holder: The International Institute of Islamic Thought (IIIT)/*American Journal of Islam and Society* (AJIS), first appeared in AJIS Year 2020 Vol. 37 Issue 1–2, pp. 67–102.

[2] Several scholars have written on new media, the transmission of knowledge, and religious authority. Gary Bunt, *Islam in the Digital Age: E-Jihad, Online Fatwas and Cyber Islamic Environments* (London: Pluto Press, 2003); idem, *Virtually Islamic: Computer-Mediated Communication and Cyber Islamic Environments* (Cardiff: University of Wales Press, 2000); Göran Larsson, *Muslims and the New Media: Historical and Contemporary Debates* (Burlington, VT: Ashgate, 2011); Jon W. Anderson, "The Internet and Islam's New Interpreters," in *New Media in the Muslim World*, ed. Dale F. Eickelman and Jon W. Anderson (Bloomington: Indiana University Press, 1999), 45–60; Francis Robinson, "Technology and Religious Change: Islam and the Impact of Print," *Modern Asian Studies*, 27, no. 1 (1993), 229–251.

In his article "The Death of Expertise," Tom Nichols argued that today, any assertion of expertise produces an explosion of anger and is immediately dismissed as an appeal to authority. He argues that it is not that there are no more experts, but that there is a collapse of any distinction between those of any accomplishment in an area and those of none at all. This line is blurred by individuals second-guessing experts and focusing on the errors and fallibility of specialists to deconstruct their expertise. In such a climate, claims of expertise are viewed as an obvious effort to use credentials to stifle dialogue.[3] Perhaps this is most obvious in the practice of dismissing facts and expert opinions as "fake news."

This "death of expertise" is a result of globalized communication removing gatekeepers in publications. Prior to the internet, journals and op-ed pages were often strictly edited. Participation in public debate required submission of an article, which had to be written intelligently, pass editorial review, and stand with the author's name attached. This process, which previously applied to even local newspapers, has been overtaken by self-published blogs, comment sections in articles, and YouTube videos that can all be anonymous.[4]

In the religious arena, the internet poses a challenge to clergy and experts in most religious traditions, but religious authority in Sunni Islam is particularly challenged by this because of its not having ordained religious authority.[5] Popular preachers existed since medieval Islam, but they did not have an outlet like the internet, cassette tapes, and printing press to promote themselves. Several medieval texts portray popular preachers as a threat to religious authority and public morality. They gain followers through charisma, emotional performances, personal appearance, and impressive clothing. Some could attract huge crowds of followers, and the jurists viewed them with suspicion because they often lacked training or

[3] Tom Nichols, "The Death of Expertise," *The Federalist*, January 17, 2014, http://thefederalist.com/2014/01/17/the-death-of-expertise/#disqus_thread, last accessed August 21, 2015. Nichols later published a book with the same title. Tom Nichols, *The Death of Expertise* (New York: Oxford University Press, 2017). Citations of *The Death of Expertise* throughout this work are from his book unless the citation is not accompanied by a page number. On the internet and religious authority see Heidi Campbell, "Who's Got the Power? Religious Authority and the Internet," *Journal of Computer-Mediated Communication*, 12, no. 3 (2007), 1043–1062.

[4] T. Nichols, "Death of Expertise."

[5] Nabil Echchaibi noted that unlike the political arena, the religious allowed for more individual autonomy and maneuvering of structures. Individual Muslims feel summoned to use the internet as a place of mediated *da'wa* to contribute to the reconstruction of their communities as well as the Muslim *umma*. See Nabil Echchaibi, "From Audiotapes to Videoblogs: The Delocalization of Authority in Islam," *Nations and Nationalism*, 17 (2009), 20.

education in law and theology. Although premodern jurists might have expressed anger over the influence of popular preachers, the construct of the *'ulamā'* was stable despite the existence of some popular preachers. Traditionalists maintained the right and responsibility to interpret Islam for the Muslim community and this remained undisputed until the modern period.[6] Prior to print and the internet the *'ulamā'* were able to confine scholarly texts and material among themselves.[7] The internet has changed this drastically, and Traditionalist *'ulamā'* who train in highly didactic systems are particularly challenged by it.

SALAFI AUTODIDACTS

Over the past few centuries, several reformers have emerged who studied Islam without formal religious training. The primary differences between these reformers and Traditionalists was not always the content of what it means to be an observant Muslim, but rather the way Islam is learned and understood. This is not to say that reformers, especially the Salafi ones, do not distinguish themselves in how they engage with daily acts as observant Muslims. Rather that they primarily disagreed on the necessary conditions for the production of authentic scholarship. Traditionalists consider it essential for knowledge to have been obtained through reliable teachers who link themselves back to earlier scholars. Salafis such as Albānī, 'Abd al-Qādir al-Arna'ūṭ (d. 2004), 'Alī al-Ḥalabī, and Ḥuwaynī are primarily self-taught and do not have any formal religious training. Although they do not explicitly encourage self-learning, they do believe that "proper" knowledge could be obtained outside of the teacher–student link.

Much of the criticism toward Albānī was due to the fact that he was self-taught. It contrasted with much of the entire Traditionalist educational and authoritative system because without particular expectations of qualifications through the teacher–student link, non-Traditionalists can claim scholarly authority. Albānī is known to have very few *ijāza*s from scholars and was distinguished in religious circles for how few *ijāza*s he held. Besides attending the lessons of his Ḥanafī father, Albānī never studied under a single scholar for a long period of time. Albānī's critics often try to discredit

[6] Jonathan Brown, "Is Islam Easy to Understand or Not?: Salafis, the Democratization of Interpretation and the Need for the Ulema," *Journal of Islamic Studies*, 26, no. 2 (2014), 119–120.

[7] See Jonathan Berkey, *Popular Preaching and Religious Authority in the Medieval Islamic Near East* (Seattle: University of Washington Press, 2001). Also see 'Abd al-Raḥmān Ibn al-Jawzī, *Kitāb al-Quṣṣāṣ wa-l-Mudhakkirīn* (Beirut: Dār al-Mahriq, 1971).

his scholarship by mocking him for being a watch-repairer and self-taught. Ḥabīb al-Raḥmān al-Aʿẓamī states:

> Whoever knows Albānī and is familiar with his history, knows that he did not receive knowledge directly from the mouths of the scholars. Neither did he sit before them to benefit. Knowledge is by learning, what is it then with him and knowledge, when he did not learn? It has reached me that the extent of his knowledge is *Mukhtaṣar al-Qudūrī*,[8] and that he was best skilled in repairing watches. He acknowledges that without shame and a consequence of that is that he, by God, does not know what a single student who works studying ḥadīth in our schools knows.[9]

Another stern critic of Albānī is the Ashʿarī Sufi Gabriel Fouad Haddad, who said:

> Nasir al-Albani is the arch-innovator of the Wahhabis and "Salafis" in our time. A watch repairman by trade, al-Albani is a self-taught claimant to hadith scholarship who has no known teacher in any of the Islamic sciences and has admitted not to have memorized the Book of Allah nor any book of hadith, fiqh, *ʿaqîda, usûl*, or grammar. He achieved fame by attacking the great scholars of *Ahl al-Sunna* and reviling the science of fiqh with especial malice towards the school of his father who was a Hanafi jurist.[10]

Although his critics mocked his being a watch-repairer, Albānī was not ashamed of his employment, arguing that he was better off than his opponents because he lived off his own work. He states: "And for the record: I was never an employee for anyone at all, officially or unofficially. By God, except three years in the Islamic University of Medina."[11] Albānī also explains: "God's blessings upon me are many, I cannot count them. Perhaps the most important of them are two: my father's migration to Greater Syria, then his teaching me his profession in repairing watches."[12] Despite other attempts to discredit his scholarship, the teachings of Albānī spread across the Muslim world and he became one of the twentieth century's most authoritative Salafi figures.

Despite his lack of formal training, one cannot deny Albānī's encyclopedic knowledge. His ability to locate all of the chains of narrations for thousands

[8] The author was Abū al-Ḥusayn al-Qudūrī (d. 428/1037), his work *Mukhtaṣar al-Qudūrī* is one of the most celebrated introductory manuals in Ḥanafī *fiqh*. See A. Qudūrī, *Mukhtaṣar al-Qudūrī* (Beirut: Dār al-Kutub al-ʿIlmiyya, 1997); Moh. Ben Cheneb, "al-Ḳudūrī," in *Encyclopaedia of Islam, First Edition (1913–1936)*, ed. M. Th. Houtsma, T. W. Arnold, R. Basset, and R. Hartmann, https://referenceworks.brillonline.com/browse/encyclopaedia-of-islam-1, last accessed June 2, 2020.

[9] H. Aʿẓamī, *Shudhūdhu*, 9–10.

[10] G. F. Haddad, *Albānī*. Also see idem, *Albānī & Friends*.

[11] Ibn Taymiyya, *Kalim al-Ṭayyib*, 34.

[12] M. Shaybānī, *Ḥayāt*, 48.

of ḥadīth and analyze them demonstrates that he was not as ignorant as his critics make him out to be. Albānī authored hundreds of books, referenced manuscripts and books that are very challenging to index, and even discovered many *isnād*s that were previously unknown. This illustrates that those who tried to deny his scholarship often did so because they disagreed with his methodology. Traditionalists attack Albānī's scholarship not only because his lack of "correct" knowledge, but because the method in which he obtained it poses a threat to their authority. If everyone followed Albānī's self-taught method of acquiring knowledge it would open the door for many people to claim scholarship without studying with scholars.

What makes studying with a teacher and the *ijāza* system different from self-learning? In the *ijāza* system, there is a student–teacher relationship that is established as well as a level of respect for scholarly authorities. However, if an *ijāza* is one scholar's recognition of the qualifications of a student, how does that differ from other scholars recognizing someone's scholarship, as in the case of Albānī? Although Albānī has few *ijāza*s, many scholars have characterized him as one of the leading scholars of the twentieth century. This is important because his scholarship is in fact legitimized by other scholars citing him as an authority in the field of ḥadīth. Traditionalists, however, do not acknowledge his learning strategy as a legitimate one because he did not learn from a teacher.

TRADITIONALIST EDUCATION

How does one become a scholar? What are the essential requirements, if any, for one to be deemed an expert of Islam? What is the difference between studying with a teacher and self-learning? In traditional Islamic circles, knowledge was primarily meant to be transmitted through the teacher–student *isnād*, not solely through books.[13] Authentic knowledge was stored in scholars, and the art of memory was among the most highly prized arts; scholars were masters of mnemonic tricks.[14] Education through a teacher is what made knowledge trustworthy. The value and authority of knowledge were not in knowledge itself as much as it was in its being obtained through "proper" methods. The traditional methods of transmitting knowledge, especially in Islamic law, have become crystallized in the Islamic legal

[13] The *isnād* is a record of transmission and is not the instrument of pedagogy. However, the record of transmission could be used to establish a relationship. In other words, the word *isnād* here refers to the student–teacher relationship.

[14] F. Robinson, "Technology," 231.

schools. These schools do not only establish the transmission of texts between successive generations, but more importantly the understanding of those texts and a methodology for understanding secondary and primary sources.

This is not to suggest that Traditionalists had a single or monolithic understanding of scripture. Throughout the Muslim world, Traditionalists have a wide range of opinions on a host of Islamic topics. However, they have also been careful about uniting that diversity within a comprehensive umbrella, at the root of which is the connection between the teacher and student.

When the chain of Muslim teachers who trace their learning back to the earliest Muslim schools of theology and law are bypassed, whether through self-study or studying in western universities, knowledge loses its authenticity and authority. Muslim scholars believe that the transmission from a teacher to a student creates and transfers authority. It is the living tradition that passes on sacred learning. To innovate one's own commentary on tradition, without the collective commentaries of generations explained by a teacher, was considered inauthentic.[15]

THE TEACHER–STUDENT *ISNĀD*

In this chain, the teacher was expected to gradually guide the student in the studying of texts through a curriculum. Without the teacher, students would be left on their own and may arbitrarily study advanced texts they are ill-equipped to deal with. Muḥammad ʿAwwāma, a Syrian ḥadīth scholar, explains that today people approach classical sources and proof-texts directly without studying the basics of Islam. This often results in them considering their opinions to be superior to the four *madhhabs*.[16] In traditional Islamic learning, students were given the tools to understand scripture before approaching scripture directly. Consequently, the core of the curriculum was the study of *fiqh* works, whereas *ḥadīth* collections and commentaries on the Qurʾān were studied only as supplements to the law.

[15] Jonathan Brown, *Ḥadīth: Muhammad's Legacy in the Medieval and Modern World* (Oxford: Oneworld, 2009), 273–274. Despite going through this system, some Traditionalists still arrive at conclusions that are condemned by the vast majority of Muslim scholars. For instance, the Egyptian scholar ʿIzzat ʿAṭiyya gave a controversial fatwa that if a woman can breastfeed her male coworker, they would establish a family bond that would make their seclusion in the workplace permissible. This caused a great deal of backlash and he eventually withdrew his fatwa.

[16] M. ʿAwwāma, *Adab al-Ikhtilāf*, 159.

A teacher was essential in this process of learning. Students typically began with memorizing the Qur'ānic and learning from local scholars. If they proved themselves capable, they would then travel from city to city learning from scholars of different specialties. As students completed the study of a book with a teacher, they would receive an *ijāza* (license to teach) testifying to their accomplishments (more on this later).[17] A student's knowledge was evaluated based on the number of certificates he obtained as well as the scholars he received them from.[18]

Unlike the modern university system, it was not where one studied that was important in traditional Islamic learning, but rather with whom they studied. This is noted from the biographical dictionaries of medieval scholars which tell us little about where the person studied and are virtually silent about the schools in which a young scholar received his training. It is not that information about one's education was unavailable, but what was important was one's teachers. Historians and biographers regularly provided long lists of scholars' teachers, a sort of curriculum vitae. One of the most critical elements of this curriculum vitae consisted of the names of those on whose authority one transmitted Islamic texts.[19]

In their earliest stages, students would learn the Qur'ān and Sunna through the scholarly class. It was understood that novice students, let alone laity, cannot extract rulings from these sources independently, this job was limited to the *mujtahid*. Lay Muslims having direct access to scholarly texts without the tutelage of a teacher would prove catastrophic for the scholarly class. Traditionally trained scholar Yusuf Talal DeLorenzo argues that, for instance, very few people are equipped to deal with Bukhārī's

[17] On curricula and the *ijāza* system see Jan Witkam, "The Human Element between Text and Reader: The Ijāza in Arabic Manuscripts," in *Education and Learning in the Early Islamic World*, ed. Claude Gilliot (Burlington, VA: Ashgate, 2012), 149–162. On *ijāzas* see Ṣalāḥ al-Dīn al-Munajjid, "Ijāzāt al-Samāʿ fī-l-Makhṭūṭāt al-Qadīma," *Majallat Maʿhad al-Makhṭūṭāt al-ʿArabīya/Revue de l'institut des manuscrits arabes* (Cairo), 1 (1955), 232–251; Qāsim Aḥmad al-Sāmarrāʾī, "Al-Ijāzāt wa-Taṭawwuruhā al-Taʾrīkhīya," *ʿĀlam al-Kutub*, 2 (1981), 278–285; Yūnus al-Khārūf, "Al-Samāʿāt wa-l-ilāzāt fī-l-Makhṭūṭāt al-ʿArabīya," *Risālat al-Maktaba* (Jordanien), 10 (1975), 16–22; Devin J. Stewart, "The Doctorate of Islamic Law in Mamluk Egypt and Syria," in *Law and Education in Medieval Islam*, ed. Joseph Lowry, Devin Stewart, and Shawkat Toorawa (Cambridge: E. J. W. Gibb Memorial Trust, 2004), 45–90.

[18] B. Metcalf, *Islamic Revival*, 18–20. Also see George Makdisi, "Institutionalized Learning as a Self-Image of Islam," in *Islam's Understanding of Itself*, ed. Speros Vryonis, Jr. (Los Angeles: University of California Press, 1983), 73–85; Dale Eickelman, "The Art of Memory: Islamic Education and Its Social Reproduction," *Comparative Studies in Society and History*, 20, no. 4 (1978), 485–516.

[19] Jonathan Berkey, *The Transmission of Knowledge in Medieval Cairo: A Social History of Islamic Education* (Princeton, NJ: Princeton University Press, 1992), 23.

Ṣaḥīḥ, a work that is readily available online in Arabic and translation. He points out that in traditional learning circles the *Ṣaḥīḥ al-Bukhārī* came only after a student had spent years learning the classical disciplines such as Arabic, rhetoric and literature, the rational sciences of logic, Islamic legal theory, the many Qurʾānic sciences from elocution (*tajwīd*) to Qurʾānic exegesis (*tafsīr*), and the science of ḥadīth. Only after a student had demonstrated his mastery of these subjects was he allowed to attend the lessons, which were usually given by the most learned and respected of all teachers, on the *Ṣaḥīḥ* of Bukhārī.[20]

DeLorenzo goes on to state that in the traditional educational scheme, there were many reasons for this postponement. The status accorded to Bukhārī's *Ṣaḥīḥ* was so elevated that only those who had mastered the classical disciplines were considered prepared to take on its study. The *Ṣaḥīḥ* is so full of technical nuances related to principles of ḥadīth (*uṣūl al-ḥadīth*) and the biographical handbooks (*ʿilm al-rijāl*) that a thorough understanding of those subjects is required if they are to be entirely appreciated. Similarly, unless one has mastered other classical disciplines, there is much learning and meaning that will be overlooked.[21] DeLorenzo explains that bypassing a teacher and studying texts directly results in profound misunderstanding of scripture. He writes:

> The word I recall the shaykh using to describe what results when the unprepared non-scholar attempts to read the hadith literature was *fitnah*, or a trial, in the sense that the person would be so confused and overcome after undertaking such an uninformed and one-dimensional reading of that literature (i.e., in translation without the presence of a shaykh to guide him/her through the obstacles) that he or she would face a crisis in their religion, a trial of spiritual proportions.[22]

The insistence on learning from a teacher was meant to supervise the student's methodology and interpretation of scripture. Without the supervision of a teacher, knowledge was not considered legitimate. ʿAwwāma explains that even those who have reached great scholarly achievements are still in need of a teacher or peer to provide feedback for knowledge to be authentic.[23] Studying with a teacher and having a group of scholars to

[20] Yusuf Talal DeLorenzo, *Imam Bukhari's Book of Muslim Morals and Manners* (Alexandria, VA: Al-Saadawi Publications, 1997), i–iii.

[21] Y. DeLorenzo, *Imam Bukhari's*, ii.

[22] Y. DeLorenzo, *Imam Bukhari's*, ii–iii.

[23] Muḥammad ʿAwwāma, "Ḥadīth al-Dhikrayāt maʿ al-Shaykh Muḥammad ʿAwwāma," www.youtube.com/watch?v=6cgbKunEEQY, last accessed February 27, 2014. ʿAwwāma was one of ʿAbd al-Fattāḥ Abū Ghudda's main students. Abū Ghudda was a strong critic of self-learning

consult is necessary even for the greatest of scholars. Studying with a teacher for a few years and then resorting to self-study without scholars is insufficient.[24]

In order to obtain legitimacy as scholars, students were required to spend a significant period of time learning from scholars. The completion of the study of the book would involve a reading back of the text along with its explanation. If this were done to the teacher's satisfaction, the student would then be given an *ijāza*. The *ijāza* system was a scholar's method of licensing others to teach his works and serves as a testimony to the student's scholarship. The student was left in no doubt that he was a trustee in his generation as part of the long tradition of Islamic learning handed down from the past, and he was now responsible for continuing this chain to the next generation.[25]

This method of learning often includes reading an entire text line by line in the presence of a teacher who provides guided commentary on each statement. Often, there is a very careful grammatical analysis of why each word was selected and what it implies. The teacher would shed light on what kind of theological and legal messages the author is delivering in his choice of words. This didactic fashion of teaching is often accompanied by students' questions and teacher–student debates. This form of active learning was meant to yield increased structure, feedback, and interaction, prompting students to become participants in constructing their own knowledge rather than passive recipients. For Traditionalists this was the only way to read a text and retain its uncertain authority.[26]

In ḥadīth circles whenever a student finished explaining a ḥadīth to his teacher the student would place a mark next to the ḥadīth to distinguish it from ḥadīth that were not yet read to the teacher. Even when a student knew ḥadīth through books, he was not entitled to use those ḥadīth for teaching or his own compilation until he received them through properly recognized methods of learning. This supervision served as a form of peer-review. Ḥadīth scholars labeled such a person as a *sāriq al-ḥadīth* (ḥadīth thief). Despite the fact that the information was accurate because it was taken from

and also the student of Muṣṭafā Ṣabrī (d. 1954) the last Shaykh al-Islam of the Ottoman Empire. He experienced first-hand the frustration and decline of Traditionalist authority and spent his life trying to revive it.

24 M. ʿAwwāma, *Adab al-Ikhtilāf*, 149.

25 F. Robinson, "Technology," 236.

26 Timothy Mitchell, *Colonising Egypt* (Berkeley: University of California Press, 1991), 133. On active learning see Annie Murphy Paul, "Are College Lectures Unfair?," *The New York Times*, September 12, 2015, Gray Matter Science and Society sec., www.nytimes.com/2015/09/13/opinion/sunday/are-college-lectures-unfair.html, last accessed September 15, 2015.

the teacher's book, the individual was not considered an authority in the ḥadīth because of the method by which he obtained it.[27]

Learning a text with a teacher was meant to ensure that texts were not distorted or severely misconstrued. At a practical level, many Arabic texts, whether individual ḥadīth or entire books, were written without many vowels and diacritic marks. Reading a book properly required learning it from a teacher who heard it read aloud.[28] Muhammad Mustafa Al-Azami (d. 2017) argues that at times, Muslim scholars have intentionally used difficult words or script to force students to learn directly from scholars. He states that even the third Caliph ʿUthmān made certain the Qurʾān was written in such a fashion that it would ensure that a student would learn the Qurʾān directly from a scholar and not on his own. Although they existed and were used at the time, skeletal dots and diacritical marks were both absent from ʿUthmān's compilation of the Qurʾān. By its consonant-heavy and dotless nature, ʿUthmān's Qurʾān was shielded from the guiles of anyone seeking to bypass oral scholarship and learn the Qurʾān on his own; such a person would readily be detected if he ever dared to recite in public.[29] Among the arguments that Traditionalists make is that scripture was always sent with a Prophet to explain its contents. Many Prophets were sent without scripture, but scripture was never revealed without a Prophet.[30] This rationalization is based on the notion that people would not have the capability to properly understand scripture without the teaching of a Prophet.[31] The Prophet's explanation of the Qurʾān was meant to preserve its meaning, without which the text would be misunderstood. Part of the preservation of scripture and text is to preserve and pass down its "proper" understanding. As a result, traditional religious authority is characterized through established, supervised approaches to texts. When learning and

27 Muhammad Mustafa Al-Azami, *Studies in Hadith Methodology and Literature* (Indianapolis, IN: Islamic Teaching Center, 1977), 30. Azami notes that this is similar to modern copyright laws in which one could buy a thousand copies of a book but may not print even one copy without permission. Similarly, Muslim scholars would not allow someone to use the material in a book by simply obtaining it. Also see ʿAbd al-Fattāḥ Abū Ghudda, *Al-Isnād Min al-Dīn* (Aleppo: Maktabat al-Maṭbūʿāt al-Islāmiyya, 1996), 146.

28 J. Brown, *Ḥadīth*, 273.

29 Muhammad Mustafa Al-Azami, *The History of the Qur'anic Text from Revelation to Compilation: A Comparative Study with the Old and New Testaments* (Leicester: UK Islamic Academy, 2003), 147–148.

30 Muhammad Ibn Adam, "Learning from a Teacher & the Importance of Isnad," *Daruliftaa*, September 3, 2004, www.daruliftaa.com/node/5795?txt_QuestionID, last accessed September 15, 2015.

31 See D. Brown, *Rethinking*.

education take place outside of this supervised system it can become haphazard. Traditionalists like ʿAwwāma characterize modern auto-didacticism as educational disorder (*al-fawḍa al-ʿilmiyya*).[32] Ultimately, the teacher–student link was intended to prevent non-experts from speaking on behalf of religion. Traditionalists believe that it is only those who have undergone particular training that have the right to interpret scripture.

SCHOLARS AS HEIRS OF THE PROPHETS

Sunni Muslims hold the Prophet's Companions in the highest regard because they are believed to have embodied his teachings and etiquette.[33] The Andalusian literalist scholar ʿAlī Ibn Ḥazm stated that no one can ever surpass the generation of the Companions who are unrivaled in their righteousness.[34] The status they were given in Sunni doctrine is a result of their being the nearest to the Prophet in time as well as their application of Islam. Education at the hands of scholars who link themselves back to the earliest generations is an attempt at attaining a portion of the Prophetic inheritance. Therefore, Traditionalists hold the scholarly class in high esteem because they collectively embody knowledge and characteristics that can be traced back to the Prophet.[35]

Scholars attempted to embody the teaching methods of the Prophet because his pedagogical techniques were considered to have the greatest impact. A famous *ḥadīth* describes scholars as "heirs of the Prophets," and Traditionalist *ʿulamāʾ* viewed themselves accordingly.[36] This manifested itself in the manner in which a scholar's closest students were called his *aṣḥāb* (companions). George Makdisi explains that earlier scholars intentionally modeled their relationship with their students on that of the Prophet and his Companions. He states, "Just as the Prophet was the leader with followers, each school consisted of a leader, imam, with followers, *ṣāḥib*,

[32] M. ʿAwwāma, "Ḥadīth al-Dhikrayāt."

[33] On the history of the status of the Companions, especially in ḥadīth literature, see Scott C. Lucas, *Constructive Critics, Ḥadīth Literature, and the Articulation of Sunni Islam: The Legacy of Ibn Saʿd, Ibn Maʿīn, and Ibn Ḥanbal* (Boston: Brill, 2004), 221–282.

[34] ʿAlī b. Aḥmad Ibn Ḥazm, *Al-Faṣl fi-l-Milal wa-l-Ahwāʾ wa-l-Niḥal* (Beirut: Dār al-Jīl, 1996), 4: 185–188.

[35] A. Abū Ghudda, Lecture in Turkey.

[36] Muḥammad b. ʿĪsā al-Tirmidhī, *Al-Jāmiʿ al-Kabīr Sunan al-Tirmidhī* (Beirut: Dār al-Gharb al-Islāmī, 1996), Bāb Al-ʿIlm, 4: 414 no. 2682. Ibn Rajab al-Ḥanbalī has a treatise on this ḥadīth where he defines who a scholar is and how one is to properly attain the level of scholarship. See Ibn Rajab Abū al-Faraj Abd al-Raḥmān, *Majmūʿ Rasāʾil Ibn Rajab al-Ḥanbalī* (Cairo: Al-Fārūq al-Ḥadītha li-l-Ṭibāʿa wa-l-Nashr, 2001), 1: 5–60.

pl. *aṣḥāb*."[37] Scholars attempted to replicate the Prophet–Companion/teacher–disciple mode of transmission in all of the Islamic sciences. The importance of the Prophet as a pedagogical role model is noted from the many *ḥadīth* collections that contain chapters that specifically describe how Muhammad taught his community. These *ḥadīth* collections can be seen as handbooks of prophetic pedagogy.[38]

Imitating the Prophet's pedagogical methods was not only important because of the knowledge the teacher transmits to the students, but also for the personal characteristics the students inherit from their teachers. Education is not merely information or knowledge, but it consists of fostering morally upright individuals. The traditional educational paradigm emphasizes the importance of specific religious rituals, behaviors, and norms of attaining knowledge. Kasper Mathiesen notes that being a student in traditional learning circles "implies *suḥba*, studying with and being in the presence of *ijāza*-holding scholars in order to absorb their spiritual *ḥāl* (state of heart and being)."[39]

The teacher–student relationship was meant to ensure that students learn from their teacher's spiritual state. By shadowing a scholar, a student was expected to absorb his spiritual state in intellectual exchanges and in mundane activities. This provided the student with a model of scholarly etiquette and instilled a reverence for the scholarly class. The spiritual element of learning necessitates the insight of a teacher and cannot be accomplished by self-learning. In some cases, such as *ḥadīth* transmission, it was not common for students to have a close relationship with the *ḥadīth*-master they transmitted from. Nevertheless, the student would learn to observe the scholars in general. In other words, it was not always necessary to accompany one particular scholar but learning from multiple scholars can still have a similar impact.[40]

Muslim scholars from the third century AH until today have produced a large number of books on the guidelines for knowledge acquisition.[41]

[37] George Makdisi, *The Rise of Colleges: Institutions of Learning in Islam and the West* (Edinburgh: Edinburgh University Press, 1981), 7.

[38] Laury Silvers, "The Teaching Relationship in Early Sufism: A Reassessment of Fritz Meier's Definition of the Shaykh al-Tarbiya and the Shaykh al-Taʿlīm," *The Muslim World*, 93, no. 1 (2003), 72.

[39] K. Mathiesen, "Anglo-American," 204.

[40] K. Mathiesen, "Anglo-American," 204.

[41] For example see Muḥammad b. Jamāʿa, *Tadhkirat al-Sāmiʿ wa-l-Mutakallim fī Adab al-ʿĀlim wa-l-Mutaʿalim* (Beirut: Dār al-Bashāʾir al-Islāmiyya, 2012); Burhān al-Islām al-Zarnūjī, *Taʿlīm al-Muttaʿallim Ṭarīq al-Taʿallum* (Beirut: Al-Maktab al-Islāmī, 1981); Yūsuf b. ʿAbd Allāh Ibn ʿAbd al-Barr, *Jāmiʿ Bayān al-ʿIlm wa Faḍlihi wa mā Yanbaghī fī Riwāyatihi wa Ḥamlihi* (Cairo: Dār al-Kutub al-Ḥadītha, 1975); Abū Bakr Aḥmad b. ʿAlī Al-Khaṭīb al-Baghdādī, *Al-Jāmiʿ li*

The existence of these guidelines demonstrates that in contrast to most modern education systems, in traditional Islamic learning a teacher is primarily a *murabbī* (mentor). Yedullah Kazmi argues that emphasis in education has shifted from who the teacher is to what the teacher teaches. In other words, the knower is distinguished from what he knows so that the scholar is simply a transmitter of information. Describing this phenomenon Kazmi writes: "What a teacher is expected to bring to the class is what he/she knows and not what he/she is. What a teacher is is purely an accidental quality with little or no relevance to his/her competence as a teacher as long as he/she has the necessary credentials and no criminal record."[42]

The shift from who the teacher is to what he teaches closely relates to the purpose and nature of education. Islamic sciences were not distinct from spirituality. Jon Anderson makes the interesting observation that the modes of transmission, master–pupil relations, and cohort networks of Sufism and Traditionalists *ʿulamāʾ* are very similar.[43] Many Sufis were not only spiritual seekers, but scholars of *ḥadīth* and jurisprudence. Those who were not such scholars were nevertheless learned to some degree in religious sciences.[44] Even *madrasas* built exclusively for training *ʿulamāʾ* were often paired with *khanqahs*. Scholarship was usually a central part of the spiritual endeavor. The process of traveling and learning from a scholar was considered a spiritual experience in itself, one that was based on nostalgia and longing for a connection with the Prophet.[45] Scholars and *ḥadīth* narrators wanted to be as close to the Prophet as time allowed. They used *isnāds* as a means to teleport back to the Prophet, and the shorter *isnāds* were better not only because they decreased the likelihood for error in transmission, but because they became a means of close connection to the Prophet's blessings. In Sufism, the *isnād* was the chain of transmission for the Prophet's blessings, teachings, and esoteric knowledge.[46]

Akhlāq al-Rāwī wa Ādāb al-Sāmiʿ (Al-Dammām: Dār Ibn al-Jawzī, 2011). Also see ʿAbd al-Fattāḥ Abū Ghudda, *Namādhij Min Rasāʾil al-Aʾimmat al-Salaf wa Adabi-him al-ʿilmī* (Beirut: Dār al-Bashāʾir al-Islāmiyya, 1996), 61–62.

42 Yedullah Kazmi, "The Notion of Murrabī in Islam: An Islamic Critique of Trends in Contemporary Education," *Islamic Studies*, 38, no. 2 (1999), 231.

43 See J. Anderson, "The Internet," 42.

44 L. Silvers, "Teaching," 73.

45 For instance, Muḥammad b. Ismāʿīl al-Bukhārī composed his *Tarīkh al-Kabīr* while sitting next to the Prophet's grave. He organized the names in alphabetical order but began with the Prophet and then those named Muḥammad out of love and reverence for him. See Muḥammad b. Ismāʿīl al-Bukhārī, *Kitāb al-Tarīkh al-Kabīr* (Beirut: Dār al-Kutub al-ʿIlmiyya, 1986), 1: 6–11.

46 J. Brown, *Ḥadīth*, 273.

Kazmi argues that there are two kinds of knowledge: theoretical and personal. In traditional learning circles, it was only when they were combined that knowledge was considered authentic and proper. Theoretical knowledge is what we normally associate with the term *knowledge*: "It is abstract, formal, impersonal, universalizing and almost completely objectifiable in language, either natural or artificial or a combination of the two."[47] Personalized knowledge is incapable of being fully formalized or objectified and is entirely dependent on linguistic communication and, more importantly, through styles and strategies for living.[48] Although these two forms of knowledge are distinct, for traditional scholars they cannot be separated; when they are, knowledge loses its legitimacy.

This personalized knowledge is communicated not only through language but also, among other things, through strategies for living and orientation to knowledge and the world. Obtaining knowledge only through reading texts is considered insufficient since it does not produce the essential processes of self-transformation and moral and spiritual purification that are at the core of Islamic education.[49] The teacher–student relationship is based on presence, closeness, and fellowship. The passing of information and knowledge can occur over the internet, but it takes place in a space that fosters distance and disembodiment.

Not having studied through this system, Albānī does not maintain the same reverent attitude as Traditionalists. Albānī critics accused him of not adhering to the etiquette of scholarly discourse because he often resorted to insults and harsh words. However, his students loved his personality because he so strongly held on to what he believed was true. He preferred the truth of politeness or political correctness. What outraged Traditionalists about Albānī was not necessarily the fact that he differed with earlier scholars. Rather it was the manner in which he spoke of them. This is what motivated Ḥasan b. ʿAlī al-Saqqāf to author his work *Qāmūs shatāʾim al-Albānī* (*Dictionary of Albānī's Slandering*), where he compiles many of Albānī's alleged slandering of scholars.

Because Traditionalists do not believe all texts to be clear they consider debate and dialogue to be a natural part of Islamic law. Therefore, they emphasize proper etiquette in cases of disagreements. Consequently, they do not consider debate and disagreement to be negative, but they believe the lack of etiquette that sometimes accompanies them is problematic.

[47] Y. Kazmi, "Murrabī," 213. [48] Y. Kazmi, "Murrabī," 213.
[49] K. Mathiesen, "Anglo-American," 204.

Magnanimity in criticism is a great virtue and Muslim scholars have produced many books on the rules for acquiring knowledge. For the uninitiated reader, many of Albānī's actions and choices of words may seem normal and unproblematic; however, his critics are appalled by his lack of mannerisms. Even some of Albānī's students and fellow Salafi scholars pointed out his caustic and contentious personality.[50]

In his effort to reform Islamic tradition Albānī was met with plenty of resistance from scholars throughout the Muslim world, many times these disputes were full of maligning and harsh insinuations. In order to maintain unity Muslim jurists have adopted etiquettes or rules for discussion and engagement. Albānī's lack of conformity to this etiquette was perhaps due to the fact that he believed that there can only be one valid interpretation and answer to everything.[51] Albānī notes that some peers have questioned his harshness toward those who disagree with him such as Būṭī; he justifies himself by saying:

> I believe with full certainty that I did not do anything except what was permitted according to the Sharia, and there is no room for the objective person to criticize us. How [can they criticize], when God, Glory and Mighty, says in his Honorable Book while describing His believing servants: *And those who, when aggression afflicts them, defend themselves. And the retribution for an evil act is an evil one like it, but whoever pardons and makes reconciliation then his reward is from God. Verily, He does not like wrongdoers. And whoever avenges himself after having been wronged, those do not have any blame. Blame is only on the ones who wrong the people and aggress upon the earth unjustly. They will have a painful punishment. And whoever is patient and forgives then that is of courageous conduct.*[52]

He justifies his harshness against Būṭī and other critics because they attack Salafis and insult them. However, Traditionalists maintain that a scholar must be above retribution and revenge, instead he must pardon, be patient, and forgive, which are the higher standards mentioned in the verse. For Salafis, *ijāza*s and degrees are worthless if the person produces material that contradicts the teachings of the Prophet found in authentic ḥadīth. For instance, when criticizing Būṭī, Albānī says: "He has revealed by all his

[50] J. Brown, *Canonization*, 325.

[51] Albānī mocks the concept of there being two valid interpretations on one issue. See Muḥammad Nāṣir al-Dīn al-Albānī, "Fī l-Mas'ala Qawlān," lecture from www.islamway.com, last accessed January 10, 2012.

[52] Q. *Al-Shūrā*, 42:39–43, this and all subsequent Qur'ānic translations are my own. N. Albānī, *Difā'*, p. ḥā [numbered in Arabic *abjād* scheme].

arguments that these high degrees and what they call doctorate does not give its bearer knowledge, analysis, and manners."[53]

THE DISENFRANCHISEMENT OF THE TRADITIONALISTS

By the nineteenth century, Islamic scholarship had reached a mature level and many legal issues had been thoroughly reviewed. Changes that took place were usually slow and gradual, thus they did not require a great deal of new scholarship that was not already found in the works of earlier scholars. Therefore, later generations sufficed themselves with writing commentaries or abridged manuals on the works of earlier scholars. With the swift technological and scientific changes that took place around the world, perhaps the greatest challenge of Traditionalists was their inability to make crucial changes in *fiqh* discourse in order to remain relevant in a fast-changing world. The Traditionalist educational system did not train scholars to think outside the box, or tackle issues in an unorthodox manner. Many of them, even though they were eminent scholars, could not fathom giving a fatwa that went against the scholars of their *madhhab* or an opinion held by all four legal schools. Traditionalists did not want to break away from their orthodox ways. They were very skeptical of western influence and supposed that the best way to preserve their societies was by completely rejecting the west and its advancements. As Traditionalists were losing authority in the Arab world, the Salafi movement began to gain momentum.

The fall of the Ottoman Empire, colonization of Muslim lands, and the rise of secular governments in the Muslim world further contributed to the decline of the traditional pedagogical methods necessary to become a religious authority. Modernization, the institutionalization of religious knowledge, and breaking up the "old" order of learning have produced a disruption, or rather "democratization" of knowledge acquisition and transmission. There were several sociopolitical events that served as points of entry that led to the deterioration of the infrastructure of Islamic educational institutions that undermined and neutralized the teachers who were perceived as a threat to secular governments. These include the push to modernize the Ottoman Empire, imbalance of political powers, and the weakening of traditional elites like the *ʿulamāʾ*.[54] The caliphate served as an embodiment of Muslim unity, not only politically, but also in terms of scholarship. Those who had religious authority, and therefore spoke for

[53] N. Albānī, *Difāʿ*, p. bā [numbered in Arabic *abjād* scheme].
[54] M. Hassan, *Longing for the Lost Caliphate*, 10.

Islam, were traditionally trained scholars who held influential positions in government and education. In the Ottoman Empire, the role of the scholars expanded as the respective bureaucracies evolved. It was the scholars who were responsible for the education of the nobility, who staffed various levels of judiciary, and who oversaw the charitable establishment of the Empire. Leading members of the scholarly class ranged from those who led prayers in small towns to the most prestigious courtiers.[55]

Through their positions as judges, muftis, guardians of religious endowments, scribes, and market inspectors, the *ʿulamāʾ* served as the mouthpiece for various branches of Islamic tradition. They held the recognized authority to interpret scripture and define the religious outlook of society.[56] The secularization of governments in the Muslim world brought about a class of secular elites who usurped the powerful positions previously held by traditional *ʿulamāʾ*. There developed a vacuum in religious authority, and it was not clear who spoke for the religion. Scholars such as Muṣṭafā Ṣabrī who held powerful positions in the Ottoman Empire, were sidelined by the new secular government. Initially, Ṣabrī and several others strived to restore the fallen caliphate but were eventually defeated. They shifted from their influence in government to trying to preserve the cognitive frameworks of Islam for a new generation of Muslims.[57] This fragmented the authority of the *ʿulamāʾ* as the sole authoritative voice of Islam and opened the door for reformers who were critical of the scholarly class to challenge the *ʿulamāʾ*.

Sweeping transformations produced by modernization programs as well as European imperialism were leaving their impact on the position of Traditionalists, facilitating the emergence of new spokesmen for Islam. Since Traditionalists were supported by the Ottoman Empire, many of their institutions lost funding with the Empire's demise. Traditionalists were unprepared for the fall of the Ottoman Empire and the changes of modernity. Prior to the Industrial Revolution, changes between centuries were few and slow. In the early twentieth century, Traditionalists faced heavy setbacks by the fall of the Islamic caliphate and world wars, followed by the rise of secular governments in the Muslim world. Most importantly, Traditionalists lost their economic backbone. Those who sought to continue in scholarship often faced the choice between obtaining Islamic knowledge and earning a living. Mona Hassan explains: "Faced with the disappearance of a traditional Islamic caliphate as represented by the Ottomans,

[55] B. Metcalf, *Islamic Revival*, 18–20. [56] S. Farouki and B. Nafi, *Islamic Thought*, 6.
[57] M. Hassan, *Longing for the Lost Caliphate*, 244.

a Pandora's box of possibilities had opened up by the 1920s."[58] Islamic Modernists took over institutions such as al-Azhar, imposing western systems of education and changing the classical forms of education.

THE UNIVERSITY SYSTEM

Reformers emerged who believed that the traditional pedagogy led to exaggerated reverence for teachers which resulted in blind and uncritical imitation of scholarship. Traditional education was criticized as being limited to the memorization of texts and the study of commentaries of law books that were no longer adopted by the state and had little bearing on the contemporary world. Reformers such as the Egyptian Mohammad ʿAbduh deemed traditionally trained *ʿulamāʾ* to be backward, irrelevant, and out of touch with contemporary issues because they were studying manuals, commentaries, and glosses that were not able to address the issues of modern times. He considered the conventional way of learning as unable to address the main concerns of modern times, and he sought to introduce new methods that would provide solutions to the problems of the Muslim world.

ʿAbduh's first experience with learning by rote, memorizing texts and commentaries of laws for which he was given no tools of understanding, was critical to his later commitment to a thoroughgoing reform of the Egyptian educational system.[59] ʿAbduh then went to al-Azhar in hopes for a better experience, but encountered the same method of overemphasis on memorization rather than comprehension. At the time, students had to read texts that could not be understood without their commentaries, glosses, and super glosses. Despite ʿAbduh's traditional training, he shifted away from it and started studying other sciences.[60]

ʿAbduh was at the forefront of replacing traditional learning methods with the modern university system. To meet the threat of European-style institutions, many Islamic educational institutions were compelled to introduce western methods such as formal curricula, new subjects, entrance and course examinations, formally appointed faculties, and budgets that were subject to external governmental control.[61] The Tunisian scholar Ṭāhir b. ʿĀshūr (d. 1973) was also influenced by the efforts to reform education

[58] M. Hassan, *Longing for the Lost Caliphate*, 260.

[59] Yvonne Haddad, "Muhammad Abduh: Pioneer of Islamic Reform," in *Pioneers of Islamic Revival*, ed. Ali Rahnema (London: Zed Books, 1994), 31; ʿUthmān Amīn, *Rāʾid al-Fikr al-Misrī: al-Imām Muḥammad ʿAbduh* (Cairo: Maktabat al-Anjlū al-Miṣrīyah, 1965), 25.

[60] U. Amīn, *Muhammad ʿAbduh*, 26.

[61] D. Eickelman, "The Art of Memory," 488–489.

in Egypt and the opinions of ʿAbduh expressed in the *Manār* journal. Scholars like ʿAbduh and Ibn ʿĀshūr were products of the nineteenth-century Euro-Ottoman culture of modernization. They sought to reform what appeared to be a lack of dynamism and innovation in Traditionalist organizations. For these individuals, the formulation of a defined plan by the *ʿulamāʾ* who are aware of the requirements of the time and place is the first step toward educational reform.[62] In this regard, Islamic Modernists took Traditionalists to be the objects of reform rather than its agents.[63]

Traditionalists often criticize ʿAbduh for his role in discounting the works of classical scholars. Muḥammad ʿAwwāma rebukes ʿAbduh for criticizing most of the books that were being taught at al-Azhar. ʿAwwāma bemoaned ʿAbduh's belittling of those books because it led many young intellectuals to also label them as outdated and as a result also dismiss the scholars themselves. He states that this was the first rupture that disconnected Muslims from scholarly tradition. This is not an exaggeration according to ʿAwwāma because ʿAbduh and others like him were the first in Islamic history to petition for a method of studying Islam that was critical and dismissive of classical scholarship.[64] For instance, Ṭaha Ḥussein (d. 1973), a distinguished figure in Egypt's modernist movement, was inspired by ʿAbduh's criticism of previous scholarship. He promoted the idea that Islamic scholarship and most of its sciences were full of inaccuracies and fabrications. Ḥussein contended that pre-Islamic poetry was fabricated by later Muslim scholars for several reasons, one of which was to give credence to Qurʾānic myths.[65] Hussein's views attracted significant backlash which led him to abandon some of his more radical claims. Nevertheless, his highly critical approach left a significant impact.

Moreover, modern education brought with it new disciplines and methods of teaching, depriving the *ʿulamāʾ* of the centuries-old monopoly over the educational process. This produced new types of professionals and intellectuals who considered traditional Islamic knowledge irrelevant.[66] Since the *ʿulamāʾ* were supported by the Ottoman Empire, many of their institutions lost funding with the Empire's decline.

[62] Basheer Nafi, "Ṭāhir Ibn ʿĀshūr: The Career and Thought of a Modern Reformist ʿālim, with Special Reference to His Work of Tafsīr," *Journal of Qur'anic Studies*, 7, no. 1 (2005), 13.

[63] B. Ingram, *Revival from Below*, 17.

[64] M. ʿAwwāma, *Adab al-Ikhtilāf*, 161–162.

[65] M. ʿAwwāma, *Adab al-Ikhtilāf*, 162–163. Also see "Ṭāhā Ḥusayn," *Encyclopedia Britannica*, November 10,
2018, www.britannica.com/biography/Taha-Husayn, last accessed May 28, 2019.

[66] S. Farouki and B. Nafi, *Islamic Thought*, 6.

Essentially, traditional scholarship and education declined when the state stopped supporting them.[67]

With the world rapidly changing, from technological and scientific perspectives, many in the Muslim world aspired to catch up with the west and the traditional method of learning became more unpopular. Today, Sharia sciences are considered to be the domain of the underachiever. A degree in Islamic sciences, generally speaking, does not lead to a well-paid career. The Tanzimat reforms of Ottoman Sultan Maḥmūd II adopted some aspects of western law, and thereby initiated a challenge to the supremacy of Islamic law. However, the fall of the Empire resulted in replacing the entire Islamic legal system with western substantive law. Consequently, the government, which was previously the major employer of Traditionalist scholars, no longer needed experts in Islamic law.[68] Colonial governments' overall control of education further marginalized Islamic knowledge. Along with a shift in education, Muslim legal systems were largely replaced by the introduction of European codes. David Waines notes that, "In both cases it meant that those trained in traditional Islamic knowledge, the *'ulama'*, were disenfranchised and replaced socially by a new secularized Muslim elite."[69]

The shift away from employing the *'ulamā'* in governmental positions is important to understand the rise of intellectuals who did not undergo traditional training. However, their unemployability is also important for understanding how the *'ulamā'* viewed themselves. The notion that the *'ulamā'* were merely "religious" professionals was rather new. Prior to the rise of secular states, the primary function of the *madrasas* was the education of scholars for state employment.[70] Although Sharia is institutionally inoperative, it remains as a moral resource.

Legal education was redefined in the Muslim world in the past century with the adoption of European codes, procedures, and courts. Although Islamic law has been largely excluded from the curricula of modern law schools, Islamic legal theory has been retained, but on a highly reduced scale. Moreover, Islamic legal theory is taught through modern textbooks, which means that students do not directly access classical works.[71] New educational

[67] See Rudolph Peters, "Religious Attitudes towards Modernization in the Ottoman Empire: A Nineteenth Century Pious Text on Steamships, Factories and the Telegraph," *Die Welt des Islams*, 1. no. 4 (1986), 76–105.

[68] Monique Cardinal, "Islamic Legal Theory Curriculum: Are the Classics Taught Today?," *Islamic Law and Society*, 12, no. 2 (2005), 268–269.

[69] David Waines, "Islam," in *Religion in the Modern World: Traditions and Transformations*, ed. Linda Woodhead (New York: Routledge, 2002), 224.

[70] B. Ingram, *Revival from Below*, 40–44.

[71] M. Cardinal, "Curriculum," 224.

systems paralyzed Traditionalist institutions. Scholars and students who studied in the Traditional system for years were out of work and not recognized by the state. Most students entering college sought to become doctors, engineers, teachers, or lawyers. It was students who could not get into any of these schools due to poor grades that would study Islamic sciences. The state and public accepted them as religious authorities because they had degrees from modern universities. This outraged Traditionalist scholars, who went through a much more rigorous curriculum and educational system, and now had little hope in a career or being accepted anywhere outside of Traditionalists circles.[72] Göran Larsson explains that "Slowly, it became more rewarding to hold a doctoral degree from a Western university than to have a similar degree from an Islamic educational institution."[73]

The adoption of the modern university system over the traditional educational helped diminish the authority of the *'ulamā'* and paved the way for those who studied outside the traditional method to be considered authorities. Eickelman explains that the introduction of mass higher education in the Middle East has eroded the positions of Traditionalists. He notes: "Religious authority in earlier generations derived from the mastery of authoritative texts studied under recognized scholars. Mass education fosters a direct, albeit selective, access to the printed word and a break with earlier traditions of authority."[74] 'Awwāma laments that the shift in educational methods produced a new generation of professors who teach Islam based on what they think, even if that disagrees with the four schools of law or ḥadīth scholars such as Bukhārī or Muslim.[75]

The style of religious training through the university system constitutes a significant break with the earlier emphasis on the written word, mediated by an oral tradition and geared toward a mastery of accepted religious texts acquired through studying with recognized religious scholars. The university system delineates subjects and prescribed texts are taught by a changing array of teachers, and competence is measured by examination.[76] Göran Larsson points out that even the prestigious Al-Azhar university was forced to abandon its age-old policy of requiring complete memorization of the Qur'ān as a prerequisite for admission.[77]

72 A. Abū Ghudda, Lecture in Turkey.

73 G. Larsson, *Muslims and the New Media*, 41.

74 Dale Eickelman, "Mass Higher Education and the Religious Imagination in Contemporary Arab Societies," *American Ethnologist*, 19, no. 4 (1992), 646.

75 M. 'Awwāma, *Adab al-Ikhtilāf*, 164.

76 D. Eickelman, "Mass Higher Education," 650.

77 G. Larsson, *Muslims and the New Media*, 37.

Ultimately, the post-Ottoman political, educational, and religious context facilitated the contestation of traditional *'ulamā'* and the issue of religious authority took center stage. Colonization, modernization, and globalization all contributed to creating a plethora of religious movements all claiming authenticity and contesting the authority of traditional *'ulamā'*. Traditionalists responded to the diversification and fragmentation of authority in the contemporary world by insisting following the *madhhab*s protects individuals and the community from inconsistent application of Islamic law. In their view, bypassing traditional learning opens the door to legal anarchy and disorder.[78]

With the introduction of secular schooling systems in the Muslim world the *'ulamā'* lost their positions as gatekeepers of Islamic knowledge. Individuals who studied Islam in these universities did so outside the circles of Traditionalist *'ulamā'* and often positioned themselves against them. Individuals emerged who argued that Islam is simple and easy to understand. Self-taught Muslim intellectuals began offering themselves as alternative voices of Islamic interpretation. Traditionalists held that bypassing traditional Islamic education will result in chaos and extremism and they considered Salafism to be the fruit of anticlericalism.[79]

THE PRINTING PRESS AND NEW MEDIA

With the rise of the new media, the mass consumption of Islamic knowledge is at people's fingertips. Before the internet, anyone looking for information on Islam had to consult a scholar or search through books. The overload of Islamic information available today has allowed people to learn without leaving their homes. While access to information is a great benefit to many, it comes with some pitfalls. The introduction of the printing press in the Muslim world also played a role in the decline of traditional education because it was the increase in the availability of books that made it easy to learn without studying directly with a scholar. The printing press threatened to release scripture from the structure of discipline and authority that governed its social existence and ensured its moral reception.[80] This challenged traditional pedagogical methods and provided an outlet for others to redefine Islam by taking its interpretation out of the hands of the *'ulamā'*

[78] Fachrizal Halim, "Reformulating the *Madhhab* in Cyberspace: Legal Authority, Doctrines, and *Ijtihād* among Contemporary Shāfi'ī 'Ulamā'," *Islamic Law and Society*, 22, no. 4 (2015), 433.

[79] J. Brown, "Is Islam Easy to Understand," 119–120.

[80] G. Larsson, *Muslims and the New Media*, 343.

and appropriating for themselves the authority to interpret Islam. Because scholarship in the Ottoman Empire was primarily based on the *ijāza* system those who claimed scholarship outside this system were not considered credible.

The decline of traditional Islamic education had been drastically altered as early as the late 1700s. Napoleon Bonaparte's invasion of Egypt and the introduction of the printing press were important factors in changing religious authority.[81] Printed books attacked the very heart of Islamic systems for the transmission of knowledge; relying on books alone attacked what was understood to make knowledge trustworthy and authoritative.[82] In many modern western societies, writing is more reliable than speech. However, in the *ijāza* system oral expression was essential to ensure correct understanding. When a scholar was unable to obtain knowledge directly from an author, he strove to get it from a scholar whose *isnād* from the original author was thought to be most reliable.[83] The printing press facilitated the emergence of self-taught Salafis because they provided them the tools needed to bypass scholars. Cassette tapes and the internet created another dimension of communication where students of Salafi scholars were able to record and disseminate thousands of lectures.

The printing press and cassette tapes allowed Salafi autodidacts such as Albānī to access and share knowledge without studying with scholars. While print enabled Traditionalists to extend their influence in public affairs it was also challenging their authority. With the mass printing of classical works, scholars were not always around when these texts were read. Their monopoly over the transmission of knowledge was depleted. Books which they possessed and transmitted with a whole series of mnemonic aids to memory, could now be consulted by anyone who would make what they will of them. The force of 1,200 years of oral master–disciple transmission became increasingly ignored.[84] Modern documentary culture vilifies memorization as irrational and superfluous. For Traditionalists, memorization was not thoughtless repetition, but it was a learning skill that enhanced memory and instilled virtues for which memory was essential.[85] This is not to say that Traditionalists did not use texts, but texts were not studied alone without a teacher. "Proper scholarship" consisted of a slow study of texts in the presence of a teacher.

[81] D. Eickelman, "The Art of Memory," 487–488. [82] F. Robinson, "Technology," 234.
[83] F. Robinson, "Technology," 237. [84] F. Robinson, "Technology," 245–246.
[85] S. Haj, *Reconfiguring Islamic Tradition*, 12.

Traditional educational methods consisted of a developed and layered scholastic tradition of religious interpretation, which otherwise constrains and regulates, in a rigorous fashion, the output of opinions. With the minimization of this method through the fall of the traditional institutions and the rise of print and the internet, it is striking how relatively easy it is to become an authority. The rise in new forms of communication, such as books, audio cassettes, television, and the internet, gave laity an outlet to share their understanding of Islam even if they did not have formal training in Islamic sciences.[86] The use of audio cassettes in the 1960s and 1970s was even used by scholars to reach the masses. For example, the tapes of the famous Egyptian preacher ʿAbd al-Ḥamīd Kishk (d. 1996) were distributed all over the world. Mass higher education, print, and the internet provided unprecedented access to Islamic texts and subjected their interpretation to techniques outside the framework of Traditionalist education.[87] This expanded the pool of people who could participate in religious education and hence challenged the authority of the *ʿulamāʾ*.

In the history of Muslim thought and belief, new media very often played a key role in the introduction and distribution of new religious interpretations. The introduction of the printing press in the Middle East in the nineteenth century led to the emergence of a new class of Muslim intellectuals who were successfully able to challenge the authority of religiously established *ʿulamāʾ*. Had they not had the possibility to spread their ideas through new channels of communications that could not be controlled by the *ʿulamāʾ*, the reformers of the nineteenth and twentieth centuries would hardly have had the same impact.[88] For instance, print was essential to Albānī's popularity. In 1957, Zuhayr al-Shāwīsh, a Damascene Salafi, established a publishing house in Damascus, al-Maktab al-Islāmī, which built a reputation for itself in its early years as a scholarly press that published critical editions of classical works that bolstered the Salafi mission, including many of the writings of Ibn Taymiyya and his student Ibn Qayyim. These publications were distinguished because they contained detailed tables of contents and indexes, few printing errors, and, most importantly, rigorous

[86] On cassette tapes and Islamic revival see Charles Hirschkind, *The Ethical Soundscape: Cassette Sermons and Islamic Counterpublics* (New York: Columbia University Press, 2009). Also see Jakob Skovgaard-Petersen, "New Media in the Muslim World," *Oxford Encyclopedia of Islam and Politics*, ed. Emad El-Din Shahin (Oxford and New York, 2014), 183–188.

[87] J. Anderson, "The Internet," 49.

[88] Jan Scholz, Are Selge, Max Stille, and Johannes Zimmermann, "Listening Communities? Some Remarks on the Construction of Religious Authority in Islamic Podcasts," *Die Welt Des Islams*, 48, no. 3–4 (2008), 460. Also see J. Anderson, "The Internet," 48.

documentation of ḥadīth. It was in this latter capacity – as the ḥadīth editor – that Shāwīsh hired Albānī and through which Albānī's scholarship would be showcased.[89]

Previously, Albānī's writings were published through a Damascene reformist journal, *al-Tamaddun al-Islāmī*, which had limited circulation. Shāwīsh published many of Albānī's earlier writings with al-Maktab al-Islāmī, and, with his distribution networks, established Albānī's name and reputation among Salafi publics in the Gulf and elsewhere. Indeed, it was Albānī's writings through al-Maktab al-Islāmī that attracted the attention of leading Salafis in Saudi Arabia such as the former mufti ʿAbd al-Azīz b. Bāz. Al-Maktab al-Islāmī was Albānī's exclusive publisher for decades until he had a falling out with Shāwīsh in the 1990s and the two parted ways. Shāwīsh's pivotal role in spreading the teachings of Salafis such as Albānī was best expressed by ʿAlī al-Ṭanṭāwī (d. 1999), who said, "Were it not for Zuhayr, the views of Nāṣir [al-Dīn al-Albānī] would not have circulated."[90] Shāwīsh and al-Maktab al-Islāmī helped spread a form of Salafism that focused on ḥadīth verification, authenticity, and basing all Islamic teachings thereon that shaped and authenticated modern Salafi Islam.

For centuries, the *ʿulamāʾ* had the exclusive role of scriptural interpreters and religious authority. Laity had no role in the interpretation process, nor did they have the tools to challenge religious authority because texts and outlets to share opinions were very limited. However, the mass proliferation of religious texts through print and the internet have changed this considerably.[91] A clear example is the rise in Qurʾānic translations over the last twenty years.[92] Using the internet, one can find hundreds of previously

[89] Jawad Qureshi, "Zuhayr al-Shāwīsh (1925–2013) and al-Maktab al-Islami: Print, Hadith Verification, and Authenticated Islam," presentation of an unpublished paper at the American Academy of Religion, November 21, 2016. ʿAlī Jumʿa also attributes Albānī's popularity to Shāwīsh: see "Wallāhu Aʿlam: Al-Duktur ʿAlī Jumʿa Yataḥaddath ʿan Adawāt al-Albānī fī Taḍʿīf al-Aḥādīth," www.youtube.com/watch?v=yhiYnXx2d9Q, last accessed April 11, 2018.

[90] J. Qureshi, "Zuhayr."

[91] On the rise and impact of print in the Muslim world see G. Larsson, *Muslims and the New Media*, 21–45.

[92] For example, there were a total of four English translations in the seventeenth to nineteenth centuries. Conversely, there were approximately forty translations in the twentieth century, and thirty in the twenty-first century. Charles Hirschkind argues that the authority and transmission of the Qurʾān were based on both hearing and listening. It is not possible to obtain religious authority through a single medium because it interconnects the ear, heart, and voice. See Charles Hirschkind, "Media and the Qurʾān," in *The Encyclopedia of the Quran*, ed. Jane McAuliffe (Leiden: Brill, 2003), 342. On the Qurʾān and new media also see G. Larsson, *Muslims and the New Media*, 167–193.

nonexistent Qurʾān translations as well as ḥadīth corpuses in multiple languages.

It is important to note that none of these sites is specifically autodidactic, but their collective presence has increased the disparity between teacher–student education and literary/electronic resources. When such translations were not readily available the only way laity could gain access to the meaning and interpretation of the Qurʾān was through a scholar. Charles Hirschkind notes that "the printing press threatened to unleash the sacred text from the structure of discipline and authority that governed its social existence and ensured its ethical reception."[93] This challenged traditional pedagogical methods and provided an outlet for autodidacts to redefine Islam by taking its interpretation out of the hands of the *ʿulamāʾ* and appropriating for themselves the authority to interpret Islam. Once a book was printed it was now beyond the sphere of a scholar's direct authority. It was no longer possible for him to influence the readers' attitude toward the text. Additionally, the reader who lost communication with the scholar frequently ignored the commentary and focused solely on the original.[94]

Laity's independence from religious scholars and their direct access to scripture pose a significant challenge to the *ʿulamāʾ* because they are often asked by lay Muslims to explain the authenticity of the proof-texts they use as well as their method of coming to religious judgments. Göran Larsson explains that new information and technology are the agents that started the process in which the authority of Traditionalist *ʿulamāʾ* came to be questioned. This paved the way for scholars who preferred *ijtihād* over *taqlīd* because the importance of the individual was stressed rather than putting the scholar at the center.[95] For instance, reformers like Albānī, a self-taught Salafi scholar, may have inspired a "do it yourself" form of Islam among the laity. Albānī considers the teacher to be important in the learning process, but his criticism of *taqlīd* and over-reverence of the scholarly class contributed to having the laity challenge scholars.[96] In particular, he insisted that laypeople always ask scholars to provide proof-texts (*dalīl*s), this empowered lay Muslims with the decisive belief that they must take the interpretation and reconciliation of scripture into their own hands.[97]

[93] C. Hirschkind, "Media and the Qurʾān," 343.

[94] Reinhard Schulze, "The Birth of Tradition and Modernity in the 18th and 19th Century Islamic Culture – The Case of Printing," *Culture and History*, 16 (1997), 48.

[95] G. Larsson, *Muslims and the New Media*, 44.

[96] On Albānī's encouragement of laity to challenge scholars see E. Hamdeh, "Salafi Polemic." On Albānī's life and autodidactic education see E. Hamdeh, "Formative Years."

[97] See J. Brown, "Is Islam Easy to Understand."

The internet and searchable online religious libraries make it easy for lay Muslims to perform this "*ijtihād*." The availability of sources is what led the Salafi Muḥammad Sulṭān al-Khujnadī (d. 1960) to promote a "do it yourself" where one does not need the four legal schools. One needs only the Qur'ān and major ḥadīth collections to understand the religion.[98] Fachrizal Halim refers to this as the phenomenon of "instant experts." These are intellectuals who may not be trained in Islamic legal knowledge in the same manner as traditional *'ulamā'*, but who are nonetheless capable of accessing the substantive content of legal knowledge.[99] The internet positions *'ulamā'*, who are often indulged in the study of complex Islamic sciences, to be in constant competition with the random results of Google searches. Therefore, there exists an easy avenue to challenge established religious interpretation and share it with the public who most likely would not have come in contact with the sender's views without the internet.[100] Intellectual Muslim reformers, *dā'īs*, lay preachers, as well as entertainers, offer themselves as the alternative voices of religious authority.

Everyday Muslims do not need to rely on their local scholars as means of knowledge, because websites like Islamqa.info and Askimam.com allow them to ask a question comfortably without leaving their home or revealing their identity.[101] The removal of the human element from the educational process also provides a number of obstacles for traditionally trained scholars. For instance, they worry that untrained people are prepared to interpret Islam without proper education. Peter Mandaville correctly notes that one

[98] Muḥammad Sulṭān al-Khujnadī Ma'ṣūmī, *Hal al-Muslim Mulzam bi-ittibā' Madhhab Mu'ayyan Min al-Madhāhib al-Arba'a?*, ed. Salīm Hilālī (Amman: al-Maktaba al-Islāmīya, 1984).

[99] F. Halim, "Reformulating the *Madhhab*," 425.

[100] J. Scholz et al., "Listening Communities," 462.

[101] The importance of knowing the identity of the questioner is more important in a fatwa than it is in transmitting knowledge. Fatwas are often geared toward the specific questioner and not meant to be general. However, these fatwas are available online for others to access and apply to their particular case, even if the mufti may not have intended it for them. This poses a problem to scholars because it sometimes results in people choosing fatwas that best suit their personal interests or what they find easiest. This process is often referred to as "fatwa shopping." In the past, "fatwa shopping" was not as easy because it required traveling, or communicating via phone or mail with numerous scholars to obtain numerous opinions. In some cases, scholars refused to give fatwas if the question was tied to a local cultural issue that they did not have knowledge of. The internet removes the time, locality, and particularity of the fatwa. Hence, search engines like Google provide a large database of information that supplies common people with a wide array of fatwas and religious teachings, but not the tools to properly deal with it. On the internet and the process of decision making and construction of Islamic knowledge see Vit Sisler, "The Internet and the Construction of Islamic Knowledge in Europe," *Masaryk University Journal of Law and Technology* , 1, no. 2 (2007), 205–217.

can never really be sure whether the advice received on the internet "is coming from a classically trained religious scholar or a hydraulic engineer moonlighting as an amateur *ʿalim*."[102]

The phenomenon of seeking religious insight from nonexperts through new media can be seen in the rise of Muslim televangelists and YouTubers. For instance, the shows of Egyptian televangelist Amr Khaled are watched by millions across the world. Khaled has over thirty million fans on Facebook and over three hundred thousand subscribers on YouTube. In 2007, he was named the thirteenth most influential person in the world by *Time* magazine. Khaled broadcasts his religious advice, admonishments, and opinions on scripture to young viewers throughout the world. Ironically, Khaled is not a trained scholar of religion. He never studied at al-Azhar or any clerical institution or seminary but is rather an accountant by training.[103] Despite his lack of training, and Traditionalist criticism of his authority, Khaled's message appeals to a large number of Muslims who want an easy way to understand Islamic tradition. Khaled's set is similar to Oprah Winfrey's and his style and method models that of Billy Graham and Joel Osteen.[104] Khaled and other YouTube scholars appeal to modern sensibilities that are often consumed with a flagrant sense of certainty. The antihierarchical, individually empowering, and simplistic hermeneutics of their methods appeal to many Muslims, but they stand in stark contrast to Traditionalism that provides a more complex and comprehensive approach to Islamic scripture.

In the standards of traditionally trained scholars, Khaled is not qualified and has no right to express his opinions on Islam. Many *ʿulamāʾ*, including Yūsuf al-Qaraḍāwī have questioned whether Khaled possesses the qualifications of what Muslims should do.[105] Nevertheless, Khaled is not the only one who has usurped the role traditionally reserved for the *ʿulamāʾ* as the sole interpreters of Islam. As Reza Aslan notes, "All over the world, a slew of self-styled preachers, spiritual gurus, academics, activists, and amateur intellectuals have begun redefining Islam by taking its interpretation out of the iron

[102] Peter Mandaville, "Reimagining Islam in Diaspora: The Politics of Mediated Community," *International Communication Gazette*, 63, no. 2–3 (2001), 183.

[103] Reza Aslan, *No God but God* (New York: Random House, 2011), 281.

[104] Peter Mandaville, *Islam and Politics* ,2nd ed. (New York: Routledge, 2014), 394. Khaled has also been dismissed by groups such as the Muslim Brotherhood for being out of touch with the reality and struggles of everyday Egyptians. They dismissed him as being representative of what Haenni and Tammam have called "air-conditioned Islam." See Patrick Haenni and Husam Tammam, "Egypt's Air-Conditioned Islam," *Le Monde Diplomatique*, September 2003, https://mondediplo.com/2003/09/03egyptislam, last accessed May 20, 2020.

[105] P. Mandaville, *Islam and Politics*, 395.

grip of the Ulama and seizing for themselves the power to dictate the future of this rapidly expanding and deeply fractured faith."[106]

The internet has reconfigured traditional structures of authority and new authorities are emerging. Opportunities to acquire knowledge about Islam have emerged through YouTube, online universities, social media, and search engines such as Google. Millions of people use the internet as their primary source of information about Islam. By asking questions to "Shaykh Google," students no longer have to spend money to travel in search of knowledge and experience the challenges and culture shock that accompanied it. Instead, they can simultaneously search themes and terms in the Qurʾān, ḥadīth corpus, and thousands of Islamic texts in an instant. The internet also allows laypeople to convey their own understanding of Islam. This has serious implications for the way in which Islam is learned, given the diverse material and perspectives available online, as well as the random and nonsystematic method in which this information is accessed.[107]

Traditionalists often position themselves as masters of an Islamic tradition that is complex. The internet and search engines create a culture of immediacy. All answers are within the press of a button or a quick search. Traditionalists are often viewed as out of touch because of the difficulty in communicating the complexity of Islamic legal tradition without diluting it or undermining their authority.[108] In addition, they are in constant competition with popular preachers who attract large followings with simplistic, but appealing presentations of Islamic subjects.

RESERVATIONS AGAINST SELF-LEARNING

Traditionally trained scholars often caution about the many educational pitfalls of learning without a teacher. It was problematic if the student obtained knowledge from books rather than through a teacher because on their own, books were a threat to the epistemological basis on which Islamic revelation and traditional educational methods stood.[109] Traditionally trained scholars found self-learning problematic because it threatened the entire educational and authoritative system. Without particular expectations of qualifications through the teacher–student link, the untrained could effortlessly claim scholarly authority. Abū Isḥāq al-Shāṭibī (d. 790/1388)

[106] R. Aslan, *No God but God*, 281. [107] G. Bunt, *Virtually Islamic*, 3.

[108] B. Ingram, *Revival from Below*, 213.

[109] Paul Heck, "The Epistemological Problem of Writing in Islamic Civilization: al-Ḫaṭīb al-Baġdādī's (d. 463/1071) 'Taqyid al-ʿilm'," *Studia Islamica*, no. 94 (2002), 86.

argues that when this link is interrupted, heresy (*bidʿa*) occurs, because abandoning the adherence to a teacher is an indication of following an evil innovation in religion.[110] In other words, Shāṭibī considers knowledge acquired outside of this link to lack authority and validity.

A person might graduate from the most prestigious western university, but if he did not learn Islam from a qualified Muslim teacher through the *ijāza* system, his knowledge is not considered authentic by Muslims who believe in the traditional system.[111] The production of a scholar in the traditional system would not be possible by self-learning, intensive weekend seminars, or online classes. Studying directly with a teacher for extended periods was vital because it allowed the teacher to vouch for the student at the scholarly, spiritual, and personal level. Those who do not follow the traditional method of learning tend to do away with the entire system. They consider the Muslim community to have gone wrong and believe it their job to put it right. They attempt to retrieve the "true" teachings of Islam from the oppressive institutions that caused centuries of stagnant scholarship and blind imitation of scholarly authority. They create a do-it-yourself method where one will come to an authentic reading of scripture by putting tradition to the side and approaching Islamic texts with a fresh reading.[112] The emergence of reformers over the last few centuries who insisted the texts are easy to understand opened the floodgates of individuals who dismissed the importance of scholarly expertise in textual interpretation.

Muḥammad Saʿīd Ramaḍān al-Būṭī explains that there are certain unequivocal texts whose meanings are easy to understand for both scholars and nonscholars. However, there are also verses that the common Muslims could not properly understand, such as those relating to divorce, inheritance, prayer, and charity. In this case, it is only the *ʿulamāʾ* who have the right to

[110] Abū Isḥāq al-Shāṭibī, *Al-Muwāfaqat*, Vol. 1 (Al-Khubar: Dār Ibn ʿAffān, 1997), 145.

[111] On a separate, but related issue, ʿAbd al-Fattāḥ Abū Ghudda explains that while some Orientalists who study Islam are objective and well intentioned, their knowledge is still not considered authentic because it lacks the methodology and spirituality that is passed down in Traditionalists circles. He explains that Orientalists often err because:

> They acquire knowledge from other than its people, they acquire it from books, and they study it in a language other than their own. They are studying sciences without having a spiritual connection to them and base their study on faulty methodologies established by their predecessors. On top of that, there is still the influence of their upbringing and beliefs which overcomes them, and they end up diverging from genuine knowledge.

See Aḥmad Shākir, *Taṣḥīḥ al-Kutub wa Ṣunʿ al-Fahāris wa Kayfīyat Ḍabṭ al-Kitāb wa Sabq al-Muslimīn al-Afranj fī Dhālik*, ed. ʿAbd al-Fattāḥ Abū Ghudda (Cairo: Maktabat al-Sunna, 1994), 13.

[112] J. Brown, "Is Islam Easy to Understand"; M. Zaman, "The ʿUlamāʾ," 8.

interpret these texts. Traditionally trained *'ulamā'* often defend their expertise and sole right to interpret scripture by comparing themselves to experts in other fields, and warn of the chaos that would ensue if common people bypassed those experts.[113] An analogy often given by Traditionalists is that of physicians being challenged by patients brandishing internet opinions about treatments and diagnoses. Physicians will point out the dangers of people practicing medicine based only on their online research.[114] However, the analogies provided by Traditionalists are often dismissed by popularist preachers as appeals to authority.

'Abd al-Fattāḥ Abū Ghudda describes the phenomenon of interpreting religion without proper qualifications as "the affliction of modern times" (*muṣībat al-'aṣr*). He states that some people think they can surpass previous scholars using only books, the Qur'ān, Sunna, and their reason. Abū Ghudda explains that autodidacts argue that a plethora of information is now available through books and the internet that was not available to scholars in the past. Like other *'ulamā'*, Abū Ghudda argues that there are things beyond the texts, such as the interpretation of the scholarly community, that are lost when one studies alone. In his view, it is dangerously misleading to approach texts and discuss them outside of their historical, cultural, and linguistic contexts.[115] In the Traditionalist scheme, education is about the reference to scripture, but understanding them according to scholarly methods. Ismā'īl al-Anṣārī observes that there are other problems with studying only from texts. Texts commonly have typographical errors; without a teacher to identify these mistakes the person will follow them unknowingly. Self-taught individuals bypass teachers in hopes of not performing *taqlīd*, but instead, they end up performing *taqlīd* of printed books. He states, "This is what blameworthy *taqlīd* produces from the one who blames praiseworthy *taqlīd*!"[116]

The internet often produces more confusion than knowledge. Although people may think they are learning when they search the internet, they are more likely to be immersed in yet more data they do not understand. As Tom Nichols points out, "Seeing words on a screen is not the same as understanding them."[117] Put differently, what often happens online is an avoidance of reading in the traditional sense. It is not reading with the aim of learning but reading to win an argument or confirm a preexisting belief.

[113] M. Būṭī, *Al-Lā Madhhabiyya*, 146.
[114] G. Bunt, *Islam in the Digital Age*, 3.
[115] A. Abū Ghudda, Lecture in Turkey.
[116] Ismā'īl al-Anṣārī, *Ibāḥat*, 106.
[117] T. Nichols, *Death of Expertise*, 119.

Experts who insist on a systematic method of learning and logic cannot compete with a machine that always gives readers their preferred answers.[118]

The late-Ottoman Ḥanafī jurist Ibn ʿĀbidīn (d. 1258/1842), who was also the most distinguished scholar of his time, explains that the absence of a teacher to correct misunderstandings results in lay readers not fully grasping technical terminology.[119] Superficiality is what often accompanies self-study and is perhaps amplified in today's era of immediacy of information and instant gratification.[120] Muḥammad Ḥasan Hitou, a Syrian Shāfiʿī jurist who studied in al-Azhar, gives an example of one of his own students who read a text that says *Yandub saddu furja fī al-ṣaff*, which means that one who is praying can fill in the gap. The dots on the last letter in the word *furja* were missing as is common in many Arabic texts. The student mistakenly read it as *Yandub saddu farjihi fī al-ṣaff*. which means that one should cover their private parts when standing in line for prayer. When asked to explain the text the student said that during prayer one should place a tissue in their underwear to ensure no urine gets on their clothes during prayer. Hitou notes that this student should not be chastised because he was learning with a teacher and was happily corrected for his misunderstanding. However, autodidacts do not have anyone to correct their misunderstanding of texts. What is worse, Hitou explains, is that they also want to enforce their misunderstanding of texts on everyone else.[121]

Muṣṭafā al-Sibāʿī (d. 1964), a prominent Syrian politician and ḥadīth scholar, makes a similar point. He gives an example of a layperson who refrained from getting a haircut on Friday morning for several years because he had read a ḥadīth that prohibited *ḥalq* before the Friday prayers. Eventually, he learned that the ḥadīth was actually talking about having groups sit in circles in the mosques (*ḥilaq*) because they disrupt and inconvenience the congregants.[122]

There is also a context often missing when one relies only on texts. For instance, one can be misinformed by a misprint. Muḥammad ʿAwwāma points out that sometimes there are different narrations where the Arabic

[118] T. Nichols, *Death of Expertise*, 115–120.

[119] Muḥammad Amīn ibn ʿĀbidīn was a prominent Ḥanafī scholar who lived in Damascus. He is sometimes considered the school's final verifier (*muḥaqqiq*). This work is important, because it is considered the final word on most Ḥanafī legal issues. See Ed. EI2, art. Ibn ʿĀbidīn.

[120] Muḥammad Amīn Ibn ʿĀbidīn, *Radd al-Muḥtār ʿalā al-Durra al-Mukhtār Sharḥ Tanwīr al-Abṣār* (Riyadh: Dār ʿĀlim al-Kutub, 2003), 139.

[121] Muḥammad Ḥasan Hitou, *Al-Mutafayhiqūn* (Syria: Dār al-Farābī, 2009), 26–27.

[122] Muṣṭafā al-Sibāʿī, *Al-Sunna wa Makānatuhā fī al-Tashrīʿ al-Islāmī* (Beiruit: Al-Maktab al-Islāmī/Cairo: Darussalam, 2006), 367.

short vowels differ. Consequently, this results in different *fiqh* opinions, because the variation in short vowels change the meanings. Concerning this, ʿAwwāma shares an incident between the Syrian scholar ʿAbd al-ʿAzīz ʿUyūn al-Sūd (d. 1978) and the young Albānī:

> A man who I did not know entered upon me in the mosque before the afternoon call to prayer, then someone told me his name – then our shaykh told me his name, and it was shaykh Nāṣir al-Albānī! – so he sat and waited for the call to prayer. When the caller to prayer said: Allāhu Akbara[123] Allāhu Akbar – with a "a" after the "r" – this man said in revolt and anger: "This is wrong, this is an innovation!" Our shaykh [ʿAbd al-ʿAzīz ʿUyūn al-Sūd] said: "What is wrong and an innovation?" Albānī said: "This contradicts what is in the *Ṣaḥīḥ* of Muslim!" Our shaykh repeated the question: "What is in the *Ṣaḥīḥ* of Muslim?" [Albānī] said: "What is in the *Ṣaḥīḥ* of Muslim is Allāhu Akbaru Allāhu Akbar – with a 'u' after the 'r'" – our shaykh then said to him in his known mannered and calm way: "Did you acquire Muslim's *Ṣaḥīḥ* from your teachers, from their teachers, back to imam Muslim [learning so] that he narrated the ḥadīth with a 'u' after the 'r', or was it based on what is printed in an edition?!" Our shaykh then said: "He kept silent, so I kept silent, and he prayed and took off."[124]

ʿAwwāma intends to highlight that there is a lot of meaning lost when relying only on books. ʿAwwāma goes on to say: "This man [Albānī] does not have any shaykhs except one shaykh – from the scholars of Aleppo – through *ijāza*, not by *talaqqī*, acquiring it, companionship, and following [the scholar]."[125] Other Traditionalists have also pointed to the mistakes Albānī made as a result of relying on print. For instance, Ismāʿīl al-Anṣārī notes that in a printed version of Ṭabarī's *tafsīr* there is a chain of narration that mistakenly says "Alqama *narrated from* Marthad" rather than "Alqama *the son of* Marthad." Based on this Albānī looked up Marthad and found that al-Dhahabī said that he does not have any known narration. Anṣārī states:

> This is a mistake! Albānī performed *taqlīd* of the printers!! The correct chain says "From ʿAlqama b. Marthad"... Furthermore, had Albānī pondered over Dhahabī's statement "He does not have a known narration" he would have been guided to the correct answer, because had that narration been from Marthad from Mujāhid, he would have had a known narration! However, this is what blameworthy *taqlīd* produces from the one who blames praiseworthy *taqlīd*![126]

[123] Ending the word with the *fatḥa* short vowel. [124] M. ʿAwwāma, *Athar*, 47.
[125] M. ʿAwwāma, *Athar*, 47. [126] I. Anṣārī, *Ibāḥat*, 106.

Traditionalists lament about a new generation who have a superficial understanding of Islam but are nevertheless in positions of leadership. Calls for *ijtihād* and reform include the nontrained layperson. Hitou notes that this call to *ijtihād* evolved into a dismissal of *fiqh* that tens of thousands of the greatest scholars of the *umma* contributed to in order to build an Islamic system that governed the Islamic world for fourteen centuries. He says: "This call to *ijtihād* is actually an invitation to destroy this great structure." He goes on to say that self-learning results in thinking that the early scholars were mistaken and accusing them of not following scripture. "They tell people not to follow the great classical scholars, but to follow the Sunna of the Messenger of God, as though the classical scholars were enemies of the Sunna."[127] Traditionalists consider the call to return to the Qurʾān and Sunna instead of the *madhhab*s an implicit accusation that the *madhhab*s follow something other than the Qurʾān and Sunna. What is meant by calls to prefer scripture over scholarly opinions is that the *madhhab*s should not be followed when they contradict a text. However, this is problematic because it is directed toward the scholars, but lay Muslims are often included in this invitation to evaluate legal opinions in light of scripture. Consequently, lay Muslims begin questioning scholarly opinions in light of scripture despite their lack of expertise.

Abū Ghudda notes that *ijtihād* cannot be accomplished by only reading texts. It is a challenging endeavor for which most people are unqualified. Abū Ghudda responds to autodidacts who claim to bypass the legal schools and follow the Qurʾān and Sunna, "So does that mean that Abū Ḥanīfa, Mālik, Aḥmad, and al-Shāfiʿī follow the Bible?! Some people think if they read a few books on *ḥadīth* they become *muḥaddith*s!"[128] In other words, by claiming to use only their reason and scripture autodidacts insinuate that *ʿulamāʾ* followed their personal opinions rather than scripture.

When autodidacts discard traditional learning methods it is more than just cutting corners, but it is a rejection of scholarly institutions and their authority. For traditionally trained *ʿulamāʾ*, education is not only the ability to cite scripture, but also to understand it according to their principles of interpretation. The internet created a democratization of Islamic knowledge that breaks down the standard notions of religious authority. This democratization of knowledge was not viewed positively by everyone. Jonathan Brown explains that although there are frequent calls for a "Muslim Martin Luther," Traditionalist *ʿulamāʾ* would suggest that much of the

[127] M. Hitou, *Al-Mutafayhiqūn*, 2–3. [128] A. Abū Ghudda, Lecture in Turkey.

turmoil and extremism in the Muslim world results precisely from unlearned Muslims deciding to break with tradition and approach their religion Luther-like, by scripture alone.[129] For example, while condemning ISIS, Hamza Yusuf, a famous American Muslim, complained how "stupid young boys" have dismissed scholarly tradition which requires years of training for the superficiality and errors of internet searches.[130]

Similarly, Hitou notes that self-learning leads lay intellectuals to think that they have mastered texts, and they give fatwas that contradict scholarly consensus.[131] This undermines traditional scholars because autodidacts use texts found on the internet to overshadow thousands of scholars trained within the traditional system. Abū Ghudda mockingly refers to the computer as *ḥāfiẓ al-ʿaṣr* (the greatest scholar of modern times), where people leave real-life teachers and resort to a machine for information.[132] Like Abū Ghudda, the American scholar Yasir Qadhi described the advent of online culture and its lack of appreciation for genuine knowledge as one "of the biggest tragedies of the modern era."[133]

Qadhi explains that most people cannot distinguish between a scholar, a student of sacred knowledge, an eloquent preacher who lacks knowledge, and a misguided individual. Although all of these categories of people exist offline, in the online world they are all obscure and indistinguishable for many. He cautions his Facebook followers that listening to lectures online in a haphazard manner, and from various disciplines, might give the false impression that one is grounded in Islamic sciences. However, he warns that most of these individuals have not even studied a single science of Islam from cover to cover. Why is it challenging for people to distinguish between a lay preacher and a scholar? The internet allows people to mimic intellectual accomplishments by indulging in what Nichols calls an "illusion of expertise" supported by an unlimited amount of facts. Oftentimes, these facts are not even facts because the freedom to post anything online floods the internet with misinformation. Even then, facts are not the same thing as knowledge and scholarship. Typing words into a search engine is not research, rather it is asking programmable machines that do not actually

129 J. Brown, *Misquoting Muhammad*, 7.

130 See Hamza Yusuf, "The Crisis of ISIS: A Prophetic Prediction," www.youtube.com/watch?v=hJo4B-yaxfk, last accessed May 28, 2019. Also see M. Hassan, *Longing for the Lost Caliphate*, 254–255.

131 M. Hitou, *Al-Mutafayhiqūn*, 17.

132 A. Abū Ghudda, *Lecture in Turkey*.

133 Yasir Qadhi's Facebook page, www.facebook.com/yasir.qadhi/posts/10153261512888300, accessed August 16, 2015.

understand human beings and the questioner.[134] Qadhi proposes that the best way to prevent misunderstanding is to have a real-life attachment to an actual scholar. Requesting that Muslims consult scholars in person is important from the Traditionalist perspective because it allows scholars to provide context beyond information found online. It also gives individuals the opportunity to ask questions rather than passively receive information.

The Pakistani *madrasa* teacher ʿAdnān Kaka Khel suggests that misguidance in religion is guaranteed when there is an absence of personal transmission. In his view, opinionated modern scholars claiming to reform Islam using new methods of learning are actually carrying axes and demolishing the knowledge that Muslims preserved for over a thousand years. Kaka Khel claims that these individuals do nothing but sow doubt about Islam.[135] Online learning poses a threat to Traditionalist expertise because it creates a space where laity mistakenly equate a moving sermon or post on social media with a rigorous studying of Islam under a genuine scholar. Qadhi echoes the concern of many Muslim scholars throughout the world when he states, "there is no substitute for going through the proper and professional training of scholarship that has been the hallmark of this religion from the earliest of times."[136]

Ultimately, print and the internet changed the way modern Muslims learn and interact with Islamic knowledge. Many teaching institutions and individuals are adopting new modes of learning through the internet and print media that are against the heart of traditional learning. Whereas previously it was the *ʿulamāʾ* who spoke for Islam, new media created a space where everyone can share their views about Islam through books, audio recordings, blogs, and social media outlets. Traditionalists are sometimes critical of learning only from the internet because it creates a space where laity can not only study Islam without a teacher but can also participate in teaching it and reshaping scholarly authority. Traditionalists have ultimately embraced print and the internet in order to remain relevant and compete with others who espouse to speak on behalf of Islam. Despite their caution about new media, in order to reach large audiences, Traditionalists find it necessary to partake in the very tool they criticize.

This new mode of learning causes a shift away from the status and cruciality of the teacher in Islamic education. The internet would have then

[134] T. Nichols, *Death of Expertise*, 106–110.

[135] Ebrahim Moosa, *What Is a Madrasa?* (Chapel Hill: University of North Carolina Press, 2015), 59.

[136] Y. Qadhi's Facebook page.

produced a new form of Islamic learning, one in which the teacher is a distant, unpersonalized, and customizable figure in the hands of the consumers of information in cyberspace. This technological transformation creates competition over religious authority between Traditionalists who are trained in Islamic sciences, and religious activists or autodidacts whose authority is based upon persuasion, charisma, and the interpretation of texts they primarily access through print and the internet. Although traditional learning is alive in many Muslim communities, traditional education and authority have often become displaced by individuals whose primary method of studying Islam is through text.

Part II

Islamic Law

4

Can Two Opposing Opinions Be Valid? Legal Pluralism in Islam

TRADITIONALISTS AND PURIST SALAFIS HAVE HAD MANY differences and disputes over the validity of particular principles of Islamic legal theory. They often had conflicting views about the proper method of interpreting scripture. As a result, purist Salafis garnered the image of being anti-*madhhab*. The purist Salafi legal methodology is a simplified, yet appealing, call to follow only scripture and the *salaf*. Because purist Salafis believe that scripture is clear, their legal texts are filled with verses and ḥadīth with limited commentary. This chapter analyzes the divergent approaches toward Islamic law between purist Salafis and Traditionalists. I shed light on why they differ with regards to the validity of *ijmāʿ* and *ikhtilāf*.

CERTAINTY IN ISLAMIC LAW

As with most legal systems, Islamic law leaves many legal questions unresolved and open for jurists to make judgments using their intellectual efforts. A brief look at any *fiqh* encyclopedia makes it evident that most issues in Islamic law have a wide range of understandings that are extracted from the Qurʾān and Sunna. The central aim of all legal works is to determine which opinion is most sound. In Islamic legal theory, the main difference is not between Shīʿī and Sunni thought, but between what Aron Zysow refers to as "materialists" and "formalists."[1] Materialists insist that every law must be certain in order to be valid. Formalists are committed to a framework in which norms are created, particularly the skills of the jurist to perform *ijtihād*. Materialists necessitated that legal analysis attains results that were

[1] Aron Zysow, *The Economy of Certainty: An Introduction to the Typology of Islamic Legal Theory* (Atlanta, GA: Lockwood Press, 2013), 3.

certain. Conversely, formalists were content with results that are probable, but not certain, to be true. In the history of Islamic legal theory, most jurists have been unwaveringly formalists. However, materialist tendencies have increased in modern Islamic thought. This rise could be due to increased exchange with other legal systems, or a rejection of them. The notion that a legal rule is only probable or only the result of an individual scholar's fallible legal reasoning, is proving less persuasive both intellectually and popularly.[2] The purist Salafi legal approach appeals to many Muslims because it follows this materialist tendency and promises to deliver certainty.

Traditionalists are formalists in the sense that they do not claim absolute certainty in their legal conclusions. They distinguish between the law and its sources and this distinction assumes that the law, which is a collection of divinely ordained rules, is not entirely self-evident from the sacred texts. If it were, the scripture would not be the source of law, but the law itself. Law is the result of juristic interpretation and therefore stands at the end of the interpretive process, not the beginning. What a jurist says is not authoritative because he says it, but because his authority rests in the validity of his methodology. The question is whether the jurist has properly or validly performed *ijtihād*.

Although the Qurʾān and Sunna are not law as such they nevertheless contain what jurists refer to as *dalīls*. A *dalīl* is an indication of what God intended, but unless it is conclusive (*qaṭʿī*) then the jurist's inference of what God intended is only probable and cannot be ascertained to be the absolute intent of God. A jurist uses a *dalīl* as a guide to infer what he thinks is the correct ruling for a specific legal matter. Jurists will naturally differ since they have distinctive methods with which they try to understand God's law. Because difference of opinion and dissent are the norm in Islamic law, consensus and agreement bring certainty. Considering that legal matters are probable inferences about what might be God's intent, there are sometimes multiple opinions that Traditionalists consider valid. Since these opinions are probable, a jurist must choose one as more probable, or closer to the truth, than others.

For Traditionalist jurists, the results of *ijtihād* are classified as conjectural (*ẓann*), not conclusive knowledge (*ʿilm*). If all laws were self-evident, there would be no need for interpretation because there is nothing to interpret.[3] Put differently, while the sources needed to be known with certainty,

[2] See Robert Gleave's introduction to A. Zysow, *Economy*, 3.

[3] Bernard Weiss, "Interpretation in Islamic Law: The Theory of *Ijtihād*," *The American Journal of Comparative Law*, 2, no. 26 (1978), 199–200.

the legal conclusions drawn from them need not be more than probable, or more likely true than not.[4] Traditionalists entertain the notion of having valid differences of opinion because most legal texts are conjectural (*ẓannī*) as opposed to conclusive (*qaṭʿī*). Premodern Muslim jurists restricted the scope of differences by distinguishing between two types of legal elements, those that are foundational (*uṣūl*) and others that are substantive (*furūʿ*). These have serious consequences on the scope of legal interpretation. The Shāfiʿī scholar Abū al-Maʿālī al-Juwaynī (d. 478/1085) noted that the *uṣūl* are known by reference to reason, to proof-texts, or both. When it concerns the *uṣūl*, reason or proof-texts convey certainty and contribute to core values on which no debate is allowed, and interpretation is not required. In other words, these fundamentals are immune from uncertainty. To validate conflicting perspectives on the fundamentals of the religion threatens the truth claims about the religion.[5] For instance, the oneness of God, the five pillars of Islam, and prohibition of adultery are not open to difference of opinion.

Conclusive knowledge is equated with certainty, to be unable to entertain any doubt concerning it. On the other hand, juristic opinion or *ẓann* means that it is probable, but not certain. In other words, knowledge is correlated with certainty and opinion is correlated with probability. Most Sunni jurists believe the truth to be one and there is only one correct rule on particular actions. Therefore, when jurists disagree on an issue, they cannot all be right. However, because all of these opinions are based on *ẓann*, there is no way of asserting which opinion is unquestionably correct.[6]

Reasonably, only one of these opinions can be correct and jurists cannot claim with certainty that such an issue is the absolute correct understanding of God's will unless there is consensus. When consensus does not exist, jurists cannot claim absolute truth because of the inherent subjectivity in understanding the text. Albānī holds that conclusive knowledge or certainty can be obtained in Islamic law and he rejects the plurality of valid opinions. This conviction affected his approach toward differences of opinion, the validity of *ijmāʿ*, and the fallibility of their interpretation of scripture.

These conflicting viewpoints raise an important question: when is an interpretation based on an objective process and when is it subjective? If

[4] Wael Hallaq, *The Origins and Evolution of Islamic Law* (Cambridge: Cambridge University Press, 2005), 130.

[5] Anver Emon, "To Most Likely Know the Law: Objectivity, Authority, and Interpretation in Islamic Law," *Hebraic Political Studies*, 4, no. 4 (2009), 425–429. Abū al-Maʿālī Al-Juwaynī, *Kitāb al-Ijtihād min Kitāb al-Talkhīṣ*, ed. ʿAbd al-Ḥamīd Abū Zunayr (Damascus: Dar al-Qalam, 1987), 25.

[6] B. Weiss, "Interpretation," 203.

subjectivity means that because jurists are not God their interpretation will reflect, in one way or another, some of their unique subjectivities, then such subjectivity is insignificant. If it means that all readings are equally valid then it is problematic because indeterminacy undermines the value of legal systems. Traditionalists recognize that subjectivity and bias exist, but they do not believe that truth does not exist and that all interpretations are equal. If truth and facts are to be proven, they must be established empirically. Law is ultimately based on the notion that truth and facts exist. If all legal opinions are equal, then legal systems become futile. If the notion of truth is discarded, particularly in the context of law, then law has no further ability to function. Traditionalists believe that their legal opinions are the truth, but they assert epistemic humility about the truth claims they make.

Rejecting truth in law results in a morass of arbitrary rule in which law is applied. Here, relativism in law becomes the best ally of a scoundrel. Any sustained community requires the positivist interpretation of some shared text, taken as law. Otherwise, community dissolves into the subjective points of view of each of its members and there is a regression to an epistemic state of nature. If the Qurʾān and Sunna do not carry any meaning that can be discovered, then they would be empty vessels in which each person brings their own interpretation. Therefore, there would be no community based on these texts. On the other hand, a positivist approach to scripture privileges scripture to determine the nature of the Muslim community.

There will always be tension and ongoing discussion in the Muslim community about how to correctly interpret scripture. This is only possible on the shared premise that the text itself has a meaning and that interpretation is a matter of discovery rather than imposition. Therefore, Traditionalists' disagreement does not refute but affirms the text's status as positive. Hence, the Traditionalist approach to law does not remove the need for due process and courts. The fact that law does not apply itself but must be applied by people engaging in an interpretive exercise, does not entail that the text of the law itself does not have meaning, but is quite the opposite. Traditionalists are threatened by the notion that texts have no meanings outside of what is subjectively imposed by the reader, even if it is subjectively imposed by a collectivity of readers. This results in the scholarly community being dissolved into smaller epistemically isolated individuals each speaking for himself about what Islam is or is not. It can result in a subcommunity, or even an individual, to impose intentionally obscure or unorthodox interpretations on the larger community.

Legal pluralism has always been an integral part of Islamic legal tradition. The absence of a clerical hierarchy that could impose a particular legal code across all Muslim societies gave rise to a multiplicity of different opinions. In the history of Sunni legal history, there were very few, most notably the Muʿtazalīs and the Ẓāhirī school, who rejected probability in Islamic law. Muslim jurists were aware of the impartibility of extreme legal pluralism and therefore attempted to limit the differences of opinion by arguing for the dearth of legal skills required to perform *ijtihād.* Islamic law retained much of its differences of opinion among and within the four *madhhabs.*[7] Traditionalists recognized that subjectivity is an inherent part of the process of interpretation and, as a result, scholars will naturally disagree in cases when scripture is not conclusive and definitive. By definition, *ijtihād* cannot be based on clear-cut texts because such texts do not require significant effort to understand. Furthermore, *ijtihād* only takes place in cases when scripture is unclear and is not valid in cases when scripture is explicitly clear or on well-established parts of the religion. Accordingly, Traditionalists hold that it is not permitted to condemn others for following a position based on valid *ijtihād.* This means that differences of opinion (*ikhtilāf*) will always exist and no amount of insistence on following authentic ḥadīth will unify them. Purist Salafis criticize *ikhtilāf* and consider it the result of the over-utilizing of personal reasoning (*raʾy*). They argue that *ikhtilāf* can be significantly reduced if jurists abandon the *madhhab*s and only follow the Qurʾān and Sunna.

Traditionalists consider the rendering of legal opinions as extraneous from the Qurʾān and Sunna to be inaccurate because, by definition, all valid *ijtihād* is based on an explicit or implicit understanding of a Qurʾānic verse or Prophetic tradition. What purist Salafis really mean when they differentiate between scholarly opinions and scripture is that when scripture contradicts a scholarly opinion, the scholarly opinion cannot be considered a valid interpretation of scripture.

Although many differences of opinion were the result of valid interpretational methods, Traditionalists also recognize that the notion of legal pluralism can result in individuals manipulating the meaning of scripture. In the estimation of purist Salafis, legal pluralism can also lead to individuals picking interpretations that suited their whims. Traditionalists would also reject the cherry-picking of scholarly opinions, but the picking and choosing based on whims is sometimes the combined result of legal pluralism and mass literacy of laity. Traditionalists tried to curb this by only considering

[7] Ahmed Fekry Ibrahim, "Legal Pluralism in Sunni Islamic Law: The Causes and Functions of Juristic Disagreement," in *Routledge Handbook of Islamic Law*, ed. Khaled Abou El Fadl, Ahmad Atif Ahmad, and Said Fares Hassan (New York: Routledge, 2019), 209.

certain opinions as valid, primarily based on the methodological considerations, not the interpretive result. Methodology mattered in the determination of what constitutes a valid interpretation.

Salafis and Traditionalists both believe that texts have intended meanings that are discoverable through scholarship. They agree that not all readings of scripture can be equally valid. Such a case would mean that scripture or texts have no meaning and are just the vessel of whatever people pour into them. *Ijtihād* is a dialectical process by which one attempts to reconcile the various interpretations and meanings of texts and refining them in light of the *uṣūl* of the *madhhab* and arguments that one develops in the course of scholarly dialectic. In that process, one's understanding of scripture is transformed as one interrogates it through the particular methodology. It is for this reason that Traditionalists such as Būṭī insist that, unless one has received scholarly training, they are required to follow the *ijtihād* of the scholars.[8] Traditionalists consider the *ijtihād* of a scholar who adheres to the legal principles of one of the four schools is valid. Purist Salafis seek to resolve *ikhtilāf* by reproducing evidence that verifies whether an opinion is based on scripture and not blind adherence to a legal school.

For instance, Albānī attempted to minimize *ikhtilāf* and unite the Muslims on what he considered authentic Islam. He rejected the notion that two contradicting opinions could be equally valid and criticized those who held this opinion. Referring to Abū Ghudda, Albānī states: "Abū Ghudda considers that two contradicting opinions, and there are so many of them in his *madhhab*, can all be part of the Sharia and that it is permissible to act upon any of them . . . is the religion according to you [Abū Ghudda], two religions; one of them easy and the other difficult?"[9]

Purist Salafis and Traditionalists had different objectives concerning *ikhtilāf*. Purist Salafis sought to demonstrate the invalidity of the many legal opinions in the four schools. Conversely, Traditionalists attempted to validate all the opinions within the *madhhab*s. Historically, the Traditionalist acceptance of legal pluralism was important because it facilitated particular legislative transactions within the premodern legal institutions. With the decline of these institutions the facilitation provided by legal pluralism was no longer relevant.

Nevertheless, Traditionalists argue that these opinions are not based on whims, but on scriptural evidence.[10] What makes an opinion valid in the

8 M. Būṭī, *Al-Lā Madhhabiyya*, 53–54.
9 N. Albānī, *Kashf*, 100–101.
10 For instance, ʿAbd al-Wahhāb al-Shaʿrānī (d. 973/1565) argued that God intentionally created two levels of law, one that was strict and another lenient. A. Ibrahim, "Legal Pluralism in Sunni Islamic Law," 216.

estimation of Traditionalists is the quality of the *ijtihād* that takes place to arrive at a legal conclusion. Accordingly, the question of whether an opinion is correct misses the point. Because most legal opinions are based on *ẓannī* texts, there is no way of determining their meanings with absolute certainty even if one believes that there is only one correct interpretation. The interpretation of a jurist is validated based on the epistemic excellence in investigation, which consequently gives authority to his opinion. Such a conclusion is often referred to as a preponderance of opinion (*ghalabat al-ẓann*). A preponderance of opinion is not certainty, but it is reaching a degree that approximates certainty. Therefore, although legal authority recognizes human fallibility, it restricts the validity of different opinions to those that met the standards of *ijtihād*. Anver Emon notes "*Ghalabat al-zann* represents the standard of evaluation that both grants authority to the *fiqh* rulings and preserves humility before an infinite God."[11]

Albānī does not deny the existence of what he considers legitimate *ikhtilāf*, but he tries to limit it. In his view, Traditionalists often invoke *ikhtilāf* to justify any opinion without a willingness to review their opinion in light of scripture. Therefore, Albānī sought to review all *fiqh* opinions in light of the Qurʾān and Sunna. He did not consider any opinion valid unless it was supported by scripture. In other words, a scholar could give a fatwa based on a *madhhab* under the condition that it is supported by Qurʾān and Sunna, not based on the opinion of his *madhhab* alone, thus returning authority to scripture rather than the *madhhab*.[12] Albānī states:

> Every mufti must support his fatwa by linking it to the book of God or ḥadīth of the Messenger of God, blessings and peace be upon him . . . When asked for a ruling, it is not permitted for a Muslim who follows a particular *madhhab* to give a fatwa according to his *madhhab*. This is because there are opinions in other *madhhab*s and he must refrain from giving a fatwa [without a proof-text]. If he gives a fatwa then he is sinful.[13]

Put differently, he wanted to minimize the human role in the interpretation and wanted every fatwa to have an explicit scriptural basis. Although Albānī sometimes quotes the opinion of a *madhhab*, in many cases he does not analyze the legal reasoning and supportive evidence behind them. In other words, he does not venture into why Traditionalists hold their opinion

[11] A. Emon, "To Most Likely Know," 436.
[12] Muḥammad Nāṣir al-Dīn al-Albānī, "Al-Taqlīd wa l-Ittibāʿ," lecture from www.alalbany.net, last accessed April 5, 2012.
[13] N. Albānī, "Taqlīd."

when they differ with him. His primary concern was that lay Muslims would accept a legal verdict based solely on the opinion of a scholar and not on the fact that it is supported by proof-texts. Therefore, only a text-driven approach to Islamic law could be correct. Traditionalists have a different understanding of what constitutes a valid interpretation. Muḥammad ʿAwwāma argues that if the scholar is a *mujtahid* and a person of knowledge, quoting him is equivalent to quoting scripture because a scholar's opinion is not based on his personal preferences, but a careful study of scripture.[14]

IS SCRIPTURE CLEAR?

Purist Salafis consider most texts to be straightforward and clear whereas Traditionalists hold texts to be complex and multivalent. Their assertion of following the direct and clear meaning of texts plays a very important role in the appeal of their message. Laypeople are untrained to absorb scholarly arguments. There is a degree of skepticism and mistrust between laypeople and Traditionalists. One the other hand, the appeal of Salafi legal methodology lies in its preference of simplicity over complexity and presenting Islam as being simple, straightforward, and easy to understand.

The scholastic discourse found within the *madhhab*s did not allow Traditionalists to make a similar claim and provide absolute answers, which was to their disadvantage. The supplying of "clear" texts to laypeople provided purist Salafis a means to challenge the authority of Traditionalists by requiring that every fatwa is supported by one of these clear texts.[15] For instance, Albānī believes there is only one truth and does not portray his opinions as *ẓann*; instead, he considers the results of his interpretation as conclusive knowledge and therefore equal to the Qurʾān and Sunna themselves. Because he considers scripture to be explicitly clear, his legal methodology often approaches the Qurʾān and Sunna as law rather than sources of law. If law is understood as a body of facts that are independent of the mind, then the interpreter simply finds or discovers these laws. However, if law is understood to be connected to historical and institutional context, then it allows for constructive creativity within the boundaries of the legal tradition.[16] In other words, was Islamic law, as a body of rules, given

[14] M. ʿAwwāma, *Athar*, 71–72.

[15] Muḥammad Nāṣir al-Dīn al-Albānī, *Silsilat al-Aḥādīth al-Ṣaḥīḥa* (Riyadh: Maktabat al-Maʿārif, 1995), 190. Hereafter *S.A.S.*

[16] A. Emon, "To Most Likely Know," 419.

to Muslims ready-made? Or were the sources of law given and Muslims then needed to use these sources to construct law and determine its underlying rationale?

For Traditionalists *uṣūl al-fiqh* is an attempt to understand the deep implications of scripture, jurisprudence, the human, and the context in which these laws are to be implemented. Conversely, purist Salafis view law as the direct meaning of scripture. The most one can venture from the apparent meaning of scripture is analyzing its authenticity, language, syntax, and similar texts. There is very little hermeneutical methodology or consideration for the social context in which law is implemented. Muḥammad ʿAwwāma criticizes Salafis for equating their *fiqh* with the Qurʾān and Sunna. Since *fiqh* means knowledge, the *fiqh* of the *madhhabs*' eponyms means their comprehension of the Qurʾān and Sunna. ʿAwwāma states:

> Accordingly, we notice a hazardous and obvious misunderstanding among people that is overlooked, and no one cautions them about it. This occurs when one of them labels his "*fiqh*" and "knowledge" and presents it to people as "*fiqh al-Sunna*" or "*fiqh al-Sunna wa-l-kitāb*." The *fiqh* of Qurʾān and Sunna means the understanding of the Qurʾān and Sunna, and whose understanding is he presenting? It is the understanding of Zayd and ʿAmr from among the nobodies of people. However, they have inflated their understanding and associated it with the "Qurʾān and Sunna" to trick people into thinking that they are presenting them with the pure and authentic versions of Islam. As a result they will distance people from the *fiqh* of Abū Ḥanīfa, al-Shāfiʿī, Mālik, and Aḥmad, may God be pleased with them, and they will establish themselves by saying to people: "Oh people, do you want the *fiqh* of Muḥammad, blessings of God and peace be upon him, or the *fiqh* of Abū Ḥanīfa and al-Shāfiʿī?"[17]

ʿAwwāma argues that Salafis can only make the *madhhab*s appear alien to Islam by attributing their *fiqh* to the Qurʾān and Sunna, and the *fiqh* of Abū Ḥanīfa to Abū Ḥanīfa and not to the Qurʾān and Sunna. He explains that while Traditionalists are explicit about their interpretational orientation and possible bias, Salafis do not because they claim to follow only the Qurʾān and Sunna directly. This gives the impression that their understanding of scripture is the final word and all other opinions are baseless or invalid. Traditionalists consider it impossible for anyone to possess the absolute meaning of scripture in all legal rulings because it denies the human element of interpretation. For Traditionalists, the claim to possess absolute truth in

[17] M. ʿAwwāma, *Athar*, 121.

legal matters is problematic because one could not possibly be certain that what they have understood is what God had intended unless there is consensus.[18]

Purist Salafis distinguish between the *madhhab*s and the Qurʾān and Sunna, making the two appear to be completely different. For instance, Albānī stated "the majority of scholars rely on one of the four *madhhab*s . . . as for the Sunna it has become long forgotten to them unless it is in their interest to consider it."[19] What Albānī actually means is that when there is a ḥadīth no saying or opinion of a scholar can compete with it. This again is based on the understanding that the texts are clear and can only carry one meaning. The *madhhab*s are an effort to understand texts when they are not explicitly clear. What Albānī might consider a clear text is not clear to other scholars and even other Salafis. Hence, there arises a difference of opinion. When texts are unambiguously clear they should result in consensus about their meaning. In the absence of this, a text and its understanding would remain conjectural (*ẓannī*).

SCRIPTURAL INTERPRETATION

For Salafis, the use of reason and anything beyond the text must be minimized when interpreting texts. Ḥadīth are to be placed at the heart of the process of finding answers not clarified in the Qurʾān itself. There is no such thing as *fiqh*, but only *fiqh al-ḥadīth*.[20] In other words, their legal methodology is only based on a direct understanding of ḥadīth while simultaneously dispensing with most interpretational tools and previous scholarly opinions that might lead to a conclusion that is at odds with the direct meaning of a text. All legal principles and maxims are to be directly drawn from the Qurʾān and ḥadīth. The intellect, independent of the primary texts, has no role in determining law and can only be used to passively understand what scripture says the law is. If one browses Salafi legal arguments, one might be surprised by the simplicity of their approach to legal questions. Their responses mostly consist of quoting proof-texts

18 M. ʿAwwāma, *Athar*, 121.

19 Muḥammad Nāṣir al-Dīn al-Albānī, Al-Ḥadīth Ḥujja Binafsi-hi fī l-ʿAqāʾid wa l-Aḥkām (Riyadh: Maktabat al-Maʿārif, 2005), 36. Albānī is referring to the difference between the four *madhhab*s and Ibn Taymiyya. The four *madhhab*s hold that declaring divorce three times in one sitting is considered as three divorces, and thus irrevocable. Ibn Taymiyya went against the four *madhhab*s by stating it counts as one, and several *fiqh* assemblies in the modern day have taken the opinion of Ibn Taymiyya.

20 S. Lacroix, "Between Revolution," 64–65.

which assumes that the texts are clear and there is no need for much legal interpretation. Since the texts are straightforward and clear, purist Salafis view the scholar's role as one who passively passes along the proof-text. Their resilient ḥadīth-oriented approach to Islamic law eschews almost all mention of inter- and intra-*madhhab* debates which are far from simple. It is less important to be familiar with the different opinions in the *madhhab*s than to understand the textual sources that the legal schools draw from.[21] Conversely, Traditionalists claim that the legal principles and maxims of the *madhhab*s are based on the Qur'ān and ḥadīth. They consider the legal methodology of purist Salafis to be one that derives rulings from ḥadīth without an understanding of legal theory.

Salafi criticism of the *madhhab*s is best understood in light of their conviction that the results of their *ijtihād* are authentic and free from the biases held by those who adhere to the *madhhab*s. A primary difference between purist Salafis and Traditionalists is that Salafis do not concede that there is an inherent subjectivity in the process of interpreting scripture. Traditionalists acknowledge that their interpretation of Islam holds the possibility of being incorrect, although they consider that possibility might be slim. Traditionalists rarely claim absolute certainty in *fiqh*. This is evident from their application of operative terms such as the relied-upon opinion (*al-mu'tamad*), the stronger opinion (*al-aqwā*), the more correct opinion (*al-aṣṣaḥ*).[22] Implicit in the Salafi claim that those who follow scholars are not following the Qur'ān and Sunna is that they are denying scripture itself. Although they refrain from excommunication, their position represents a slippery slope to excommunication and anathematization. Accordingly, their Traditionalist detractors consider purist Salafism to be an unhealthy trend that breeds a culture of intolerance.

They argue that Salafis cannot possibly be following the Qur'ān and Sunna without a process of interpretation. Ḥabīb al-Raḥmān al-A'ẓamī states that despite Albānī's claiming to follow the direct meaning of scripture, he actually follows his interpretation of the text. For example, Albānī considers all images, whether they are three-dimensional statues or two-dimensional pictures and drawings, to be prohibited. There is a narration in which Aisha, the wife of the Prophet, says that she saw the Prophet reclining on a pillow that had an image on it. The Companion states: "Verily, I saw him reclining on one of them and it contained an image." This ḥadīth

[21] R. Gauvain, *Ritual Purity*, 48.

[22] See Wael Hallaq, *Authority, Continuity and Change in Islamic Law* (Cambridge: Cambridge University Press, 2005), 121–140.

contradicts Albānī's prohibition of images and therefore he interprets it as follows: "Perhaps the image that is mentioned in the end of the ḥadīth "Verily I saw him reclining on one of them and it contained an image" was cut in the middle so that it lost its shape."[23] Aʿẓamī attacks Albānī for this interpretation:

> If this kind of interpretation was done by one of those who follows a *madhhab*, he would have accused him of violating the ḥadīth for the saying of his imam and preferring an opinion over the words of the Prophet or his actions, God's blessings and peace be upon him. If he had even the slightest understanding and shame, he would not have allowed himself to reject this ḥadīth with this twisted interpretation. If that image was cut down the middle, its upper half would have been on one pillow and its lower half would have been on another pillow, and it is incorrect to use the word image to describe either of them.[24]

Aʿẓamī seeks to establish that since Albānī interprets scripture like everyone else, his understanding is equally subjective and fallible. Aʿẓamī argues that although the Qur'ān and Sunna may be "infallible," the understanding of them is not. Salafis either deny the human aspect of interpretation and consider their understanding of scripture to be direct, similar to how the Prophet would have understood it. Or they conceal their methodology to infuse their opinions with a sense of objectivity in order to further market their brand of Salafism. If purist Salafis conceded that they were following their interpretation of scripture rather than scripture itself, they would risk losing credibility because it would mean that he was recreating the wheel and simply starting another *madhhab*.

Trying to understand the direct meaning of scripture without a process of interpretation is not possible. Every text that is read and every understanding obtained is achieved through the human agent of interpretation, which is impacted by modern and historical scholarship and contexts. Nevertheless, because purist Salafis believe that God's intention is clearly spelled out in scripture they maintained that scripture has one valid interpretation and they reject legal pluralism.

REMOVING *IKHTILĀF*

Because Albānī believes, at least in rhetoric, that Traditionalists have a blind loyalty to the *madhhabs*, he takes it upon himself to reexamine everything in

[23] N. Albānī, *Ādāb*, 188–189. [24] H. Aʿẓamī, *Shudhūdhu*, 55–56.

the light of scripture. He believes that the *madhhab*s' views are not founded on the Qur'ān or Sunna because they include reason based on evidence rather than an exclusive emphasis on the authority of scripture. He views every *fiqh* opinion that does not conform to the "clear" meanings of scripture to be incorrect. That is why he refers to Salafism as the "authentic" and "correct" understanding of scripture. In fact, purist Salafis understand Salafism to be nothing more than Islam in its pure and original form.[25]

Purist Salafis consider differences of opinion to be the result of Muslims straying from the original and clear meanings of proof-texts. They maintain that these differences are destructive to the Muslim community and are a source of division and strife. They argue that if the followers of the *madhhab*s truly wished they could have limited their differences on most issues by referring to the proof-texts, then after that they could forgive each other over minor differences. Albānī asks why Traditionalists would make such an effort if they consider *ikhtilāf* to be a source of mercy?

Disagreement on *ikhtilāf* has profound implications that go far beyond theology and law. If one does not accept the validity of *ikhtilāf* one views those who differ with them as going directly against God. On the other hand, validating conflicting views on the foundational elements threatens the essence of the religion. Albānī's criticism of differences of opinion stems from a concern about the authority of scripture. If all opinions are valid, and differences are a mercy, that means that Islam suffers from a lack of clear direction.

Leading purist Salafis such as Albānī acknowledge that uniting everyone on a single opinion is not possible, but he seeks to minimize the number of different opinions by opposing anything that contradicts proof-texts. Therefore, he does acknowledge the use of human reason and its necessity in legal reasoning. The problem, in his view, is that the differences among Traditionalists are not due to legitimate reasons, but because they blindly follow the schools of law.

Traditionalists accuse purist Salafis of being irreverent and methodologically rebellious toward the imams by claiming that their opinions are based on blind following of the *madhhab*s (*taqlīd aʿmā*). However, Traditionalism also has its share of scholars who might have recognized the subjectivity in their approach but have nevertheless claimed that others are absolutely incorrect. For example, the Ḥanafī Ibn ʿAbidīn stated "Our *madhhab* is correct and has the possibility of being wrong. When we are asked about the

[25] E. Hamdeh, "Salafi Polemic," 20.

madhhab of others, we say it is all wrong."[26] Albānī blames Traditionalists for having double standards because they accuse Salafis of being irreverent for declaring others to be absolutely wrong, yet they remain silent when leading Traditionalists like Ibn ʿĀbidīn do it.[27]

In purist Salafi thought, reverence for scholars does not prevent them from reviewing some of their opinions in the light of scripture. They consider it to be their scholarly responsibility to correct and circumvent their opinions when they contradict a saying of the Prophet or verse of the Qur'ān. Traditionalists' acceptance of differing opinions reflects their understanding of the nature of the scholarship and how the different times and circumstances lead scholars to come to different conclusions. Traditionalists consider Salafi efforts to erase difference of opinion as futile because they try to provide certainty in an area that offers none. In contrast, the authentic and conviction-driven Salafism appeals to modern sensibilities that are often consumed with a flagrant sense of certainty.[28]

One of the most influential Salafi works that attempts to promote this type of certainty is Albānī's *Aṣl Ṣifat Ṣalāt al-Nabī Min al-Takbīr ilā al-Taslīm Ka'anna-ka Tarā-hā* (The Original Description of the Prophet's Prayers, Blessings and Peace Be upon Him, from the Beginning to the End as Though You See Him). This is one of the most famous works in Salafi circles and has been translated into several languages. For instance, in the 1980s many Salafi women in Britain were praying according to the Ḥanafī *madhhab*, but when Albānī's book became available in the 1990s they started praying according to the "authentic" Sunna. This book was popular because it provided them certainty concerning the prayer, one of the most important elements of Islam.[29]

Nevertheless, due to the allegations it made against the madhhabs, this book was also very controversial. Traditionalists have even taken offense to the book's title. For instance, the American Traditionalist Hamza Yusuf notes that Mālik b. Anas (d. 179/795) had a direct link to the Prophet because his teacher Nāfiʿ was the student of the famous Companion Ibn ʿUmar. The title of Albānī's book implies that if one follows Mālik or the eponyms of the other schools, he is not praying according to how the Prophet was observed, despite Mālik having a direct link to the Prophet.[30] In Albānī's estimation,

[26] ʿAmr ʿAbd al-Munʿim Salīm, *Al-Fatāwā al-Manhajiyya li-Faḍīlat al-Shaykh Muḥammad Nāṣir al-Dīn al-Albānī* (Cairo: Dār al-Ḍiyā', 2008), 66.

[27] A. Salīm, *Al-Fatāwā al-Manhajiyya*, 66. [28] N. Albānī, *Kashf*, 94.

[29] Anabel Inge, *The Making of a Salafi Muslim Woman: Paths to Conversion* (Oxford: Oxford University Press, 2016), 35.

[30] Hamza Yusuf, "The Four Schools (Madhabs) or Albānī," www.youtube.com/watch?v=FUigJfAcKgE, last accessed February 28, 2018.

only one opinion concerning the prayer can be correct. He explains why he authored the work:

> I wrote this book because the knowledge of [the details of prayer] are indecipherable to most people, even among many scholars because of their *taqlīd* of a specific *madhhab*. It is known to everyone who works in serving the pure Sunna, gathering and understanding it, that in every *madhhab* there are Sunnas that are not found in the other *madhhabs*. And they all contain that which cannot be correctly attributed to the Prophet, blessings and peace be upon him.[31]

In other words, if one prays according to any of the four legal schools, they will be following something outside of scripture because they have opinions that differ with the Sunna. Traditionalists find this problematic because prayer is one of the most important pillars of Islam and thousands of scholars have written on the topic. Their critique of Albānī partly stems from his frankness in declaring his book to be the one that best captures the Sunna. He explains:

> Since I did not find a book that contains everything on this topic, I considered it obligatory upon myself to provide my Muslim brothers, whose concern is to follow the guidance of the Prophet in their worship, with a book that is as comprehensive as possible for everything related to the description of the prayer of the Prophet.[32]

Albānī's conviction is so total that it implies the immediate disappearance of other perspectives as the ideal outcome. His detractors do not necessarily disagree with the content of the book, but rather the attitude Albānī has in it. They accuse him of considering his book to be the final criterion on the correct manner of praying and criticizing the *madhhabs* for holding opinions that contradict his conclusions. For instance, Albānī takes issue with followers of the Mālikī *madhhab* who pray with their hands to their sides instead of holding them together. His understanding is that they do so solely because the *madhhab* says it and not based on scriptural proof-text. Albānī states "Why [do they pray like this]?! Because that is the *madhhab*!"[33] Although most non-Mālikī jurists, including Albānī, disagree with the Mālīkī opinion, Traditionalists argue that the reason Mālikīs do not hold

[31] Muḥammad Nāṣir al-Dīn al-Albānī, *Aṣl Ṣifat Ṣalāt al-Nabī Min al-Takbīr ilā al-Taslīm Ka'anaka Tarā-hā* (Riyadh: Maktabat al-Ma'ārif, 2006), 15.

[32] N. Albānī, *Aṣl Ṣifat*, 18.

[33] Muḥammad Nāṣir al-Dīn al-Albānī, *Al-Taṣfiya wa l-Tarbiya wa Ḥājat al-Muslimīn Ilay-hā* (Riyadh: Maktabat al-Ma'ārif, 2007), 16.

their hands in prayer cannot be reduced to only following a *madhhab*, but because they believe it is the way the Prophet performed prayer. This is based on their understanding of Sunna to include the living tradition of the people of Medina immediately following the death of the Prophet. If the people living in Medina immediately after the Prophet were praying a particular way, that must mean that they were following the Prophet who was among them. For the Mālikīs, this living tradition is prioritized beyond a single narration.

Albānī notes that the scholars of ḥadīth were unable to find a single ḥadīth, even if it is weak or fabricated, that states the Prophet did not hold his hands during prayer.[34] Instead one finds the ḥadīth books full of narrations describing the Prophet as holding his hands during prayer. Albānī does not recognize or engage with the principle of *ʿamal ahl al-Madīna* and does not excuse Mālikī scholars for following a principle that they considered legitimate nor does he do that for any other *madhhab*.[35] Moreover, Albānī differed with the Mālikī school because of his methodological insistence that the Qurʾān and ḥadīth are the only authoritative sources. Whenever the Qurʾān and Sunna give specific guidelines, there is no need to resort to the actions or customs of people. He states that even if there is an opinion of a scholar or a Companion, such statements cannot override the statements of the Prophet.[36] Interestingly, not all Traditionalists took interest in refuting Albānī's arguments against the *madhhab*s such as his disapproval of Mālikīs praying with their hands to their sides. Instead, they usually call for an ending of the discussion because they did not consider Albānī's unconventional opinion important in the light of centuries of scholarship.

WHY DO SCHOLARS DIFFER?

The reasons and causes of *ikhtilāf* are at the heart of the debate between Traditionalists and purist Salafis. Both groups understand that to some degree there will always be differences of opinion. However, they have varying understandings of the explanation behind differences of opinion. Purist Salafis argue that differences of opinion are usually the result of not knowing a specific proof-text or its authenticity. They maintain that differences of opinion among the legal schools and jurists are due to the ignorance

[34] For a discussion on this point and *ʿAmal* in the Mālikī school see Yasin Dutton, "ʿAmal v Ḥadīth in Islamic Law: The Case of Sadl al-Yadayn (Holding One's Hands by One's Sides) When Doing the Prayer," *Islamic Law and Society*, 3, no. 1 (1996), 13–40.

[35] N. Albānī, *Taṣfiya*, 17. [36] N. Albānī, *Taṣfiya*, 22–23.

combined with dogmatic adherence (*taʿaṣṣub*) to their *madhhabs*. Therefore, purist Salafis argue that these opinions should be disregarded, and Muslims should return to the primary sources of Islam, the Qurʾān and Sunna. In their view, if a sincere scholar of the Qurʾān and Sunna was aware of the particular proof-text and its authenticity, then he would arrive at the same conclusion as purist Salafis.

Most Traditionalists believe that every legal opinion found in the *madhhabs* is rooted in textual and rational evidence. Moreover, jurists from among each *madhhab* are aware of the arguments of their opponents and have responded to them using the principles of textual criticism and the legal theory of their school. When a number of texts related to the same issue appear to contradict each other, the *mujtahid* employs the principles of legal theory to resolve the perceived contradiction. As a result, he may interpret some texts to be qualified and restricted by other texts. If all attempts of resolving between the various texts prove futile, the *mujtahid* must give preference to the texts that are sounder, after ascertaining the authenticity of all the reports using the principles of textual criticism. This process itself can lead to different opinions, because authenticating a report is a matter of *ijtihād*. Alternatively, the *mujtahid* may conclude that one text is abrogated by the other.

Ibn Taymiyya explains that *ikhtilāf* can occur for several reasons such as a text being understood in multiple ways, a dispute in the text's authenticity, abrogation or lack thereof, or whether it is directly related to the issue under discussion. He argues that earlier scholars also had better knowledge and understanding of the Sunna than later scholars because much of what has reached them, and what they considered authentic, might not have reached later scholars except through an unreliable narrator, a defective chain, or it may not have reached them at all.[37] However, purist Salafis consider it impossible for a ḥadīth to have not reached later scholars because God promised to preserve scripture. If scripture is lost, then the Qurʾān would be commanding Muslims to follow something that does not exist.

Therefore, purist Salafis leave minimal room for difference of opinion. Accordingly, they do not consider other interpretations as possibly valid, but rather they consider them to contradict proof-texts. Ḥabīb al-Raḥmān al-Aʿẓamī argues that purist Salafis like Albānī have a simplistic understanding of the reasons for *ikhtilāf*. He notes that some other scholars, such as the literalist Ibn Ḥazm, also claimed to follow only the Qurʾān and Sunna, yet

[37] M. Būṭī, *Al-Lā Madhhabiyya*, 131. Also see Taqī al-Din Ibn Taymiyya, *Rafʿ al-Malām ʿan al-ʾAʾimmat al-Aʿlām* (Beirut: Dār Al-Kotob al-ʿIlmiyya, 2003), 4–23.

both Ibn Ḥazm and Albānī differ on several issues. Albānī explains that these differences are due to Ibn Ḥazm's lack of expertise in the area of ḥadīth.[38] A'ẓamī turns the tables on Albānī by noting that if Ibn Ḥazm's incorrect opinions were due to his lack of expertise in ḥadīth, would he also say the same about Ibn Taymiyya and Ibn Qayyim? In his introduction to Ibn Taymiyya's *al-Kalim al-Ṭayyib*, Albānī advises anyone who reads the book to not rush in acting upon the ḥadīth found in it until they verify their authenticity, which he does in his commentary.[39] A'ẓamī writes:

> The intelligent Muslim, therefore, has no choice but to follow you and to submit his intellect to be guided by you. If he performs *ijtihād* on his own, he will unquestionably violate the Sunna. If Ibn Taymiyya, Ibn Qayyim, Ibn Ḥazm, and those who were greater than them were not absolved from violating the Sunna then he cannot be absolved from violating it either. If he acts upon what they have verified in their books which goes against your advice he will also violate the Sunna. So, he has no choice then but to return to you, and this is what is meant by your statement: "Otherwise he should ask those who are qualified." Because when Ibn Taymiyya and Ibn Qayyim are not qualified in ḥadīth, then who else can be qualified other than you, imam Albānī?![40]

A'ẓamī argues that differences do not occur because scholars disregard the Qur'ān and Sunna and "anyone who claims that does so due to stupidity and a deficiency in his understanding."[41] Differences of opinion are consistent with human reasoning and bound to exist because people are at different intellectual and scholarly levels, not because they intentionally disregard the Qur'ān and Sunna.[42] Albānī agrees, at least in theory, that differences may be the result of understanding a text in a varying light.[43] In an attempt to refute Albānī, A'ẓamī points out that one also finds differences of opinion among those who claim to follow only the Qur'ān and Sunna. He notes that both Albānī and Ibn Ḥazm claim to follow the direct meaning of scripture, but they both differ. He writes:

> You say that a ḥadīth is a conclusive text in a certain issue and Ibn Ḥazm would certainly say your statement is a lie. First, please explain to me who the liar among you is. Second, for my own benefit, are both of you following the ḥadīth or only one of you? If both of you are following the ḥadīth then this necessitates that the two different understandings are from

[38] N. Albānī, *S.A.S.*, 1: 187. [39] T. Ibn Taymiyya, *Kalim al-Ṭayyib*, 54–55.
[40] H. A'ẓamī, *Shudhūdhu*, 80–81. [41] H. A'ẓamī, *Shudhūdhu*, 78.
[42] H. A'ẓamī, *Shudhūdhu*, 78.
[43] Muḥammad Nāṣir al-Dīn al-Albānī, *Ṣalāt al-Tarāwīḥ* (Beirut: Al-Maktab al-Islāmī, 1985), 26.

> the Sunna, and that the ḥadīth simultaneously commands two opposite things. If it is only one of you, then how do we know the truthfulness of one of you and the lie of the other? And how do we know who is more deserving of the claim to be following the ḥadīth?![44]

Because of their varying attitudes toward the legitimacy of *ikhtilāf*, Traditionalists view legitimate differences as a source of mercy for the Muslim community while Albānī considers *ikhtilāf* to be a source of division and punishment.

DIFFERENCES AS A SOURCE OF MERCY

In a famous tradition, the Prophet is reported to have said "Differences of opinion in my nation are mercy."[45] Traditionalists use this tradition to argue that *ikhtilāf* is not only a natural part of law, but an intended and positive component of it.[46] Many ḥadīth scholars including Albānī respond to this by explaining that this ḥadīth is fabricated and has no basis in Islam. They also argue that the meaning is also problematic because if differences of opinion are a source of mercy, then that necessitates that unity, such as *ijmāʿ*, must be punishment.

In his voluminous work titled *The Series of Weak and Fabricated Ḥadīth and Their Negative Impact of the Muslim Community*, Albānī notes that this fabricated ḥadīth legitimizes the many differences found in the *madhhab*s and the Muslim community. When differences are not only legitimized, but considered to be positive, then there will never be a need to reexamine positions in light of the Qurʾān and Sunna. This will then result in Muslims simply accepting their state of division and do nothing to resolve it. Muqbil al-Wādiʿī furthers Albānī's argument by noting that *ikhtilāf* between the *madhhab*s has never led to mercy, but always resulted in divergences and disputes.[47] Albānī and Wādiʿī understand *ikhtilāf* and division (*tafrīq*) to be the same thing. Differences of opinion do not necessitate division but can be the source of it when differences are not tolerated.

According to Albānī, *ikhtilāf* cannot be from God because the Qurʾān states "Had it [the Qurʾān] been from other than God they would have found in it many contradictions."[48] He comments on this verse by writing,

[44] For instance, Ibn Ḥazm permitted singing and musical instruments while Albānī prohibited them. See H. Aʿẓamī, *Shudhūdhu*, 66–75.

[45] Muḥammad Nāṣir al-Dīn al-Albānī, *Silsilat al-Aḥādīth al-Ḍaʿīfa wa l-Mawḍūʿa wa Atharu-hā al-Sayyiʾ fi-l Umma* (Riyadh: Maktbat al-Maʿārif, 1992), 1: 141–142. Hereafter *S.A.D.*

[46] Muḥammad ʿAwwāma, *Adab*, 95.

[47] Muqbil al-Wādiʿī, *Ijābat*, 316.

[48] Q. al-Nisāʾ, 4:82.

"The verse is clear that contradictions are not from God. How then can the *madhhabs* all be considered part of God's law and a mercy sent down from God?!"[49] ʿAwwāma objects to this and states that besides this verse being in the context of war, the words "differences" or "contradictions" in it refer to differences in the principles of religion, not secondary issues. There is nothing in the context of the verse that indicates that it is addressing the branches of law. Because people vary over the meaning of one verse does not mean that the verse is no longer from God. Furthermore, differing in the understanding of a proof-text is not the same as intentionally violating a proof-text or a contradiction in scripture.[50]

Traditionalists argue that since the majority of scripture is *ẓannī*, it means that God has deliberately employed words that can be interpreted in more than one way, even though He could have used other words that would make the purport of the text conclusive (*qaṭʿī*). In their estimation, this illustrates that disagreement among scholars is not only inevitable but ordained by the divine will. Yet, these differences were not intended to cause division, but help remove hardship. For instance, in the Traditionalist assessment, *ikhtilāf* can be utilized to accommodate different societal and individual needs.

ʿAwwāma uses historical context to point out that differences of opinion have always existed, even dating back to the Companions. The fact that the Companions had different understandings of the Qurʾān and Sunna is evidence that variation in secondary issues is permissible. ʿAwwāma argues that the *ikhtilāf* of the earliest generations is the clearest evidence that differing on secondary issues is permissible.[51] What then is the distinction between the *ikhtilāf* that occurred among the Companions and that of those who follow a *madhhab*? Albānī sees this as a question of intention. He states that there were no deliberate differences between the Companions, but they had varying interpretations because they naturally understood things differently. Additionally, he explains that the Companions differed because some of them were unaware of particular ḥadīth. Despite their variations, even though the Companions and early Muslims differed, this did not lead to disunity in their application of the religion.[52]

In other words, Albānī views the difference between the *ikhtilāf* of the Companions and later Muslims to be that for the Companions it was natural *ikhtilāf* and they did their best to avoid it. However, Traditionalists vary and accept differences even though they are capable of removing most of them. Albānī does not excuse Traditionalists for their *ikhtilāf* because the evidence

[49] N. Albānī, *S.A.D*, 1: 141–142. [50] M. ʿAwwāma, *Adab*, 108. [51] M. ʿAwwāma, *Adab*, 106.
[52] N. Albānī, *Aṣl Ṣifat*, 40–45.

from the Qurʾān and Sunna is clear to them. These evidences are often found in an opposing *madhhab*, but they disregard the proof-text simply because it contradicts their *madhhab*. Albānī believes that some of the adherents of the *madhhab*s consider their *madhhab* to be equivalent to the religion, and the other *madhhab*s are abrogated religions.[53]

The Salafi argument that adherents of the *madhhab*s are contradicting or purposefully disregarding proof-texts is difficult to determine because it presumes knowledge of their motives. Although this might be accurate for some adherents of the *madhhab*s, it is quite possible that others followed the *madhhab* because they believe it to be the correct interpretation of scripture. Since the *madhhab*s are made up of thousands of scholars throughout the centuries, it is a substantial generalization to assume that they differed because they disregarded the texts they considered to be divine, or that they were uncritically following a school of law. It was the purist Salafi belief that the texts were clear and that there could be no other "correct" understanding that led them to such a conclusion.

Purist Salafis explain that they want to unify the Muslim community, but their critics view them as agitators who incite arguments among the Muslims. ʿAwwāma sarcastically calls Albānī "the pseudo-*mujtahid* of the modern era" (*mutamajhid al-ʿaṣr*) and questions Albānī's understanding of differences among scholars.[54] He writes:

> If differences of opinion are evil, then why do you deviate from scholarly consensus? If you do not accept that you are deviating from consensus, then you must certainly admit that you hold "rare views," such as prohibiting circular gold for women! If differences are evil, then why did you cause division in many of the Muslim communities that you visit by calling them to many things that cause division about Islam's established teachings such as this issue [of circular gold]? You also cause division in the community by saying that Abū Ḥanīfa is weak in ḥadīth and you empower the untrained and ignorant people to the status of *ijtihād* so that they oppose the imams and the scholars.[55]

ʿAwwāma shifts the argument from areas of differences of opinion to the area of *ijmāʿ*. He states, "And this one who claims to follow the proof-text by not following the imams, he falls into saying that which no one has previously said without realizing it. Nay, he even claims that he is a champion of the Sunna (*Nāṣir li l-Sunna*), and calls to it!"[56] Traditionalists acknowledge

[53] N. Albānī, *Aṣl Ṣifat*, 40–41. [54] M. ʿAwwāma, *Adab*, 98. [55] M. ʿAwwāma, *Adab*, 98–99.
[56] M. ʿAwwāma, *Athar*, 106.

the fallibility of the interpretation or understanding of a single jurist, but when jurists collectively agree on an issue the understanding is raised to the level of infallibility. This belief is based on the concept that the Muslim community cannot agree on an error. However, the purist Salafi certainty-based approach to legal issues also led them to disagree with the practicality of consensus.

CONSENSUS

The primary sources of Islam are the Qurʾān and the ḥadīth. While Muslims believe the Qurʾān to be the direct word of God, ḥadīth are the words of the Prophet inspired by God. Both the Qurʾān and the words of the Prophet were recorded in the form of a text. Muslim jurists attempt to understand these texts to discover God's law. This forms what is known as *fiqh*. Juristic disagreement was the norm in Islamic law, but there were a few issues that all leading jurists of a particular generation agreed on and this is referred to as consensus (*ijmāʿ*). Consensus means that all jurists of any generation after the Prophet are certain that what they have understood is actually what God intended. The theory of consensus holds that it is inconceivable for the entire Muslim community to agree upon falsehood.

Bernard Weiss notes that whenever all living jurists agreed on a particular formulation of the law, this consensus raised the formulation to an infallible representation of divine will. The possibility of error concerning formulations of law only existed when jurists disagreed. However, when they agreed on an issue the fallibility of individual jurists was erased through the supervening principle of the infallibility of consensus. Consensus set boundaries on disagreement in the formulation of law. For Muslim jurists, consensus must be regarded as sacred because it is the product of divine guidance bestowed on the community, safeguarding it from error.[57] Weiss states, "Whenever the mujtahids are in agreement, the rule of law on which they are agreed becomes written on tablets of stone as an infallible expression of divine law that may never be set aside by any future mujtahid."[58]

Weiss is correct in noting that the reopening of cases on which there is consensus amounts to questioning certainty. However, he also notes that this questioning of certainty includes conclusive texts in the Qurʾān and the Sunna.[59] Weiss is not the only scholar to make this claim; others have also

57 B. Weiss, "Interpretation," 201.

58 Bernard Weiss, *The Spirit of Islamic Law* (Athens: University of Georgia Press, 2006), 122.

59 See Wael Hallaq, *An Introduction to Islamic Law* (Cambridge: Cambridge University Press, 2009), 22.

argued that the Qur'ān and ḥadīth are primarily authoritative because that authority has been vouchsafed for them in consensus.[60] They argue that consensus guarantees the authenticity and authority of scripture. In other words, consensus guarantees that the Qur'ān as we know it is the very Qur'ān that was taught by the Prophet Muhammad.[61] Weiss writes, "If the consensus of jurists determines what is of God and what is not, then God can be hardly regarded as anything more than a rubric. Any system of thought which assigns to a human consensus the authority to determine what shall be the sources of law cannot be regarded as inherently positivist."[62]

Aron Zysow correctly points out that an examination of classical texts does not support such a conclusion. He notes, "It would be a pathetic example of incompetence if the Islamic jurists had failed to observe so obvious a circularity as is suggested."[63] How can *ijmāʿ* be the basis of the authenticity of Islamic scripture when several Muslim jurists reject *ijmāʿ* altogether? It is not *ijmāʿ*, but rather *tawātur* that provides Islamic scripture with its historical basis. Furthermore, the consensus of jurists is also something that must be transmitted. The interpretation of the Qur'ān and ḥadīth rests on an understanding of a language that is prior to consensus.[64] The skepticism of purist Salafis toward the scholarly competence of Traditionalists is related to the issue of *tawātur* because the same scholars played a role in both the formation of *fiqh* as well as the transmission of Islamic scripture.

The Islamic sciences, even ḥadīth tradition and the science of ḥadīth, were passed down by Traditionalist scholars. Purist Salafis approach *fiqh* with a level of skepticism because it was passed down through Traditionalist institutions, but they simultaneously accept the scripture they preserved and transmitted. Hence, by implying that these scholars are not trustworthy in one regard, they are implicitly, and perhaps unknowingly, attacking the authenticity of the Qur'ān and Sunna themselves. Even though they do not trust Traditionalists and accuse them of being blind followers, by putting their faith in the science of ḥadīth, they are implicitly placing their faith in Traditionalist institutions.

[60] See H. A. R. Gibb, *Mohammedanism*, 2nd ed. (New York: Oxford University Press, 1962), 96; Jerome N. D. Anderson and Norman J. Coulson, "Islamic Law in Contemporary Cultural Change," *Saeculum*, 18 (1967), 26.

[61] Bernard Weiss, "The Primacy of Revelation in Classical Islamic Legal Theory As Expounded by Sayf al-Dīn al-Āmidī," *Studia Islamica*, 59 (1984), 79.

[62] B. Weiss, "The Primacy," 80.

[63] A. Zysow, *Economy*, 114.

[64] A. Zysow, *Economy*, 155.

THE (IM)PRACTICALITY OF CONSENSUS

Salafis require that the evidence of *ijmāʿ* be definitive in authenticity and meaning. The majority of Traditionalists hold that the source of consensus can be presumable, such as a solitary narration or *qiyās*. However, as soon as *ijmāʿ* is established, *ijmāʿ* is elevated to being equivalent to a conclusive proof-text (*qaṭʿī*). It was primarily the Ẓāhirī school that was skeptical about the validity of *ijmāʿ*. Like Ibn Ḥazm, Albānī cast doubt about the practicality of consensus and points out how it is often erroneously claimed when there is in fact none.[65] Traditionalists do not object to the idea that *ijmāʿ* might be erroneously claimed, but they do not consider such a practice to be a valid reason for rejecting the practicality of *ijmāʿ* altogether. Albānī does not reject *ijmāʿ* in theory, but he rejects its practicality in order to warrant his unconventional opinions. Therefore, his stance is such that theoretically consensus might be valid, but it is impossible to prove, and he therefore places several requirements that must be met in order for *ijmāʿ* to be valid. He highlights several reasons why *ijmāʿ* cannot be established in practicality.

First, it is impossible to prove that *ijmāʿ* actually occurred on any issue other than that which is necessarily known about the religion (*al-maʿrūf min al-dīn bi-l-ḍarūra*).[66] Albānī argues that it is inconceivable for a large group of people to agree on an issue that lends itself to different interpretations. He uses the statement of Aḥmad b. Ḥanbal, "Whoever claims *ijmāʿ* is a liar, how does he know that they did not differ?" to demonstrate that a large group of people cannot agree on anything that was not already of certain validity.[67] However, if such a proof-text or source existed, *ijmāʿ* would serve no purpose. Most Traditionalists would reject Albānī's doubt on the practicality of *ijmāʿ* because they consider it possible for jurists to come to the same conclusion on a text despite the text lending itself to multiple interpretations. The primary purpose of consensus was to ratify what is uncertain and *ijmāʿ* has no place in a system where only certainty is admitted in the first place.[68]

Practically, knowledge of the existence of consensus on an issue was determined by looking into the past and observing that jurists were unanimous concerning a particular issue. This is similar to the manner in which the science of ḥadīth was practiced, in other words looking into the past to

[65] Muhammad Ibn Hazm, *Al-Iḥkām fī Uṣūl al-Aḥkām* (Cairo: Dār al-Ḥadith, 2005), 4: 538–595. Ibn Taymiyya examined Ibn Ḥazm's list of erroneous claims of consensus and highlighted some areas where Ibn Ḥazm also wrongly claimed consensus. See Taqī al-Dīn Ibn Taymiyyah, *Naqd Marātib al-Ijmāʿ* (Beirut: Dār al-Fikr, 1988).

[66] N. Albānī, *Ādāb*, 238. [67] N. Albānī, *Ādāb*, 44–45. [68] A. Zysow, *Economy*, 125.

examine scholarly opinions about narrators and historical matters. Therefore, rejecting consensus on the basis of probable difference of opinion also results in the rejection of *āḥād* ḥadīth because they are also established based on probability.

Ḥasan al-Saqqāf, one of Albānī's harshest critics, wrote a treatise against Albānī's position on *ijmāʿ* titled *Iḥtijāj al-Khāʾib bi-ʿIbārat man Iddaʿā al-Ijmāʿ fa-Huwa Kādhib* (The Loser's Recourse to the Phrase: "Whoever Claims Consensus Is a Liar").[69] Saqqāf argues that Albānī misuses the quote of Ibn Ḥanbal, "Whoever claims consensus is a liar," because the statement was directed at those who claimed the Qurʾān to be created. Saqqāf accuses Albānī of taking this statement that was specifically used about the claim that the Qurʾān was created and applying it to all claims of consensus. Saqqāf also notes that Ibn Ḥanbal did not reject *ijmāʿ* because he references it on several occasions.[70] For Albānī, even if it were possible to prove that there was consensus on an issue it would only be correct if it does not contradict authentic proof-text. Otherwise, it would mean that the Muslim community has gathered upon error.[71]

Albānī's second restriction on *ijmāʿ* is that it must not contradict scripture. Conversely, Traditionalists hold that consensus cannot contradict scripture, since scripture is either conjectural (*ẓannī*) or conclusive (*qaṭʿī*). If the text falls into the category of *qaṭʿī* then it is impossible for there to be a contradiction between two clear-cut issues. However, if the text is *ẓannī* and it cannot be reconciled with the consensus of scholars, then *ijmāʿ* would be given preference over the text. If consensus cannot go beyond the evidence of a text, then it is only the text that can determine whether one rule can abrogate another. In other words, all authority returns to the text and not to the jurists who are in consensus about the meaning of a text.

Ḥabīb al-Raḥmān al-Aʿẓamī states that even if there was an authentic and clear text on an issue, the consensus of the scholars on something incorrect is impossible. Therefore, *ijmāʿ* is infallible whereas the *āḥād* ḥadīth are not. Moreover, texts are only given preference over *ijmāʿ* when it is not possible to reconcile the two. For instance, there has been a long-standing consensus among jurists that circular gold is permissible for women and not men. Albānī's fatwa prohibiting it was so unpopular that it was dismissed by his critics and supporters alike. How did he arrive at a

[69] Ḥasan Saqqāf, *Majmūʿ*, 557–590. [70] Ḥasan Saqqāf, *Majmūʿ*, 551–554.
[71] N. Albānī, *Ādāb*, 239.

conclusion that contradicted scholarly consensus? Albānī describes his approach as follows:

> Among many others, this topic of prohibiting circular gold is an example that highlights the importance of this approach, which, as far as we know, we are the only ones who practiced it in these times. This method consists of determining the additions found in different narrations of ḥadīth, gathering them, and adding them to the original ḥadīth, along with investigating what is established from it. So, all praise is to God who has guided us to this, and we would not have been guided had God not guided us.[72]

As noted above, Albānī's methodology consists of gathering ḥadīth and allowing them to speak for themselves. The primary legal tool he uses is specifying a general text but does not expound on any interpretive process beyond that. Albānī breaks with consensus on the permissibility of gold for women and uses a number of ḥadīth that prohibit circular gold to justify his position. For Traditionalists, once consensus is established, it is not permitted to subject it to reexamination.

Because Albānī's approach was mainly limited to scripture, he based his case on a few ḥadīth that seem to preclude the prohibition of circular gold for women. Albānī writes that scholars who claim that these ḥadīth have been abrogated are incorrect because the ḥadīth that permit it are general, while those that prohibit it specifically speak of circular gold.[73] Albānī states that there was no consensus on the issue, although some scholars, including scholars like Muḥammad b. Aḥmad al-Dhahabī (d. 748/1348) and Ibn Ḥajar al-ʿAsqalānī (d. 852/1448) said a consensus exists. Albānī rejects the claim of consensus because it does not have textual evidence. For Albānī, unless there is another authentic abrogating text, valid consensus cannot contradict an authentic ḥadīth. The ḥadīth that allow gold for women, claims Albānī, refer to smaller items of gold items such as buttons or jewelry patterns, they do not apply to larger items such as rings and bracelets. Aʿzamī attempts to reconcile the proof-texts and *ijmāʿ* by explaining that *ijmāʿ* permits circular gold for women, while the few ḥadīth prohibiting it can be referring to those who wear gold out of arrogance and ostentation.[74]

Many scholars, whether they are Salafis or Traditionalists, either proclaimed the ḥadīth Albānī uses to be weak or understood that they apply to acts of asceticism of people. On the other hand, Albānī is the only known scholar to have prohibited circular gold. His critics interpret the ḥadīth that appear to prohibit circular gold as being abrogated or referring to women

[72] N. Albānī, *Ādāb*, 232. [73] N. Albānī, *Ādāb*, 247. [74] H. Aʿẓamī, *Shudhūdhu*, 72–73.

who did not pay *zakā* on gold.[75] Despite many classical and modern scholars highlighting consensus on this issue, Albānī rejects the validity of the consensus and argues that they were incorrect. He states that scholars adopt this method of interpretation in order to do away with the proof-text because it contradicts their *madhhab* and scholarly traditions.[76] Anṣārī states that even if there was no *ijmāʿ* on the issue, the texts themselves demonstrate that circular gold for women is permissible. Albānī weakens a narration attributed to the Successor Mujāhid b. Jabr (d. 104/722), which reads as follows: *On the authority of Sufyān, from ʿAlqama b. Marthad, from Mujāhid, that he said: An exception has been made for women concerning gold and silk.*[77]

Anṣārī notes that the word "exception" (*rukhkhiṣa*) would indicate that there was a prohibition on gold, and then women were exempted from this prohibition. Therefore, the few ḥadīth that appear to prohibit circular gold for women must be understood in this light. Much of the debate includes authenticating and weakening ḥadīth and narrations concerning the issue of circular gold. Albānī's ḥadīth method is discussed in Chapter 7, but Albānī's critics like Anṣārī do not consider his method in ḥadīth or *fiqh* to be legitimate.[78] Anṣārī tries to discredit Albānī by accusing him of dismissing the *salaf*, because none of them came to the same conclusion as Albānī on this topic.

One of the texts Albānī uses is found in the Sunan of Abū ʿAbd al-Raḥmān al-Nasāʾī (d. 303/915). Aʿẓamī responds to Albānī's use of the ḥadīth as follows:

> Even if it were a clear text, Nasāʾī did not understand it to be a prohibition of showing beautification. Even though Nasāʾī is more knowledgeable about ḥadīth narrations, and is better at understanding their numerous implications and more protective over following the ḥadīth than you and your likes of textualists.[79] Otherwise, you would have rallied against him all your violent campaigns which you wage against the followers of the *madhhabs*.[80]

Aʿẓamī argues that the Prophet encouraged some people to leave off many things out of asceticism, such as food or wealth, yet Albānī does not prohibit those items like he does circular gold. Aʿẓamī explains that none of the

75 I. Anṣārī, *Ibāḥat*, 60–67. 76 N. Albānī, *Ādāb*, 253. 77 I. Anṣārī, *Ibāḥat*, 106.
78 I. Anṣārī, *Ibāḥat*, 136.
79 The word Aʿẓamī uses is *ḥadīthīyīn*, which refers to those who irrationally follow ḥadīth without proper understanding.
80 H. Aʿẓamī, *Shudhūdhu*, 64–65.

ḥadīth Albānī uses indicate that circular gold is prohibited, which explains why Nasāʾī placed them under the chapter title of it being disliked for women to display their jewelry and gold. Aʿẓamī ends his argument by saying that if Nasāʾī and other scholars are mistaken on this issue, then what is the point of even trying to understand the text? In his estimation, if all of these great scholars are mistaken, then no one else is absolved from making similar or greater mistakes. For Traditionalists it is inconceivable that anyone will reach the level of the classical scholars in knowledge, therefore their understanding of Islam must be followed.[81]

Traditionalists also attempt to illustrate that the practice of women wearing circular gold was widespread from the earliest days of Islam until modern times. If it had been forbidden by scripture, the scholars would have prohibited it. This widespread practice along with the fact that no scholar has denounced the practice cannot be rejected on the grounds of a few *āḥād* ḥadīth that are not only questionable in terms of authenticity, but also lend themselves to multiple interpretations. Put differently, they argue that historical reality should be given preference over Albānī's interpretation of particular ḥadīth.

Conversely, Albānī believes the ḥadīth take precedence over the actions of the entire Muslim community. Even if no one acted on the ḥadīth that prohibit circular gold for women, it is not a legitimate excuse to discard acting upon them. If there was no text addressing the issue, then one can take into consideration the fact that the entire Muslim community did not prohibit circular gold. However, since there is a text, the actions of others, even if it is the entire Muslim community, become irrelevant.[82] In Albānī's view, what Traditionalists often consider to be "Islam" is merely a prominent interpretation, whereas Islam is the message delivered prior to the appearance of scholarly opinions. Consequently, scholarly opinion, even consensus, are unimportant to him if they contradict scripture. In other words, Albānī believes that most of what passes as traditional scholarship is actually just jurists regurgitating party lines about the "correct opinion" without any regard for basic scriptural analysis.

Traditionalists scholars take somewhat of the opposite approach concerning the scholarly opinions. Ismāʿīl al-Anṣārī, emphasizes the existence of *ijmāʿ* on the issue by compiling a long list of scholars who permitted gold for women and then states, "After all of this, the issue does not need Albānī's opinion!"[83] Anṣārī's responses to Albānī had an impact on the students of

[81] H. Aʿẓamī, *Shudhūdhu*, 68. [82] N. Albānī, *Ādāb*, 266–267. [83] I. Anṣārī, *Ibāḥat*, 58.

Islamic knowledge and rumors spread that Albānī had changed his opinion on the issue. When asked about whether he had retracted his opinion, Albānī stated: "No, it only increased me in my certainty, especially after I read Anṣārī's treatise."[84] The prohibition of gold rings, bracelets, and necklaces for women is an example of how Albānī approaches issues of Islamic law with the notion of complete certainty. Because he holds that his interpretation of Islam to be based on the only valid understanding of scripture, he introduces certainty to cases that have none, and introduces doubt to cases that have certainty.

By challenging the alleged *ijmāʿ* on the issue, Albānī shifted the conversation from debating the issue of gold to the validity of *ijmāʿ* itself. His approach to Islamic scholarship centers on bypassing and purging centuries of consensus building among scholars and demanding proof-texts (*dalīl*) for every religious position. Traditionalists do not simply consider this to be a different method of interpretation, but a threat to the authority of centuries of scholarly tradition that was previously accepted and trusted. Although Albānī accepts *ijmāʿ* in theory, he denies its practicality in some cases and notes that the theory of *ijmāʿ* is frequently abused. Traditionalists agree with Albānī about the theoretical validity of *ijmāʿ* but disagree with him on individual cases where he says there is no consensus. It is important to emphasize this similarity because it shifts their differences on *ijmāʿ* from being about the validity of *ijmāʿ* to its application.

Albānī examined everything anew in his endeavor to offer Muslims a version of Islam that was pure. He wrote books on topics like prayer and argued that only his book was based on the pure and authentic Sunna. He held that others must always provide scriptural evidence for their positions. Because he was reexamining everything anew, this led to him holding several unconventional interpretations that drew strong criticism from numerous scholars. These interpretations demonstrate that Albānī was someone who did not concern himself with who said what in the past, and in this sense, he was not a Traditionalist. Most Muslim scholars would be very concerned about previous scholarly opinions, but he thought it was not as important as his own understanding of a ḥadīth. If the ḥadīth said it, that was his *madhhab*. Although he was not a Ẓāhirī he did incline toward the literalism sometimes found in the Ẓāhirī school.[85]

[84] N. Albānī, *Ādāb*, 5.

[85] See N. Albānī, *S.A.S.*, 1: 430–438; idem, *Tamām al-Minna fī Taʿlīq ʿalā Fiqh al-Sunna* (Riyadh: Dār al-Rāya, 1998), 418–420.

Albānī had several unconventional opinions that he shared with the Ẓāhirī school. For instance, he believed that ejaculation through masturbation does not break the fast. In other words, if a man ejaculates through any means other than direct intercourse with his spouse, then it does not break the fast. He still considered masturbation to be prohibited but argued that it does not break the fast even if it results in ejaculation. Albānī rejects the *qiyās* comparing ejaculation to intercourse and argues that the two cannot be compared. He argues that it is far-fetched to consider one who masturbates equal to one who has intercourse. Scholars who say that ejaculation breaks the fast do so because ejaculation is the ultimate purpose and result of penetration, which breaks the fast. However, according to Albānī it is only penetration that breaks the fast, regardless of whether ejaculation occurs or not. He argues that masturbation and penetration through intercourse are two different things and therefore *qiyās* comparing the two is incorrect. However, *qiyās* can only occur between two different things that have a commonality. If both things are the same, there would be no need to draw an analogy between them. Therefore, Albānī appears to discount their commonality.

These unconventional *fiqh* opinions are important because they provide a better understanding of Albānī's hermeneutical methods and how he differed with Traditionalists. Other Salafis deal with these unconventional opinions by noting that Albānī was a scholar who made mistakes like all other scholars. However, in the estimation of Traditionalists, Albānī's unconventional opinions are not only grievous and fatal mistakes but demonstrate his lack of scholarly qualifications. They use this as evidence that the Salafi methodology results in exceptionally absurd conclusions.

5

Qur'ān and Sunna or the *Madhhabs*?

THE QUR'ĀN AND SUNNA ARE THE MAIN SOURCES FROM WHICH Muslims extract legal rulings. The twentieth century witnessed an intense tug of war between purist Salafis and Traditionalists about the legitimate and proper approach to Islamic law. Each of these groups considers itself to be the authentic and true understanding of Islam. The role of the *madhhab*s in understanding the Qur'ān and Sunna is at the crux of the debate. Traditionalists maintain that the *madhhab*s represent a collective scholarly understanding of God's intent because they are based on scholarship that was developed over centuries. On the other hand, purist Salafis consider the *madhhab*s to be fallible human institutions that often contradict the commandments of scripture and need purging. They maintain that the *madhhab*s are an innovation and something apart from the Qur'ān and Sunna.

A famous Prophetic tradition states that the Muslim community will be divided into seventy-three sects, all of which will be in hell except one. The saved group are described as those who follow what the Prophet and his Companions adhered to. Being that purist Salafis consider themselves to be the only "true" followers of the *salaf*, they identify themselves as that group. This means that their understanding of Islam is the only valid one. Therefore, the purist Salafi legal methodology is the only correct way of understanding Islam.

When purist Salafis say that they only follow the Qur'ān, Sunna, and the *salaf* they really seek to follow an Islam that is pure and unadulterated. They privilege the interpretations of the early Muslims, in particular those who lived before the third century AH. This is based on the notion that the legal injunctions in scripture are clear and unambiguous to the extent that everyone who seeks to understand them correctly will arrive at the same conclusion. Therefore, it is common to see purist Salafi scholars encouraging

Muslims to always ask jurists for their evidence. Despite requiring nonexperts to ask for a *dalīl*, purist Salafis emphasize that nonspecialists do not have the tools to interpret the legal elements of scripture independent of qualified scholars. These contradictory positions often result in confusion about the stance of Salafism toward *taqlīd* and following scholars. This chapter sheds light on the Salafi position toward the *madhhabs*, *ijtihād*, and *taqlīd*.

DEFINING *IJTIHĀD* AND *TAQLĪD*

Because purist Salafis believe that legal rulings only have one correct understanding they must maintain the position that texts are clear and unambiguous, otherwise they will be categorized as another *madhhab*. In order to maintain their argument that they were not involved in the interpretive process purist Salafis had to remain uncompromising in their positions. Compromising on their positions meant they would have to acknowledge that their conclusions were based on an interpretive process rather than the direct meaning of infallible texts. In other words, conceding that their conclusions involved an interpretive process would undermine their claim to possess the absolute truth extracted directly from scripture.

The prohibition of *taqlīd* and insistence on following scripture presents the question of how nonscholars should understand legal rulings.[1] Is it through a scholar or directly from scripture? After Ibn Ḥanbal three main positions emerged about the *ijtihād*, *taqlīd*, and *ittibāʿ* debate. The dominant one was that *taqlīd* was permitted for both laypeople and jurists unable to perform *ijtihād* (*muqallid*-jurists). The second rejected *taqlīd* for both jurists and laypeople, while the third rejected *taqlīd* for all jurists but permitted it for the laity.[2] The term *taqlīd* is used by many scholars who each have a different definition in mind, and this results in confusion. Traditionalists understand *taqlīd* to be deference to precedent and a *muqallid* can still perform *ijtihād* while adhering to precedent. On the other hand, purist Salafis consider *taqlīd* to be the uncritical adherence to a scholar or school

[1] On *taqlīd* see Abdul-Rahman Mustafa, *On Taqlīd: Ibn Al Qayyim's Critique of Authority in Islamic Law* (Oxford: Oxford University Press, 2013); S. Jackson, *Islamic Law*, 75–78; W. Hallaq, *Gate of Ijtihad*; Mohammad Fadel, "The Social Logic of Taqlīd and the Rise of the Mukhtaṣar," *Islamic Law and Society*, 3, no. 2 (1996).

[2] Ahmed Fekry Ibrahim, "Rethinking the Taqlīd-Ijtihād Dichotomy: A Conceptual Historical Approach," *Journal of American Oriental Society*, 136, no. 2 (2016), 296. On different levels of jurists, see Norman Calder, "Al-Nawawī's Typology of *Muftīs* and Its Significance for a General Theory of Islamic Law," *Islamic Law and Society*, 3, no. 2 (1996), 137–164.

of thought. They perceive *taqlīd* as being solely negative without any redeeming qualities or creative features. At the same time, purist Salafis acknowledge that laity must not interpret texts on their own. Rather they must ask scholars and seek their opinions. Therefore, they sometimes completely prohibit *taqlīd* and necessitate it at other times. As we shall see, this shifting of positions can cause confusion concerning the purist Salafi attitude toward *taqlīd*.

Purist Salafis define a *muqallid* as someone who is ignorant and unlearned in religion. *Taqlīd* is equivalent to absolute ignorance and only befitting of those who are absolutely unlettered; everyone else must ask for a *dalīl*. Albānī compares the prohibition of *taqlīd* to the consumption of pork that is only made permissible under exceptional circumstances. This definition suggests that *taqlīd* only occurs in the absence of *ijtihād*. Traditionalists reject this concept as an oversimplification of *taqlīd* because it places people as either full-fledged *mujtahid*s or completely ignorant. Traditionalists like Būṭī and ʿAwwāma maintain that there are different levels of *taqlīd* and one may be an expert in a particular *madhhab* but not at the level of full-fledged *mujtahid*. Traditionalists set the standard of full *ijtihād* so high that they often refer to themselves as *muqallid*s rather than individual *mujtahid*s, despite their expertise in Islamic law. At first glance, it may appear to be a contradiction that a *muqallid* can also be a *mujtahid*, but this is by no means the case. One who is not a full-fledged *mujtahid* can perform *taqlīd* by following the opinions or hermeneutical methodology of a *madhhab*. *Ijtihād* through *takhrīj* or *taqlīd* of the principles of a *madhhab* was a dominant interpretive feature in Islamic intellectual history. Sherman Jackson explains that in the view of someone like Shihāb al-Dīn al-Qarāfii (d. 684/1285), a *muqallid* could be said to perform more *ijtihād* than the eponym.[3] The *ijtihād* is attributed to an individual scholar, but he is performing *taqlīd* by following the legal principles of the *madhhab*.[4] Although Traditionalists refer to themselves as *muqallid*s, they do not deem themselves incapable of *ijtihād*. Jackson accurately contends that *taqlīd* was fundamentally about authority. What legal scholars appropriated from the past was not the substance of existing teachings, but the authority attached to the name or doctrine of an already established authority

[3] S. Jackson, *Islamic Law*.

[4] Wael Hallaq, "Takhrīj and the Construction of Juristic Authority," in *Studies in Islamic Legal Theory*, ed. Bernard Weiss (Boston: Brill, 2002), 320.

figure. In this regard, *taqlīd* was not a commitment to "unthinking" and was not inconsistent with the continued development of the law.[5]

If purist Salafis believe *taqlīd* is prohibited yet acknowledge the difference between laity and scholars, how can the untrained follow the teachings of Islam without performing *taqlīd*? Purist Salafis use a third term which they call *ittibāʿ*; this is a level between *taqlīd* and *ijtihād. Ittibāʿ* refers to following a scholar's opinion while being aware of the proof-text he uses. The term *ittibāʿ* is meant to distinguish Salafi laity from those who have uncritical loyalty to a *madhhab* and do not investigate the validity of the argument.[6] The debate surrounding *taqlīd* and *ittibāʿ* was a result of polemics surrounding the tension between the personal authority of the jurist and the authority of textual sources.

Purist Salafis believed it was possible for laypeople to avoid *taqlīd* by making them responsible for inquiring about the proof-text for a ruling before following it, calling this intermediate category *ittibāʿ*. This is designed to shift authority from the jurist to the text.[7] In other words, once the individual is presented with scripture then there is no need for a scholar to be the basis of one's belief. However, this presents a problem because it implies that the scholar and the layperson are equal in understanding of texts. The main difference is that the former served as the means of communicating the proof-text. As a result, Traditionalists accuse Salafis of making *ijtihād* seem like an easy task. Traditionalists consider *ijtihād* to be a lofty exercise that only very few are capable of. For instance, Abū Ghudda points out that not everyone who reads a ḥadīth immediately becomes an expert in extracting legal rulings from it. He states:

> If the likes of Yaḥyā al-Qaṭṭān, Wakīʾ b. al-Jarrāḥ, ʿAbd al-Razzāq, Yaḥyā b. Maʿīn, and those of their caliber did not dare partake in *ijtihād* and *fiqh*, then how audacious are those who claim to *ijtihād* in our time?! On top of that, they call the pious predecessors ignorant without the least amount of shame or modesty! God is our refuge from such deceit.[8]

Salafis never refer to themselves as *muqallids* because they consider it a derogatory term. They refuse to accept an opinion of a scholar if it goes against what they consider to be a clear authentic ḥadīth and petition that

[5] S. Jackson, "*Ijtihād*," 259.

[6] A similar argument was made by Ibn ʿAbd al-Barr, although Ibn ʿAbd al-Barr's criticism of *taqlīd* is directed toward the scholarly class and not the laity. He permitted *taqlīd* for laypeople because they could not understand the evidence presented to them. See Y. ʿAbd al-Barr, *Jāmiʿ Bayān al-ʿIlm*, 110–118.

[7] A. Ibrahim, "Rethinking," 288.

[8] A. Abū Ghudda, *Al-Isnād*, 68.

Muslims return to the true teachings of their religion. Albānī notes that even if a person acquires all the knowledge found in the secondary literature of the *madhhab*s, he is not a scholar. Instead, he is like a collector who has gathered everything that the scholars have said in their books, which include many differences of opinions.[9]

ANTI-*MADHHAB*ISM

Albānī dedicated his life to providing Muslims an understanding of Islam that was free from outside influences. Other Salafis have agreed with Albānī in rhetoric, but in practice they did not have strong anti-*madhhab* inclinations. Traditional Saudi Arabian Salafi scholars such as Ibn Bāz and Ibn ʿUthaymīn have admitted that the strong *dalīl* trumps the *madhhabs*' teachings, but this was primarily a rhetorical claim rather than actual practice. In practice, Ibn Bāz and Ibn ʿUthaymīn clung to the Ḥanbalī school in their *aḥkām* and fatwas. However, there were exceptions to this practice. In other words, Ibn Bāz and Ibn ʿUthaymīn were Ḥanbalī in practice but not always Ḥanbalī in rhetoric, whereas Albānī was a systematic and principled anti-*madhhab*ist in both rhetoric and practice. Additionally, Ibn Bāz and Ibn ʿUthaymīn did not campaign against the *madhhab*s and there was little to no debates between them and Traditionalists on the status and validity of following a school of law. On the contrary, Albānī was primarily known for his anti-*madhhab*ism that generated many book-length responses from Traditionalists throughout the Muslim world.

A strong anti-*madhhab* campaign lies at the heart of Albānī's Salafism. Although his anti-*madhhab*ism may have been inspired by the likes of Ibn Taymiyya, Ibn Qayyim, and Muḥammad b. ʿAbd al-Wahhāb, he had a different stance toward the *madhhab*s. While these three scholars were anti-*taqlīd* to varying degrees, they were not anti-*madhhab*. For example, Ibn Taymiyya was a Ḥanbalī who rarely engaged in legal issues without mentioning the four schools and he did not prohibit *taqlīd* for the common man.[10] By contrast, Albānī refused to present himself as a follower of any person or *madhhab* besides the Prophet. He states:

> Those who are called Wahhabis, they are Ḥanbalīs . . . as for me, I refused to be Ḥanafī, therefore, I will also refuse to be called a Ḥanbalī. Because when I affiliated with the Messenger of God, blessings and peace be upon him, it has sufficed me from all other affiliations. I worship God alone, and

[9] E. Hamdeh, "Salafi Polemic," 236. [10] B. Haykel, "Salafi Thought," 37–45.

> I follow Muḥammad alone. God has no partner in worship, and Muḥammad has no partner in following.[11]

The implication that following a *madhhab* is akin to *shirk* is an accusation that other modern Salafi scholars never made. Albānī was the century's most ardent propagator of Salafism. He is perhaps the best-known Salafi among non-Salafis due to his scripturally charged and heated debates with many Traditionalists and the controversies he generated within the world of Salafism. These disputes were not limited to scholarly circles, but large numbers of students and religious activists served as audiences. By the 1990s, Albānī's followers had grown to such a point that they actually competed in size, number, and influence with Jordan's largest Islamist movement, the Muslim Brotherhood. They were a force to be reckoned with in mosques, public gatherings, and educational institutions.[12]

Many Salafis see this influential Islamic figure as the representative of an authentic and scripture Islam. They consider his social, political, and religious stances to be based on solid scriptural proof-texts. To many Salafis, Albānī is a *mujaddid* who has arrived to return Islam to its authentic roots, which was mainly the path of the Muslim forefathers. Others, however, view him as a thinker who has gone astray (*mubtadi*ʿ) due to his bypassing of the *madhhab* institutions and dismissal of centuries of scholarly tradition. The crux of his message promotes a literalistic understanding of authoritative scriptures that are focused on secondary ritualistic aspects of Islamic law. Albānī spent his career trying to purify Islamic law and was not primarily concerned with political, social, or economic change.

He considered reliance on the *madhhab*s and a lack of close adherence to the scriptural evidence to be the reasons for the regression of the Muslim world. His critics, such as Būṭī, believe that Muslims will not be able to formulate a proper methodology for comprehending and developing the essence of Islam if they do not move beyond a merely literal understanding of proof-texts. In other words, a "proper" understanding of Islam distinguishes between eternal and unalterable texts and texts that were formulated to meet a temporary need, an existing custom or tradition, or certain circumstances that can be changed when those particular circumstances change.[13]

[11] Muḥammad Nāṣir al-Dīn al-Albānī, "Ittibāʿ Sayyid al-Umma Ṣallā Allāhu ʿalay-hi wa sallam 1," lecture from www.ar.islamway.net/lesson/47201/, last accessed November 9, 2011.

[12] M. Abu Rumman and H. Abu Hanieh, *Conservative*, 46.

[13] A. Christmann, "Būṭī," 162–163.

Since Albānī was self-educated, he did not have a school of law or a tradition of learning that gave him religious authority. It was therefore important for him to create an image of himself that contrasted sharply with his detractors' picture. He depicted his critics as blind followers of fallible legal institutions and established a self-image as an unaffiliated scholar who broke away from the *madhhab*s and followed the Prophet directly. Critics of Albānī argue that the epistemological worldview he developed ignored the contextual understanding of the reasons, circumstances, incidents, and purposes underlying the scriptural texts.

When Albānī adopted a specific position, wrote a book, or delivered a public speech, he usually did so in response to someone else's criticism of him. He took his iconoclasm with him everywhere he went, including relatively conservative countries such as Saudi Arabia. His relationship with Saudi Traditional Salafism (or Wahhabism) changed due to his experiences in Medina. He was dissatisfied with Traditionalism right from the outset; but as time went by, he declined to become part of the Saudi Traditional Salafi hierarchy because he was committed to the truth rather than to the Salafiyya, the *madhhab*s, or any particular person.

His self-created image always remained that of an unchanging detached scholar who was interested only in the truth. Unconcerned with people, he did very little to counter his iconoclastic image and thus became a very detached independent figure and Muslim thinker. With time Albānī became more independent, separated from all religious movements, and became a religious authority on his own that was natural as he successfully garnered followers. He was a defiant figure and he did not want to be part of a system; he wanted to make sure he did not end up defending the system instead of the truth even though he might end up doing just that.

Purist Salafi attempts to purge legal tradition were not viewed positively by Traditionalists. One scholar notes that although there are frequent calls for a "Muslim Martin Luther," Traditionalist *'ulamā'* suggest that much of the turmoil and extremism in the Muslim world results precisely from unlearned Muslims who have broken with tradition and approach their religion Luther-like, by means of scripture alone.[14] Traditionalists do not necessarily oppose the unconventional opinions found in Salafism, but primarily their methodology, which threatens their scholarly authority and institutions.

[14] J. Brown, *Misquoting Muhammad*, 7.

Purist Salafis maintain that Traditionalism manifests excessive reverence for scholars and uncritical acceptance of the legal schools, with the result that members of different *madhhab*s came to behave as if they belonged to different religions. This division among Muslims can only be resolved by returning to the Prophet's true and pure teachings. Legal confusion, innovation in religion, and all other problems facing Islam and Muslims are a result of not properly adhering to the science of ḥadīth.[15]

Albānī was careful not to attack the *madhhab*s directly, but rather to attack blind *madhhab*ism. Some Salafis, such as Muḥammad Sulṭān al-Khujnadī, argued that following a *madhhab* is a religious innovation, and Albānī was criticized for defending their position.[16] To answer the question of why Salafis were staunch critics of the *madhhab*s, it is vital to point out that the emergence of Salafism in the mid-1900s was preceded by political turmoil in the Muslim world. The apparent despair in the restoration of a Muslim caliphate began to sink in the minds of many. Salafis were apolitical with a political agenda. They were not concerned with politics per se but attempted to generate global changes in the Muslim world by implementing a social order that was rooted in what they considered to be the correct interpretation of the Qur'ān and Sunna. They considered the ignorance of other Muslims concerning the proper interpretation of the Qur'ān and Sunna to be the source of division and political failure. The lack of education about the correct and only interpretation of the Qur'ān and Sunna is what led to religious and then political chaos.

Purist Salafis as well as some Traditionalists believe that in order to restore political stability, religious stability must come first. The solution for Muslim unity was to meticulously implement Islamic rituals according to the Qur'ān, Sunna, and the methods of the early predecessors. There was no need to introduce new things, but only to return to the Sunna of the Prophet which would bring upon them divine power and political dominance. The Salafi discovery that so many "foreign" elements have penetrated Islamic teachings led them to construct a thorough refutation of the *madhhab*s as criticism of their own religious community for neglecting the teachings of God and the Prophet. When examined closer, the works of both Traditionalists and Salafis are a reflection of their own disappointment in the social, religious, and political circumstances of their time. Their

15 D. Lav, *Radical Islam*, 110.

16 See M. Khujnadī, *Hal al-Muslim Mulzam*. Khujnadī argues that Muslims should not follow the *madhhab*s in any way since the Qur'ān and Sunna are clear. This work was edited by Salīm al-Hilālī, one of Albānī's closest students.

frustration with "today" led them to try to bring back "yesterday," meaning the era of the Prophet and his Companions. The Salafi anti-*madhhab* rhetoric only makes sense when understood in this light, otherwise it would only be an intellectual exercise with no relevance to the circumstances of their time.

HISTORICAL VALIDITY OF THE *MADHHABS*

Traditionalists and purist Salafis appeal to history to validate their methodology. Both groups agree that the earliest Muslim generations are the ideal models for later Muslims. Purist Salafis challenge the validity of the *madhhabs* based on the fact that they did not exist during the era of the Companions. By not adhering to a *madhhab*, purist Salafis believe they are following the footsteps of the earliest Muslim generations. They consider their methodology and understanding to be aligned with the early Muslim generations that include the eponyms of the legal schools.

Purist Salafis use historical circumstances related to the emergence of the *madhhabs* to argue that the very concept of the *madhhab* is foreign to authentic Islam. They project themselves into history by trying to model their lives as they understand their historical forefathers. The history of the early Muslim community (the *salaf*) is retold according to the image that Salafis view themselves in. Essentially, every Muslim would claim that they are following the Prophet and the early Muslims, but it was modern Salafis who used the term "Salafi" and applied it to their understanding of Islam. The usage of the term "Salafi" is a "power-play," or a method used to give authority and legitimacy to their understanding of Islam.

One of the most famous ḥadīth used by purist Salafis is one that states that the first three generations of Muslims are the best. By recognizing that the first three generations are the greatest it is also understood that this era will never return. Purist Salafis consider the generation of the *salaf* to have contained Islam in its purest form, free from the corruption and evil interpolations that appeared later. The past is gone and purist Salafis can only try to relive it, but it will not come alive today as it was then. The way modern Muslims interact with their tradition has fundamentally changed. The proposition that Muslims can return to the identical state of the first three generations is problematic because it assumes that intellectual and spiritual discourses operate at an abstract level of ideas, unaffected by the circumstances different Muslims live in. It also assumes that the early Muslim generations were monolithic in their understanding of Islamic law and had a shared methodology. The Prophet's Companions differed on legal, political, and social matters. This prompted Būṭī to argues that Salafiyyah is a blessed time period, not an Islamic *madhhab*. He explained that the first three generations cannot be followed as a school of law because they never had a single methodology. Rather, different methodologies existed like that of *ahl al-ḥadīth* and *ahl al-raʾy*. He notes that if Salafism is a method of understanding the Qurʾān and Sunna according to the understanding of the *salaf*, then it struggles with the problem of the *salaf* having multiple understandings of scripture. Therefore, he claims that a Salafi methodology did not formally exist during the time of the *salaf*.[17] However, this can be resolved if we understand the efforts of purist Salafis to reduce the range of differences from the broad level of *madhhab*-based differences to the supposedly narrower level of differences in the period of the *salaf*.

Similarly, purist Salafis argue that the *madhhab*s are invalid because they did not exist during the era of the Companions. For instance, Albānī states: "We all know that there is no difference between a scholar, a student, and an ignorant person because in the time of the righteous predecessors there was not a *madhhab* called the *madhhab* of Abū Bakr al-Ṣiddīq that some people could follow and say: 'I am a Bakrī.' There was no ʿUmarī, ʿUthmānī, or ʿAlawī *madhhab*."[18] Muqbil al-Wādiʿī similarly argues that there is nothing in the Qurʾān or Sunna that requires Muslims to follow a *madhhab*.[19] Traditionalists note that although they were not called *madhhab*s, the concept of following the understanding of a particular person existed during the time of the Companions. To support the historical validity of the *madhhab*s the American Muslim scholar Hamza Yusuf notes that most Sunni Muslim scholars have affiliated with a *madhhab*.[20]

However, purist Salafis consider the eponyms of the *madhhab*s to have followed the Salafi methodology in the sense of prioritizing ḥadīth over their personal opinions. Albānī's critics accuse him of understanding texts and the statements of the eponyms of the *madhhab*s without considering their historical context. For instance, the eponyms of the *madhhab*s are recorded to have said: "If a ḥadīth is authentic, it is my *madhhab*" (*idhā ṣaḥḥa al-ḥ adīth fa huwa madhhabī*). Purist Salafis highlight these statements to illustrate that the eponyms of the schools always preferred a proof-text over their own *ijtihād*. They often understand such statements to mean that the eponyms themselves opposed the concept of a *madhhab*.

For instance, by using the statements of the eponyms of the *madhhabs*, Albānī aligns himself with the founders and portrays their followers as blind

[17] See M. Būṭī, *Salafiyya*. [18] E. Hamdeh, "Salafi Polemic," 236.
[19] M. Wādiʿī, *Ijābat*, 317–319. [20] H. Yusuf, "The Four Schools."

adherents who distanced themselves from the methodology of those they claim to follow. He challenges the authority of earlier prominent adherents to the *madhhab*s, increases the authority of the eponym of the school, and enhances his own position as the living heir of eponyms of the *madhhab*s. Albānī explains that the eponyms of the *madhhab*s did not intend for people to prefer their opinions over authentic ḥadīth.

Traditionalists understand these statements in a completely different light and argue that there are several reasons that these statements could have been made. For example, Muḥammad b. Idrīd al-Shāfiʿī (d. 204/820)'s statement could have likely been made to differentiate his methodology with that of the Mālikī school of law that preferred the actions of the people of Medina over authentic ḥadīth. Būṭī accuses Albānī of taking the above-mentioned statement ("If a ḥadīth is authentic, it is my *madhhab*") out of context, noting that if the merely apparent meaning of a ḥadīth seems to contradict the founder's opinion, it is not necessarily a contradiction. The eponyms of all four schools of law are known to have cautioned their followers about *taqlīd*. Būṭī explains that this statement does not mean that every person who encounters an authentic ḥadīth could assert that this is the *madhhab* of al-Shāfiʿī and act according to its apparent meaning. Instead, this statement is intended for the scholar who is qualified to exercise *ijtihād*. Furthermore, the person must be certain that al-Shāfiʿī did not know the particular ḥadīth or its authenticity. The task of reviewing all al-Shāfiʿī's writings as well as those of his immediate students requires a level of scholarship. Būṭī contextualizes the above-mentioned statement ("If a ḥadīth is authentic, it is my *madhhab*") and argues that a number of considerations must be made before it can be applied.

He argues that the founders of the *madhhab*s may have known a particular ḥadīth but did not apply it because they may have considered it abrogated or interpreted it in light of other evidence. By invoking the statements of the eponyms of the *madhhab*s that the authentic ḥadīth are their *madhhab*, Albānī attempts to strengthen his condemnation of *taqlīd* by using supportive statements from the very scholars that *muqallid*s claim to follow. By doing so he places Traditionalists in a position where they essentially condemn themselves.[21]

While legal verdicts or the opinions of the *madhhab*s may appear to contradict authentic ḥadīth, there is often a legal reasoning, or countering evidence, behind the opinion of the *madhhab*. Because scholars of different

[21] N. Albānī, "Ittibāʿ."

schools often debated issues of Islamic law, rarely is it the case that the scholars of the *madhhab* were unaware of a proof-text. However, critics of *taqlīd* suggest that *madhhab* scholars, despite being aware of evidence that goes against a position of their school, will actually commit themselves to defending it, despite their knowledge of its weakness. Būṭī also states that there are conditions that come along with the statements of the four imams that authentic ḥadīth are their *madhhab*. Not every authentic ḥadīth whose apparent meaning contradicts the opinion of the eponym of a school is actually a contradiction. He quotes Nawawī who explains al-Shāfiʿī's statement about authentic ḥadīth being his *madhhab* as follows:

> And what was said by al-Shāfiʿī does not mean that every person who sees an authentic ḥadīth could then say that this is the *madhhab* of al-Shāfiʿī and act according to its superficial meaning. Instead, this is for the one who has attained the level of *ijtihād* in the *madhhab* according to what was previously mentioned of the mujtahid's attributes, or something close to it. The condition is that he be most certain that al-Shāfiʿī, may God's mercy be upon him, did not encounter that ḥadīth or was unaware of its authenticity. This can only be achieved after reviewing all of al-Shāfiʿī's books and likewise the books of those who obtained knowledge from him and so on. This condition is difficult and those who meet it are few. This condition was placed because al-Shāfiʿī abandoned acting on the superficial meaning of many ḥadīth which he saw and knew. However, the evidence he had led him to criticize it, or [consider] that it was abrogated, or specific, or interpreted it, etc.[22]

At first glance, it may appear that al-Shāfiʿī's statement is not addressing the *mujtahid* because he is not in need of following an imam in the first place. Ḥabīb al-Raḥmān al-ʿAẓamī notes that there are different levels of *mujtahids* such as the absolute *mujtahid* (*mujtahid muṭlaq*) and the restricted *mujtahid* (*mujtahid muqayyad*); the latter restricts himself to *ijtihād* within the *madhhab*.[23] Būṭī states that allowing lay Muslims to extract rulings from works like Bukhārī and Muslim will lead to chaos. He notes: "Place the *Ṣaḥīḥ* of Bukhārī or Muslim in front of the general Muslims today and ask them to understand the laws of religion from the texts that are in them. Then look how much ignorance, disorder, and meaninglessness [will enter] the religion."[24]

[22] M. Būṭī, *Al-Lā Madhhabiyya*, 103. Also see Muḥyī al-Dīn al-Nawawī, *Kitāb al-Majmūʿ Sharḥ al-Muhadhdhab li'l-Shīrāzī* (Beirut: Dār Iḥyāʾ al-Turāth al-ʿArabī, 2001), 105.

[23] H. Aʿẓamī, *Shudhūdhu*, 122–123. M. ʿAwwāma, *Athar*, 71–72.

[24] M. Būṭī, *Al-Lā Madhhabiyya*, 38.

SCHOLAR OR SCRIPTURE?

A central theme in the purist Salafi charge against Traditionalists is that they disregard the Sunna by following fallible institutions. Traditionalists criticize the purist Salafi conviction that they are following the direct meaning of scripture because it allows them to absolve their own *ijtihād* from fallibility, a technique meant to give their understanding of scripture unquestionable authority. The opposition to the *madhhab*s triggered Būṭī to write his famous book *Non-Madhhabism Is the Most Dangerous Innovation That Threatens the Islamic* Sharīʿa. This work was written in response to Albānī's praise of Muḥammad Sulṭān Maʿṣūmī al-Khujnadī's book *Is a Muslim Obligated to Follow One of the Four Madhhabs?* Khujnadī argued that Islam is clear and simple; there is no need to follow anything other than the Qur'ān and Sunna.[25] He argues that *ijtihād* is easy, and every individual, regardless of their expertise, could exert effort to understand scripture. One needs no more than the Qur'ān and ḥadīth books. This straightforward approach to scripture is countered by the Traditionalist argument that simply knowing a text is not enough to extract rulings from it.[26]

Traditionalists consider the non-*madhhab* approach to be an oversimplification of Islamic law. They argue that in addition to particular ambiguities in the Qur'ān, the Sunna sometimes proves more challenging to interpret due to the vastness of ḥadīth literature spread across many books compiled in different times and places. Even when authentic ḥadīth have been filtered out from this large body of ḥadīth literature there are some narrations that appear to conflict with each other or with verses of the Qur'ān. In this regard, Traditionalists consider the role of the *madhhab*s to be essential in providing a consistent methodology for dealing with the vast body of Islamic scripture. In their estimation, non-*madhhab*ism is considered problematic because, without a consistent methodology and expertise, scripture can easily be misunderstood and thereby threaten the orthodox method of Islamic jurisprudence.

Because purist Salafis approach the *madhhab*s with suspicion, they always ask for a *dalīl.* This is done by laypeople as well, not necessarily because they understand the text, but they want to be ensured that it is not based on following fallible scholars. This created a phenomenon where nonexperts would not accept fatwas unless they were accompanied by a verse or ḥadīth explained in detail, along with its strength, chain of narration, as well as all

[25] M. Khujnadī, *Hal al-Muslim Mulzam.*

[26] M. Būṭī, *Al-Lā Madhhabiyya*, 19.

the reliability of its narrators.[27] Anti-*madhhab* rhetoric is not new, several other scholars, such as al-Shawkānī, have historically criticized following a *madhhab*. However, these critiques did not have a significant impact on the authority of the *ʿulamāʾ*. The decline of Traditionalist authority over the last several centuries created an environment where anti-*madhhab* rhetoric successfully generated a level of mistrust in traditional *ʿulamāʾ* and this resulted in them always being asked to provide details of their evidence by nonexperts. Purist Salafis were successful in encouraging lay Muslims to require proof-texts from Traditionalists and hence helped shift authority away from the *madhhabs*.

Because laypeople are untrained, Traditionalists consider it necessary that they follow a trained scholar. After the death of the Prophet, his Companions moved to different parts of the world and the locals of those regions followed the understanding of that Companion.[28] Būṭī and Albānī both agree that people have always been categorized as either scholars who are qualified to perform *ijtihād* or laypeople unqualified to perform *ijtihād* who must rely on scholars.[29] However, Albānī differs by maintaining that nonexperts must still ask a scholar for a proof-text so they can follow scripture and not the scholar. What happens when different scholars provide different proof-texts?

Proof-texts on their own remain in need of an interpreter. *Fiqh*, which means understanding, denoted the ability to extract law from the "facts" of scripture. It is a human understanding of what God intends, and therefore fallible. Purist Salafis fear that Muslim scholars stop giving answers based on the Qurʾān and Sunna, and instead start giving their own personal opinions.[30] This fear stems from mistrust in the academic honesty of those who adhere to the *madhhab* institutions. Albānī notes that if Traditionalists were truly following the four imams, they would disregard the opinions of the eponyms of the schools when an authentic ḥadīth is presented to them that contradicts the opinion of the school. However, how do we know that these scholars were unaware of a particular ḥadīth or believed it to contradict the opinion of their *madhhab*?[31]

[27] M. Būṭī, *Al-Lā Madhhabiyya*, 18.
[28] M. Būṭī, *Al-Lā Madhhabiyya*, 16.
[29] M. Būṭī, *Al-Lā Madhhabiyya*, 33.
[30] Muḥammad Nāṣir al-Dīn al-Albānī, "Al-Salafiyya wa l-Madhāhib," lecture from www.ar.islamway.com/lesson/17857, last accessed November 9, 2016.
[31] Ibn Taymiyya mentions several reasons why early scholars might have opinions that apparently contradict authentic ḥadīth. Among them is that early scholars had better knowledge and understanding of the Sunna than later scholars because much of what has reached them, and what they considered authentic, might not come to us except through an unreliable narrator, or

Both Salafis and Traditionalists claim to be objective in their following of scripture. Albānī maintains that there is an objective principle of legal meanings in scripture that are accessible to any fair-minded reader. He has several legal opinions, such as the prohibition of gold for women, that were not held by any previous scholar. Ismāʿīl al-Anṣārī responds by noting that if this were the case that the legal meanings of scripture are clear and accessible, these legal opinions should have manifested themselves in the findings of at least some earlier jurists.[32] Traditionalists consider the *madhhab*s to be objective in the sense that they are collective scholarly attempts to understand scripture based on a methodology that can be repeated. Albānī notes that many legal maxims found in the *madhhab*s do not allow *ijtihād* in the presence of a clear text, yet Traditionalist jurists do not apply these maxims and insist on holding onto opinions that contradict the Sunna.[33]

The Traditionalist claim of objectivity is based on their findings being a result of established principles that were meant to minimize mistakes. For instance, al-Shāʿfiʿī wrote his *Risāla* because he was confronted by the many disagreements found among the jurists of his time. The *Risāla* is an attempt to spell out a consistent methodology that would allow legal interpretation to be established with minimal human error. With time Muslim jurists codified their own *uṣūl* and by the late third century the overwhelming majority of Sunni scholars adhered to one of these methodologies.

Therefore, *taqlīd* resulted from the desire to place boundaries of interpretation rulings rather than intellectual stagnation. Contrary to *ijtihād*, *taqlīd* was the result of group interpretation that provided an objective basis upon which legal decisions and rulings could be described as being either substantively correct or incorrect. According to this view, *taqlīd* is intended to limit discretionary power of legal officials, especially those at the bottom of the legal hierarchy.[34] The study of the relationship between *ijtihād* and *taqlīd* has generally been dominated by an approach that privileges *ijtihād*

a defective chain, or it may not have reached later scholars. M. Būṭī, *Al-Lā Madhhabiyya*, 131. Also see Ibn Taymiyya, Raf', 4–23. However, Ibn Taymiyya's excusing the early scholars is not sufficient in answering Albānī, because he does not blame the imams themselves, he blames their followers. He would also not accept the idea that God would have revealed knowledge that is necessary for Muslims to follow, but not preserve it through authentic chains of narrations.

32 I. Anṣārī, *Ibāḥat*, 58.

33 Albānī argues that many legal maxims found in the *madhhab*s do not allow *ijtihād* in the presence of a clear text, yet the scholars of *fiqh* do not apply these maxims and insist on holding onto opinions that contradict the Sunna. N. Albānī, *Taṣfiya*, 24–25.

34 M. Fadel, "Social," 193.

over *taqlīd* on the assumption that *ijtihād* is a superior mode of legal reasoning. Fadel states:

> Most scholars who privilege *ijtihād* over *taqlīd* rarely account for the cost of this instability to the legal system. In my opinion, *taqlīd*, viewed from the perspective of the sociology of law and the legal process, is best understood as an expression of the desire for regular and predictable legal outcomes, akin to what modern jurisprudence terms the "rule of law" the idea that legal officials are bound to pre-existing rules.[35]

Sherman Jackson also argues that *taqlīd* does not contradict independent reasoning. Rather, premodern jurists saw it as functioning as that which ultimately kept Islamic law "Islamic" in the face of a potentially unending stream of originality and innovativeness on the part of individual jurists.[36] Traditionalists understand *ijtihād* to be part of the religion that must be acted upon unless it becomes clear to the jurist that he was mistaken. Traditionalists recognize that *mujtahids* make mistakes; however, the purist Salafi argument against *taqlīd* facilitates for laypeople and non-*mujtahids* to correct or bypass an *ijtihād* when they encounter a ḥadīth that might contradict the *madhhab*. According to Būṭī, laypeople do not possess the necessary training to extract laws from religious texts; they are not qualified to decide which *ijtihād* is correct.

Albānī explains that the role of the scholar is simply to provide the layperson with a proof-text from the Qur'ān or Sunna. The verse: *And ask the people of the reminder if you do not know*[37] means to ask the scholars about what God and the Prophet say, not what is said by any particular *madhhab*. Albānī states that the principle (*aṣl*) is for everyone to follow the Qur'ān and Sunna, without differentiating between the scholar, student, and unlettered. The scholar knows a ruling through studying the Qur'ān and Sunna. The unlettered knows a ruling by asking the scholars. However, laypeople should refrain from asking about the *ijtihād* or ruling of a certain scholar and instead inquire about what God and His Messenger said.[38] This argument is based on the premise that verses are clear and have one valid interpretation, hence the scholars serve as a channel that passively passes down the proof-text to the unlettered, who is then capable of understanding it in a fashion similar to the scholar. Nevertheless, this still implies that laypeople have the tools to analyze the texts provided by the scholar. In the

[35] M. Fadel, "Social," 197. [36] S. Jackson, "*Ijtihād*," 265. [37] Q. *al-Naḥl*, 16:43.
[38] N. Albānī, "Salafiyya."

case of contradicting texts, the scholar performs *ijtihād* in deciding which text to furnish the layperson with. Bernard Haykel states:

> The opponents of Salafis ridicule this argument by insisting that an unschooled Muslim is on account of his ignorance incapable of understanding the proof, and therefore ask rhetorically what use is it to him if he obtains it by asking the scholar. They also add that the system that the Salafis are proposing is highly idealized in that it presupposes the existence of *mujtahids* around every corner, an impossible scenario given the difficulty in attaining this exalted rank of scholarship.[39]

Haykel notes that the idea that there is always an endless number of living *mujtahids* assumes that the great learning found in the *madhhabs* is worthless or, even worse, a source of misguidance.[40] In other words, *taqlīd* is a social reality, because not everyone can be a *mujtahid*. This is important because purist Salafis understand *taqlīd* as accepting and believing something without knowing the evidence for it. Traditionalists do not object to providing the proof-text, but believe the evidence is only known by the *mujtahid* because knowing it includes ensuring does not contradict other evidence. This is based on the idea that *mujtahid* must search for contradicting texts. Recognizing whether a text is free from contradiction is contingent on taking all other evidence into account: a task beyond the abilities of laypeople.

In order to know the proof-text on a particular issue one must ascertain its soundness from conflicting religious evidence. When proof-texts conflict, they must go through a process of reconciliation so that both texts will be enacted in a way that resolves the apparent conflict or the jurist will exercise *tarjīḥ* to determine which one takes precedence. The initial part of this process of reconciliation is *jam'*, which is understanding the indication of each text in light of the presence of the other. Therefore, each text is implemented respective of its counterpart. Hence, a *mujtahid* must perform a process of analytic deduction of all relevant religious evidence before issuing a ruling or providing laypeople with the evidence, and laypeople are not trained to perform such a task. By being untrained, laypeople are naturally put in a position to follow the *ijtihād* of scholars, even in something as simple as which proof-text the scholar chooses to provide the common person. It is unlikely that someone with the scholarship and intelligence of Albānī was unaware of the process of *ijtihād*. Rather, Albānī was trying to place boundaries on the scope of interpretive license of his

[39] B. Haykel, "Salafi Thought," 44 [40] B. Haykel, "Salafi Thought," 44.

opponents. His emphasis on following only authentic scripture was fundamental to his attempt to place boundaries of legal interpretation.

There is another important point that is often forgotten in discussions on *ijtihād* and *taqlīd*, that is how do laypeople know who a *mujtahid* is? For most jurists, a *muqallid* can ascertain whether someone is a *mujtahid* by particular social facts. If the person gives fatwas publicly, people generally accept his fatwas, and no one challenges his credentials then people can accept him as a *mujtahid*.[41] This is quite simple when one is only aware of one *mujtahid*. However, the problem is amplified in an era when mass literacy and communication have exposed laity to hundreds of scholars and conflicting opinions. In cases where the layperson becomes aware of differences of opinion, they are not required to follow one opinion because they do not have tools to weigh the substantive merits of the different opinions. Because Islamic ethical theory does not provide an objective perspective from which anyone can conclude which opinion is correct, all opinions are rendered to be *prima facie* in the perspective of the *muqallid*.[42] However, this presents another problem, how does the *muqallid* decide which *mujtahid* to follow? The thought here is that the *muqallid* is required to settle on a choice dependent on the *mujtahid* and not by weighing the content of the different opinions. As a result, the layperson is not completely absolved from moral obligation. He should have some premise on which he can separate between a veritable researcher and an impostor. In this regard, the untrained must have a basis on which he can trust the *mujtahid*.[43] This trust is based on a relationship in which the layperson understands that the *mujtahid* will act in the *muqallid*'s best interest.

Concerning ikhtilāf, the purist Salafi stance privileged the apparent meaning of the text over any implicit or contextual meaning it may carry. Similar to political populists, purist Salafis gained greater attention among the masses by the simplicity of their arguments and juxtaposing themselves to the "tainted" institutions. This strips interpretive authority away from the scholars and allows laypeople to challenge scholars based on what they perceive to be a clear text.

In the Traditionalist assessment *ijtihād* is a perplex and challenging task and they therefore limited it to a class of *mujtahids* to restrict differences of opinion to scholars. In other words, if laypeople and those untrained have

[41] Mohammad Fadel, "*Istafti qalbaka wa in aftaka al-nas wa aftuka*: The Ethical Obligations of the Muqallid between Autonomy and Trust," in *Islamic Law in Theory: Studies on Jurisprudence in Honor of Bernard Weiss*, ed. A. Kevin Reinhart and Robert Gleave (Leiden: Brill, 2014), 113.

[42] M. Fadel, "*Istafti qalbak*," 113–114.

[43] M. Fadel, "*Istafti qalbak*," 120.

the authority to begin claiming to hold the "authentic" opinion this will widen the area of differences without any clear methodology. Purist Salafis also maintain that interpretation must be limited to the role of scholars, but they simultaneously prohibit the common people from performing *taqlīd*.

SHIFTING POSITIONS ON *TAQLĪD*

The different positions purist Salafis hold on *taqlīd* might make their position on it unclear. This confusion stems from a lack of clarity about who purist Salafis are addressing. If their prohibition of *taqlīd* is directed at scholars who have the ability to perform *ijtihād* by extracting legal rulings directly from scripture, then Traditionalists would agree that such a person should not exercise *taqlīd*. However, outside the realm of theory, Traditionalists would say that such a person does not exist in modern times. The Salafi argument appears to be addressing laypeople because no Muslim either in the past or present would argue that an absolute *mujtahid* should perform *taqlīd*. Būṭī notes that if they are addressing laypeople then what is the purpose of telling them that the Qur'ān and Sunna are infallible while the imams are not? What would be the difference between the understanding of the *mujtahid* and the understanding of a nonexpert? Does the layperson have the ability to extract an infallible understanding from the Qur'ān while the imams of the *madhhabs* do not? Būṭī understands the purist Salafi argument to imply that the eponyms of the *madhhabs* were exercising *ijtihād* from a source other than the Qur'ān and Sunna, therefore making them followers of someone other than the Prophet.[44]

Albānī has two different positions on *taqlīd*. His first position criticizes *taqlīd* and attempts to limit it as much as possible. He considers it a *bid'a* and implies that it is similar to disbelief. He also holds a contradicting position that necessitates *taqlīd* and encourages people to perform it. In Albānī's early career he had no authority or school of law to support him. What gave a scholar authority was his studying and affiliating himself with a school or teacher. Albānī was primarily self-taught and did not have any institution to repute him. His refusal to affiliate with a *madhhab* and lack of formal training provided him the freedom to adopt unconventional methods in relation to the structures that govern the formation of religious jurisprudence and their authoritative structures. His version of Salafism was

[44] M. Būṭī, *Al-Lā Madhhabiyya*, 55–57.

independent of established legal institutions and is a more publicly accessible brand of Islam.

His views were often iconoclastic and conflicted with the majority of scholars. Being that he had no school of law or teacher to support his views, he affiliated himself with scripture directly. He wrote a book that he titled *Ḥadīth Is Proof Itself in Belief and Law* (*Al -Ḥadīth Ḥujja Binafsi-hi fī l-ʿAqā'id wa l-Aḥkām*) in which he criticizes Traditionalists making *taqlīd* part of the religion. Instead of adjusting the principles of their *madhhab* to the Sunna they interpret the Sunna to suit their principles. They accept whatever part of the Sunna conforms to their rules and reject everything else. This has caused Muslims to become disconnected with the teachings of the Prophet.[45]

Albānī's opposition to *taqlīd* is a result of most Muslims following a *madhhab* at the expense of scripture which he considers to be a *bidʿa*, if not an implicit act of disbelief for intentionally preferring a *madhhab* over God's law. Furthermore, the fact that Albānī was an iconoclastic autodidact that went against the majority of scholars of his time furthered his need to criticize *taqlīd.* In order to establish himself as a scholar and validate his iconoclastic views, he needed to attack *taqlīd* and Traditionalist institutions. The aim of his anti-*taqlīd* position was not necessarily against *taqlīd*, but to turn people away from his critics. In his criticism against Traditionalists he accused *muqallids* of everything short of disbelief. He compares *muqallids* to those who intentionally follow man-made laws. Albānī notes that it makes no difference whether the person being followed is a Muslim who misunderstood a text by mistake or a disbeliever who set himself up as a legislator instead of God.[46] Although he does not explicitly excommunicate *muqallids* his criticism of them often implies that he does exactly that. He does this by accusing them of intentionally disregarding the Qurʾān and Sunna in favor of a fallible scholar. He states:

> Just as you make God the only one you worship, likewise you should make the Messenger, peace and blessings be upon him, the only one you follow. The One you worship is one and the one you follow is one. Thereby you would have successfully applied the meaning of "There is no God except Allah and Muḥammad is the Messenger of Allah."[47]

Albānī notes that he does not follow anyone in the absolute and unrestricted sense except the Prophet. "As for others, it is well known that they

[45] N. Albānī, *Al-Ḥadīth Ḥujja*, 35–38.
[46] N. Albānī, *Al-Ḥadīth Ḥujja*, 91.
[47] N. Albānī, *Al-Ḥadīth Ḥujja*, 92.

follow many people other than the Prophet."[48] Accordingly, *taqlīd* is not proper knowledge and true scholars are those who draw directly from the Qur'ān and Sunna. Being aware of the various scholarly opinions is not proper knowledge. However, not everyone can become an expert in Islamic law, so how are nonexperts to understand scripture? Albānī notes that even laypeople must not perform *taqlīd*; instead they must ask a scholar for a *dalīl* because in many cases it is easy for intelligent lay Muslims to see the evidence in a provided proof-text. *Taqlīd* is only permissible for one who is incapable of knowing or obtaining a proof-text. While acknowledging that his students are not qualified scholars, Albānī simultaneously encourages them to follow an authentic ḥadīth even if it goes against the saying of a scholar, who may or may not be a *mujtahid.*[49] Albānī's students took his anti-*madhhab* and anti-*taqlīd* statements and began applying them in their own understanding of Islam. They often did this while ignoring the *madhhabs* and their established principles of Islamic jurisprudence. Each student felt the need to reexamine proof-texts on their own, which resulted in unconventional and often conflicting legal rulings.

Albānī's second position is one that promotes *taqlīd* that he sometimes calls *ittibā*ʿ. He vehemently denies that he, or any scholar in his right mind, would encourage the laity to approach scripture directly. Instead, they must ask and follow scholars. Albānī may have developed this contradicting position after he became a leading authority in the Muslim world. He notes that sometimes the laity have no choice but to perform *taqlīd.* When a scholar is asked about an issue that requires a significant amount of reflection and research, he cannot lay out this entire process to the questioner so that he follows his proof. Albānī explains that the scholar perhaps reflects on all the verses and ḥadīth related to the issue before coming to an answer. It is not possible for him to provide these details to the lay questioner. In this case, the layperson is to trust the scholar and follow him. Even if the scholar provides the questioner with proof-texts, he does not have the ability to understand them.[50]

Albānī notes that there is no escape from *taqlīd* even for the scholar at times. He emphasizes that *taqlīd* is necessary for many laypeople. One cannot possibly explain to an uneducated layperson how a scholar arrived

48 Muḥammad Nāṣir al-Dīn al-Albānī, "Shubah Ḥawl al-Salafiyya," lecture at www.alalbany.net/?p=4075, last accessed October 14, 2013.

49 N. Albānī, *Ḥadīth*, 93.

50 Muḥammad Nāṣir al-Dīn al-Albānī, "Silsilat al-Hudā wa l-Nūr tape 331," lecture at www.alalbany.net/catplay.php?catsmktba=1269, last accessed December 7, 2016.

at a particular conclusion. Giving a detailed lecture explaining proof-texts to the unlearned Muslim is impractical. The scholar's answer to a question could include a proof-text depending on the intellectual level of the questioner. In one of his lectures Albānī notes that the answer of a scholar for the layperson is equivalent to a proof-text for a scholar. If the layperson goes against the fatwa of a scholar he is sinful[51]

Albānī states that no one can escape exercising some level of *taqlīd*, even great scholars. His praise of *taqlīd* may make Salafis appear identical to Traditionalists, but Albānī denies this is the case. He explains that Salafis perform *taqlīd*, or follow both jurists and ḥadīth scholars. Salafis follow ḥadīth but do not limit themselves to a particular ḥadīth scholar. Traditionalists on the other hand follow a particular scholar and disregard all others. He further differentiates between Salafis and Traditionalists by explaining that Salafis do not base religion on *taqlīd.*

Traditionalists affiliate themselves to a particular school of law, but purist Salafis follow ḥadīth without affiliating themselves to a particular ḥadīth scholar. In Albānī's second position on *taqlīd*, he considers it necessary but argues that one should not base religion on *taqlīd* and adhere to it in a fanatical manner. Reluctant to call the action *taqlīd*, Albānī states: "Following a scholar you trust, this is necessary regardless of what you call it. We call it *ittibāʿ* to differentiate between us and them. Based on the fact that we leave the scholar if his mistake is clear. However, they blindly follow him without thinking."[52] In another instance, Albānī states that "*taqlīd* is necessary for every Muslim" (*lā budda li kulli muslim an yuqallid*). This *taqlīd* can be in ḥadīth or law; however, *taqlīd* should not become religion in the sense that one only follows a particular scholar. In other words, one cannot disregard all other scholars and blindly follow only one, especially when the evidence shows that his scholar is incorrect.[53]

Albānī notes that the laity should ask a scholar and follow his answer without asking for evidence. However, if it becomes clear to the questioner that this answer is incorrect he should not adhere to it. Again, there is an apparent contradiction in Albānī's response. He points out that laypeople do not have the ability to understand proof-texts, so how would it become apparent to them that it is incorrect? This could be done by asking other

[51] Muḥammad Nāṣir al-Dīn al-Albānī, "Al-Farq Bayna al-Ijtihād wa al-Taqlīd," lecture from www.youtube.com/watch?v=IS2Xhr7ZBfY, last accessed February 28, 2018.

[52] N. Albānī, "Farq."

[53] Muḥammad Nāṣir al-Dīn al-Albānī, "Mā Ḥukm Taqlīd Madhhab Muʿayyan?," lecture from www.youtube.com/watch?v=pPuzToEXunQ, last accessed January 14, 2016.

scholars, but still puts the laity in a position to judge evidence provided to them. In one of his lectures Albānī points out that someone who accepts an opinion from a scholar without asking for scriptural evidence performs *taqlīd*, but an individual who requests *dalīl* is acting in compliance with *ittibāʿ* instead of in compliance with scholars.[54] However, in another lecture Albānī notes that this is the proverbial distinction without a difference: In the end the layperson must put his trust in the scholar to provide the correct scriptural evidence.[55] The very act of asking the scholar acknowledges a level of submission and trust in his knowledge and authority. This distinction is purely semantic because *taqlīd* is disguised as *ittibāʿ*.[56]

Many scholars fail to grasp the nuances of Albānī's positions on *taqlīd* and *madhhabs*, which appear to be a messy bag of contradictions. Albānī distinguishes between the learned and the unlearned and insists that the laity must seek knowledge from scholars. In the process of seeking knowledge, however, he requires laypeople to ask for proof-texts, which assumes they are learned enough to interpret these texts on their own. At times Albānī insists that his polemics are not aimed at lay Muslims, but at scholars who should know better than to uncritically conform to past judgments.[57] Unlike earlier anti-*taqlīd* scholars, by Albānī's time the *taqlīd* debate was no longer between scholars but was one that included mass Muslim literacy and therefore laypeople became participants in the debate in a way they would not have been earlier.

Albānī makes it clear that common Muslims should seek knowledge from scholars while simultaneously arguing that proof-texts are easy to understand. In other cases, such as in his famous *Ṣifat Ṣalāt al-Nabī*, lay Muslims are given the distinct impression that the statements of the eponyms of the legal schools censuring *taqlīd* apply equally to themselves as they do to qualified and seasoned jurists.[58]

The tensions in Albānī's positions cannot be properly understood outside the context of the battle he was fighting against Traditionalists as well as social factors such as increased literacy. The Salafi argument that ordinary Muslims can understand scripture as well as the Companions was an essential move designed to undermine the rigid authority of the *madhhabs*. Jonathan Brown correctly notes, "Arguing that the Muslim masses were innately competent and needed no guardian class to understand their

[54] Muḥammad Nāṣir al-Din al-Albānī, "Aḥwāl al-Ijtihād wa'l-Ittibāʿ wa'l-Taqlīd," lecture from www.islamweb.net, last accessed January 24, 2012. See E. Hamdeh, "Salafi Polemic."

[55] N. Albānī, "Farq." [56] E. Hamdeh, "Salafi Polemic," 219. [57] N. Albānī, *Ḥadith*, 80–81.

[58] E. Hamdeh, "Salafi Polemic," 220.

religion was the most effective means to neutralize the appeals to authority made by mainstream Sunni scholars, even if all ulema, even Salafi ones, knew this claim was false."[59] In other words, since both Albānī and his critics hold that scholars must be followed, the difference between the two groups is not as stark as it may appear. His criticism of *taqlīd* is a rhetorical strategy designed to undermine Traditionalist institutions. Albānī rejects the view that tradition is an essential precondition for the proper understanding of Islam.

One way Albānī's conflicting opinions could also be reconciled is to assume that Albānī is encouraging the laity to reject a fatwa that contradicts the meaning of a text that is *qaṭʿī*. However, the majority of texts are not *qaṭʿī* in nature, but Albānī believes that his positions are the absolute truth and based on *qatʿī* texts. Hence anyone who disagrees with him is going against the Qurʾān and Sunna and therefore the type *taqlīd* Albānī promotes is *taqlīd* of purist Salafism. This is evident from the many confrontations Albānī had while trying to defend the absolute truth in his position and the absolute incorrectness in the opinion of others. He holds this position even if he is going up against the consensus of Muslim scholars. This draws criticism from Traditionalists who accuse him of positioning himself as the sole bearer of absolute truth and necessitating that all Muslims follow his opinions. Ultimately, his criticism of *taqlīd* was used heavily to attempt to give himself authority, especially in his early career, and discredit his Traditionalists opponents. Once he reached a level of authority in the Muslim world his position shifted and he acknowledged that *taqlīd* is necessary, but to not appear to contradict his previous position on *taqlīd* he called it *ittibāʿ*. Although his position on *taqlīd* may have ultimately changed, his students remained very critical of *taqlīd*.

Another important point to keep in mind concerning Albānī's different statements concerning *taqlīd* is that he allowed *taqlīd* of scholars whose primary affiliation is not to a *madhhab*. Ignoring the consequences of what kind of legal culture then emerges as a result, the two positions of Albānī himself, being against *taqlīd* yet requiring laypeople to ask scholars, are actually reconcilable because for him a *madhhab*-affiliated scholar is not the type of scholar one should perform *taqlīd* of.

The source of the problem between Traditionalists and purist Salafis is one of methodology, and these differences also trickle down to their *fiqh* opinions, being that they are established upon arguably different

[59] J. Brown, "Is Islam Easy to Understand," 144.

methodologies. Salafis believe that evaluating positions on religious matters should be reduced to an examination of the soundness of texts. They are uncomfortable with petitions to a global vision of the demands of religion or to any tradition. Salafis level severe criticism against those who adhere to the *madhhabs*. Their criticism is that these individuals would bypass the words of the Prophet and establish religious law based on the words of scholars or based on the demands of their personal reasoning. Conversely, Traditionalists hold that texts need to be understood and given contexts that bring relatively distant meanings of the texts closer to the reader. It is obvious that these discussions are often very heated, but also useful because they provide alternative and incompatible readings of the same evidence. This helps one become aware of the theoretical choices these individuals made while reading scripture.

In theory, both Salafis and Traditionalists agree that anyone who is capable of performing *ijtihād* and extracting rulings directly from the Qur'ān and Sunna should not follow the opinion of another scholar. However, Salafis and Traditionalists disagree over who qualifies as a *mujtahid*. Traditionalists only consider absolute *mujtahids* (*mujtahid mutlaq*) qualified enough to be entirely independent of following a *mahdhab*. On the other hand, the Salafi criteria for a *mujtahid* are less demanding, where anyone with a basic knowledge of the Qur'ān and Sunna must follow them directly and bypass any opinion that goes against the "clear" directives found therein. Albānī's attitude toward the *madhhabs* has initiated and caused an anti-*madhhab* stereotype of Salafis. While most Saudi Salafis actually follow the Ḥanbalī school of law, Albānī's brand of Salafism has generally been classified as being against the *madhhabs*. Moreover, it was so appealing and simple that it forced Traditionalists around the Muslim world to defend Traditionalism in response to Albānī.

Traditionalists and Salafis have different definitions of *ijtihād* and *taqlīd*. For Salafis, *taqlīd* is equivalent to blind following and therefore a *muqallid* must be an ignorant person. However, their critics believe that a *muqallid* is anyone who has not reached the level of an absolute *mujtahid*. This is what led them to differ on the issue, because when Salafis criticize *taqlīd*, they are accusing scholars of being ignorant, uncritical followers of a *madhhab*. Being that Traditionalists have high standards for a *mujtahid*, any non-*mujtahid* is a *muqallid*, but could still be a scholar. Purist Salafis present Islam in a simplistic and easy to understand manner, without denying the important role of scholars. Interestingly, both groups agree that scholars are needed to properly interpret religious texts. Purist Salafis never deny instructing lay-people to interpret texts, but stress that they ask the scholars for evidence.

Why do they argue that Islam is easy to understand and that laypeople should follow "clear" texts even though they are not properly equipped to interpret Islam in any reliable way? Essentially, they use this argument as a strategy to discredit the authority of the *madhhab*s. Empowering laypeople and claiming that they are naturally able to understand the texts was the best way to negate the Traditionalist argument for the necessity of conventional *madhhab*s. Traditionalists seek to preserve a historically contingent order of religious institutions and their functions, whereas purist Salafis want to bypass these institutions to return to a version of Islam that is purely based on scripture.[60]

This explains why Albānī took it upon himself to offer new *fiqh* opinions to the Muslim community that were based on what he often terms "the pure Sunna." By avoiding the *madhhab*s and writing *fiqh* works anew using only Qurʾānic verses and ḥadīth, Albānī was essentially creating his own *madhhab* because his own *fiqh* opinions might later be "purged" by someone who has a different understanding of the "correct" teachings. Albānī offered numerous *fiqh* opinions that were unconventional, and this has furthered his image as being an iconoclastic and controversial scholar. His critics seized the opportunity to use these unconventional fatwas to discredit Albānī's entire *fiqh* methodology and scholarship.

Purist Salafis criticize Traditionalists for following the *madhhab*s, but by bypassing the methodology of the *madhhab*s, Salafis were effectively establishing their own *madhhab*. The nature of purist movements is such that they ultimately replace religious authorities with their own authorities. Independent thinkers like Albānī garner followers who closely adhere to their teachings. While doing so, they often become followers of an independent thinker rather than adhering to that individual's methodology. Albānī's students consider themselves followers of a man more qualified to understand the Qurʾān and Sunna than they, believing that everyone else is doing something different.

Purist Salafis use anti-*taqlīd* and anti-*madhhab* rhetoric primarily as a means to discredit their Traditionalist critics. However, the differences between both groups are not as staunch as they appear because Salafis also allow *taqlīd* and ultimately Salafism is also a *madhhab*. The primary argument of Traditionalists like Būṭī is not to insist that everyone needs to follow a *madhhab*, but rather to refute anyone who says one should *not* follow a *madhhab*. His definition of *madhhab*ism does not mean to follow only one

[60] E. Poljarevic, "Selective Affinities," 489.

madhhab, but one is permitted to follow one scholar or*madhhab* and change as they please. Here Būṭī conceded more than many pro-*madhhab* scholars would. The opposite of *madhhab*ism means to not follow anyone, which Albānī rejected as redundant because virtually all Muslim laymen follow *someone*, and therefore cannot be correctly labeled as *lā-madhhabī*s. Būṭī's position is that any adherence to a *madhhab* is not an obligation; however, the *prohibition* of any voluntary adherence is baseless. In fact, if observed closely, Būṭī's definition of *madhhab*ism is synonymous with *taqlīd*. Būṭī considered the purist Salafi movement to be advocating the prohibition of following a *madhhab* and the validity of adhering to one school.

Like other Traditionalists, Būṭī claims that non-*madhhab*ism disconnects modern Muslims from the classical scholars of the past. Būṭī's contention with purist Salafis is not their following of different *fiqh* opinions or methodology, but rather their claim to be the only ones to follow the Qur'ān and Sunna because it creates distrust and a rift between modern Muslims and scholars of the past. In other words, it is Albānī referring to his *fiqh* as "the Qur'ān and Sunna" that is perceived as an attack on all other *madhhab*s. Būṭī notes that the conviction of purist Salafis to possess the absolute truth leads them to focus all their energy on causing problems in mosques; they pursue every religious individual who follows a different *fiqh* opinion and chastise him. If someone uses prayer beads, sends blessings on the Prophet after the call to prayer, or prays twenty units of *tarāwīḥ* instead of eight, they will cause chaos and disputations in mosques.[61] While Albānī considers the *madhhab*s to be a source of division because they cause Muslims to follow different opinions, Būṭī views the uncompromising attitude purist Salafis have toward Islamic law to be the source of division because they compel Muslims to follow only one opinion.

Traditionalists understand Islamic sciences to be complex and one must undergo proper training before indulging in extracting legal rulings from scripture. They view purist Salafis as a threat because they empower common Muslims to question everything in light of the Qur'ān and Sunna. This gives lay Muslims a sense of religious authority and collapses any division between scholars and those who have no training. In other words, the purist Salafi approach toward *fiqh* empowers the individual because they now have the power to engage religious evidence and challenge scholars. Traditionalists were threatened by purist Salafism because it undoes the entire *madhhab* system that they had been building for centuries.

[61] M. Būṭī, *Al-Lā Madhhabiyya*, 108–109.

What made purist Salafis so popular was their promotion of a critical methodology and questioning Traditionalist authority, at a time when Traditionalists were vulnerable because they lost the support of the state and appeared outdated. Purist Salafis legitimize their unconventional opinions by promoting their brand of understanding of Islam as a product free from partisanship toward a particular *madhhab* or human influence. Traditionalists consider this to be an impossible task because the understanding of texts is a human endeavor and a product of the human mind.

Part III

Ḥadīth

6

The Pursuit of Authenticity

Reevaluating Weak Ḥadīth

Together with the purist Salafi deconstruction of Traditionalist *fiqh*, purist Salafis sought to reconstruct what they believed to be pure Islam. They primarily focused on situating ḥadīth as the primary source of Islamic praxis. They were alarmed and concerned by the lack of ḥadīth citation and authentication found among traditional jurists. This has resulted in many authors teaching and commenting on a ḥadīth at great length, unaware that it was weak or fabricated. This is important because Albānī argued that weak ḥadīth prevented Muslims from correctly understanding the teachings of Islam. In order to purify Islamic law of weak ḥadīth, purist Salafis tried to closely adhere to the method of ḥadīth verification found in classical works on the science of ḥadīth. Actually, Salafis are primarily known for their interest in the science of ḥadīth. Ḥadīth are at the core of all Salafi religious beliefs because they provide a direct link to the Prophet. Adherence to authentic ḥadīth is therefore extremely important to understanding Islam, but problems arise when determining which ḥadīth can be authentically attributed to the Prophet. To overcome this, purist Salafis primarily determine the authenticity of ḥadīth using the *isnād*, established by ḥadīth scholars.

The purpose of the science of ḥadīth was to distinguish the Prophet's authentic sayings from those that were forged. Ḥadīth generally fall into four categories: authentic (*ṣaḥīḥ*); accepted (*ḥasan*); weak (*ḍaʿīf*); and fabricated (*mawḍūʿ*). Apart from a few *mutawātir* ḥadīth, the authenticity of all other ḥadīth is probabilistic. Although as a general rule they impart only probabilistic evidence, *āḥād* ḥadīth supported by external indicators can impart certainty. Fabricated ḥadīth, as their name suggests, are forged, and not to be ascribed to the Prophet. However, weak ḥadīth are attributed to the Prophet because there is still the possibility that they originated from him. Although weak ḥadīth do not meet the conditions of complete authenticity, there is still a chance that the Prophet said them. Therefore, Muslim scholars differ on whether they can be used in the context of virtues (*faḍā'il*). An important distinction between a weak and fabricated ḥadīth is the fact that the weakness of a ḥadīth is often attributed to its *isnād*, while the fabricated ḥadīth results from a fabrication of the text (*matn*).

DOES ISLAM NEED WEAK ḤADĪTH?

Most purist Salafi scholars reject the use of weak ḥadīth in all aspects of Islam. They consider them to be the source of many superstitions and fictitious beliefs.[1] Albānī was the twentieth century's most zealous rejecter of weak ḥadīth, and many purist Salafis agreed with him. Albānī's understanding of Salafism might be best defined as an attempt to understand Islam in its purest form, free from any interpolations and foreign teachings. The only authoritative texts are the Qur'ān and authentic ḥadīth, and the interpretation of these texts must be in accordance with the understanding of the *salaf*. In this regard, weak ḥadīth are rejected because they introduce teachings into Islam that did not originally belong to it. The use of weak ḥadīth often resulted in the legislation of that which God did not permit.[2]

Using weak and fabricated ḥadīth risks intentionally attributing a lie to the Prophet, something that Muslims believe can condemn one to hell. Even though they may not have immediately intended to lie about the Prophet, Albānī considers it to be comparable to lying, because they attribute a saying to the Prophet that they knew was weak or problematic.[3] He also persuasively argues that there is a social cost that results from the use of weak ḥadīth because they spread practices that have no authentic basis in Islam. This results in Muslims performing actions that have no basis in Islamic scripture; Sufi practices such as saint worship, dancing, and whirling dervishes are examples of "foreign practices" that have been adopted by Muslims in many regions. ʿAwwāma states that scholars who use weak ḥadīth cannot be responsible for the dissemination of unorthodox practices, but rather it is people's misapplication of these texts. He states that any text, including the Qur'ān, can lead to unorthodox practices if people misunderstand them.[4]

[1] Muḥammad Nāṣir al-Dīn al-Albānī, *Al-Tawassul Anwāʿu-hu wa Aḥkāmu-hu* (Riyadh: Maktabat al-Maʿārif 2001), 21.

[2] Muḥammad Nāṣir al-Dīn al-Albānī, *Ṣaḥīḥ al-Targhīb wa l-Tarhīb* (Riyadh: Maktabat al-Maʿārif, 2000), 1: 38–39.

[3] N. Albānī, *S.A.D.*, 1: 49.

[4] Muḥammad ʿAwwāma, *Ḥukm al-ʿAmal bil Ḥadīth al-Ḍaʿīf Bayna al-Nadhariyya wa l-Taṭbīq, wa l-Daʿwā* (Jedda: Dār al-Minhāj lil Nashr wal Tawzīʿ, 2017), 161.

Traditionalists argue that weak ḥadīth also provide societal benefits such as inspiring the masses to do good. The former Egyptian Grand Mufti ʿAlī Jumʿa complains that Albānī is trying to deprive scholars of weak ḥadīth, saying that, "we need weak ḥadīth in order to teach people."[5] He attempts to justify the use of weak ḥadīth or stories that he knew had little chance of being historically accurate in order to influence the behavior of the masses. Albānī considered this problematic because it betrays the scholarly responsibility to preserve Islam in its authentic form.

Albānī considered Salafism, in essence, to be the pure, unaltered version of Islam. Therefore, heretical beliefs and actions are often based on weak or fabricated ḥadīth. Because the laity do not have the expertise required to determine the authenticity of ḥadīth, they are likely to accept weak ḥadīth without knowing. Albānī's message was appealing because he promised his followers an Islam that was grounded in authentic texts and free from the doubts that originate from the use of weak ḥadīth. Despite the many problems Albānī raises with the use of weak ḥadīth, Traditionalists continued to allow the use of weak ḥadīth because they considered them an important part of scholarly tradition.

DIFFERENT APPROACHES TO WEAK ḤADĪTH

Historically, most Sunni scholars have allowed the conditional use of weak ḥadīth, and in the third century there was a near consensus on its permissibility. Nonetheless, as Albānī rightly points out, there has always been a group of scholars within Islam who have been critical, at least in theory, of the use of weak ḥadīth. Scholars like Muslim b. al-Ḥajjāj (d. 261/875), Ibn Ḥazm, ʿAbd al-Raḥmān Ibn al-Jawzī (d. 597/1201), and Ibn Taymiyya all rejected the use of weak ḥadīth.[6] Several eighteenth- and nineteenth-century scholars followed suit. For instance, Muḥammad al-Shawkānī categorically rejected the use of weak ḥadīth in all aspects of Islam, including in the context of virtues. Al-Shawkānī's stance on weak ḥadīth directly influenced Salafi scholars that came after him, such as Ṣiddīq Ḥasan Khān, the founder of the Indian Ahl al-Ḥadīth movement, Aḥmad Shākir (d. 1958), and ʿAbd al-Raḥmān al-Muʿallimī (d. 1966).[7]

[5] ʿAlī Jumʿa, "Al-Shaykh ʿAlī Jumʿa Yaruddu ʿalā Bidʿat al-Shaykh al-Albānī," lecture from www.youtube.com/watch?v=D90xpuOvsz8, last accessed April 10, 2018.

[6] Muḥammad Nāṣir al-Dīn al-Albānī, *Ṣaḥīḥ al-Jāmiʿ al-Ṣaghīr wa Ziyādati-hi* (Beirut: Al-Maktab al-Islāmī, 1988), 50. Hereafter *S.J.S.*

[7] Jonathan Brown, "Even If It's Not True It's True: Using Unreliable Ḥadīths in Sunni Islam," *Islamic Law and Society*, 18, no. 1 (2011), 1–52.

Albānī was perhaps the twentieth century's most systematic opponent of weak ḥadīth. He was often criticized by Traditionalists for his strict rejection and discard of weak ḥadīth. ʿAlī Jumʿa criticizes Albānī noting that he is self-taught and therefore outside of the fold of scholars who God entrusted with preserving the religion. He blames him for equating weak ḥadīth to fabricated ḥadīth. He argues that a ḥadīth can be fabricated, but fabrication does not necessitate that its meaning is incorrect (*buṭlān al-dalīl lā yaʿnī buṭlān al-madlūl*).[8]

Much of the debate surrounding the use of weak ḥadīth is about the willingness, or lack thereof, to widen one's interpretational perspective. It is important to note that Traditionalists who permitted the use of weak ḥadīth did not advocate using ḥadīth they knew to be fabricated or had known liars in their *isnāds*. They did not permit the use of weak ḥadīth in legislative matters but allowed them if they mainly addressed the reward or punishment one would receive for certain actions (*faḍāʾil al-aʿmāl*). In other words, a weak ḥadīth can be used if it is limited to the realm of virtues of actions that are already legislated by authentic texts. For Albānī, all elements of Islam, regardless of whether they concern law or virtues, must be supported by authentic evidence.

If God promises a limited reward for an action, the use of a weak ḥadīth that portrayed the virtue of the deed to be greater than what God decreed, was, in a way, attributing to God that which He did not say.[9] The increased virtue, or lack thereof, of a particular action will impact people's behavior. A failure to assign the proper virtuous weight to legislated actions will result in negative religious and societal impacts. For instance, Albānī notes that his father and many other Ḥanafī scholars in Syria preferred to pray in the Umayyad mosque and considered it to have a special virtue. They were influenced by a ḥadīth found in the works of Ibn ʿĀbidīn, the late Ḥanafī jurist, which states that one prayer in the Umayyad mosque is equivalent to 70,000 prayers elsewhere. Albānī researched this ḥadīth and characterized its *isnād* as "darkness upon darkness." He states:

> May God be exalted. How do these jurists, due to their negligence of the study of ḥadīth, narrate a saying, first, even if its chain were correct it would have been considered *muʿḍal*[10] in the science of ḥadīth? What about when

[8] ʿAlī Jumʿa, "Liman Yasʾal: Hal Naʿmal bi-l-Ḥadīth al-Ḍaʿīf," www.youtube.com/watch?v=yGW9-9To8nU, last accessed January 7, 2020.

[9] N. Albānī, *S.A.D.*, 1: 653–654.

[10] A ḥadīth that has two or more narrators successively missing in the *isnād*.

the chain is, as I said, darkness upon darkness? Therefore, they harm when they wish to benefit.[11]

By allowing the use of weak ḥadīth in virtuous matters, jurists were not fulfilling their scholarly obligation to preserve the teachings of Islam in their pure form. Traditionalists distinguished between virtues and law and allowed the use of weak ḥadīth in the former. They also allowed the use of weak ḥadīth in historical and biographical accounts of the Prophet and his Companions. Traditionalists use the conditions established by Ibn Ḥajar al-ʿAsqalānī to justify the use of weak ḥadīth. These conditions indicate that in order for a weak ḥadīth to be used in the context of virtues it must meet the following criteria:

(1) It must not be very weak or contain a known liar in its *isnād*;
(2) It must fall under a general principle of the Sharia and should not contradict more authentic evidence;
(3) The individual acting on the ḥadīth should not believe it to be authentically attributed to the Prophet.[12]

Albānī explains that these conditions were not meant to facilitate the use of weak ḥadīth, but to prevent acting upon them. Concerning the first condition, Albānī says that Traditionalists follow weak ḥadīth even if they contradict Ibn Ḥajar's requirement that the ḥadīth not be very weak. Even if this were not the case, this condition does not apply to most people because it is difficult for them to discover the level of a ḥadīth's weakness due to the rarity of "true ḥadīth scholars" in modern times.

In the case of the second condition, the individual is acting on the general principle, not the weak ḥadīth. Had the general principle not existed, the weak ḥadīth could not have been applied and therefore it is not needed. Regarding the third condition, once more Albānī contends that most people are not equipped to determine a ḥadīth authenticity and therefore this condition does not apply to them. He encourages Muslims to only act on authentic ḥadīth because their content is sufficient and dispense with the need for weak ḥadīth. Without knowledge of the authenticity of the ḥadīth one risks acting on fabricated ḥadīth.[13]

Fabricated ḥadīth represent the far end of the spectrum of ḥadīth unreliability. Because scholars naturally differed on the reliability of particular

[11] Albānī sees no benefit in weak ḥadīth. Some scholars allow such ḥadīth in matters of virtues. However, this instance shows that such a practice can cause some inauthentic beliefs or practices to become widespread. On this debate see J. Brown, "Even If It's Not True."

[12] N. Albānī, *S.J.S.*, 53.

[13] N. Albānī, *S.J.S.*, 52–56. J. Brown, "Even If It's Not True," 42.

ḥadīth, there was not always a consistent distinction between ḥadīth that were forged or very weak. At times, all a scholar had to do to elevate a ḥadīth from the category of forged to weak was to strengthen it by locating another weak narration of the ḥadīth or a statement of a Companion.[14] The conditions established by Ibn Ḥajar are directed toward scholars because the laity do not have the expertise to discover the level of a ḥadīth's weakness. Abū Ghudda argues that the most reasonable path is to accept some weak ḥadīth and reject others, depending on the level of weakness and conformity of the meaning with what is authentically established.[15] Because the masses do not have the tools to determine the authenticity of ḥadīth they must rely on ḥadīth experts. Albānī considers providing the laity a ḥadīth without informing them of its level of authenticity to be a form of deception on the scholar's part. He states: "As a way of me actualizing the mentioned advice, I have written, and continue to write books which the reader can use to help him distinguish between the authentic and weak, the pure and impure which might be on the tongues of people or recorded in the heart of ḥadīth books."[16]

Albānī considered it his obligation, as well as the obligation of every scholar, to uncover the flaws in ḥadīth and warn others of them. Scholars have an important responsibility and must protect the masses by only providing them with authentic ḥadīth. One of the reasons that purist Salafis consider him to be a champion of the Sunna (*nāṣir al-sunna*) is because he seeks to provide the masses with only authentic and unadulterated versions of Islam. At the same time, Traditionalists were struggling with their perception as being one that was opposed to new ideas and encouraged uncritical following of scholarly opinions. The notion of following a pure version of Islam was very attractive and it secured Albānī a large following and further discredited Traditionalists.

DO WEAK ḤADĪTH HAVE VALUE?

In his famous book *Ṣifat Ṣalāt al-Nābī*, Albānī explains that authentic ḥadīth are sufficient to remove any need for weak ḥadīth. He states: "I believe that the authentic ḥadīth are sufficient, leaving no need for anything weak, for the latter does not amount to anything except *ẓann* (suspicion), and incorrect

[14] J. Brown, "Even If It's Not True," 16–17.

[15] Muḥammad ʿAbd al-Ḥayy al-Laknāwī, *Al-Ajwiba al-Fāḍila li l-Asʾila al-ʿAshra al-Kāmila*, ed. ʿAbd al-Fattāḥ Abū Ghudda (Cairo: Dār al-Salām, 2009), 53.

[16] N. Albānī, *S.J.S.*, 56.

ẓann at that; as the Exalted says, 'and *ẓann* is of no use against the truth'."[17] Albānī uses the linguistic meaning of the term *ẓann* (suspicion) as used in the Qur'ān in place of its technical meaning in Islamic law (conjectural). He explains that only *mutawātir* ḥadīth are definitively authentic (*qaṭ'ī*). *Ṣaḥīḥ* and *ḥasan* ḥadīth are based on high probability (*ẓann rājiḥ*). However, when it comes to weak ḥadīth he uses the Qur'ān's linguistic usage of the term *ẓann* (suspicion) criticizing the idol worshipers and applies it to weak ḥadīth.[18] *Āḥād* ḥadīth do not impart definitive certainty on their own unless supported by extraneous evidence. Most Muslim scholars only require definitive evidence for certain creedal issues such as belief in God or the hereafter. For everything else, highly probable evidence suffices. Nūr al-Dīn 'Itr (d. 2020), the Syrian ḥadīth scholar, makes a veiled attack against Albānī for not distinguishing between the linguistic and technical meanings of *ẓann*. He states:

> Some of those pseudo-*mujtahids* are surprised by the scholars' usage of this term and criticize them for it. This indicates that he cannot distinguish between certain absolute knowledge and preponderance of opinion (*ghalabat al-ẓann*) . . . This is confusing between the meaning intended by the Qur'ān, which entails following misconceptions and conjecture without any evidence or proof, and the meaning intended by scholars which is a technical term for a type of knowledge that is based on evidence, but there is a slight, but insignificant, possibility of error.[19]

Traditionalists consider weak ḥadīth to have value because, although they are weak, they are not forged. In other words, there is still a probability that the Prophet uttered those phrases. They argue that scripture is limited and not everything can be supported by definitive proof-text. As a result, Muslim jurists have resorted to certain interpretational practices to derive legislation for issues not addressed by scripture. For instance, Maḥmūd Mamdūḥ notes that the results of *qiyās* or *ijtihād* are not attributed to the Prophet, yet they are implemented and considered to have value.[20] In the context of weak ḥadīth, Traditionalists take nonscriptural evidence into consideration when examining weak ḥadīth. In other words, Traditionalists have parameters other than the soundness of the *isnād*.

[17] N. Albānī, *Aṣl Ṣifat*, 40. See Q. 53:28.

[18] Muḥammad Nāṣir al-Dīn al-Albānī, "Al-'Amal bi l-Ḥadīth al-Ḍa'īfa," lecture from www.youtube.com/watch?v=VZHWdFx5L4M&feature=youtu.be, last accessed April 13, 2018.

[19] Nūr al-Dīn 'Itr, *Sharḥ al-Nukhba: Nuzhat al-Naẓar fī Tawḍīḥ Nukhbat al-Fikar fī Muṣṭalaḥ Ahl al-'Athar* (Karachi: Al-Bushra Publishers, 2011), 46.

[20] M. Mamdūḥ, *Al-Ta'rīf*, 1: 138.

Mamdūḥ explains that simply because a ḥadīth is weak does not necessarily mean the Prophet did not say it. Rather, the probability of him saying it is not as high as an authentic ḥadīth, but there is nevertheless a likelihood that he said it. This probability is what distinguishes weak ḥadīth from those that are forged.[21] Albānī also recognizes this distinction, but what qualifies a ḥadīth as weak is that this probability is at the lower end of the authenticity spectrum. Therefore, it is safer to refrain from using it. Būṭī has a different approach to what "safer" means, arguing that because there is a chance the Prophet said it, it is safer to apply what the ḥadīth says.[22]

What is the point of scholars labeling a ḥadīth weak if it can still be used, especially when authentic ḥadīth exist?[23] Certainly, there is a possibility that a weak ḥadīth did originate from the Prophet, but since that possibility is low, is it not better to err on the side of caution? As we see, scholars differ about where to draw the line. Traditionalists accept the weak ḥadīth in virtues because it is not fabricated and therefore has value. They defend their acceptance of weak ḥadīth by noting that even the greatest ḥadīth scholars accepted them. Abū Ghudda states:

> The early ḥadīth scholars and leading critics, such as ʿAbd Allāh b. Mubārak, Aḥmad b. Ḥanbal, Bukhārī, Abū Dāwūd, al-Tirmidhī, al-Nasāʾī, Ibn Māja, and the generation of their era used to narrate the weak ḥadīth in the books they authored in order that they are acted upon and used as evidence. They did not isolate them and view them as false speech and abandon them, as some claim today.[24]

While Albānī's rejection of weak ḥadīth was viewed as an attack on Traditionalism, many Traditionalists held on to the mainstream opinion of classical scholars on the permissibility of using weak ḥadīth as a way of loyalty to premodern tradition. Traditional Sunni scholarship had bolstered the authenticity of weak ḥadīth in ways other than the *isnād.* Some Traditionalists claimed that if there was a weak ḥadīth that the majority of the Muslim community accepted and applied then it should be considered

[21] M. Mamdūḥ, *Taʿrīf*, 1: 172–174.

[22] Muḥammad Ramaḍān al-Būṭī, "Mubarāt Yafūtuhā ʿalā Nafsihī fī Hajr al-Ḥadīth al-Ḍaʿīf fī Faḍāʾil al-Aʿmāl," www.youtube.com/watch?v=MlZJ2SerzCo, last accessed April 10, 2018. Ḥabīb ʿAlī Jifrī has a similar stance; see "Dealing with Weak Ḥadīth Methodology of Traditional Sunni Scholars," www.youtube.com/watch?v=MNL14f9MVQg, last accessed April 10, 2018.

[23] N. Albānī, "Al-ʿAmal."

[24] Muḥammad ʿAbd al-Ḥayy al-Laknāwī, *Ẓafar al-Amānī bi Sharḥ Mukhtaṣar al-Sayyid al-Sharīf al-Jurjānī fī Muṣtalaḥ al-Ḥadīth*, ed. ʿAbd al-Fattāḥ Abū Ghudda (Aleppo: Maktab al-Maṭbūʿāt al-Islāmiyya, 1995), 186.

equal to an authentic ḥadīth. Therefore, they bolstered the value of a weak ḥadīth to that of an authentic one if the Muslim community accepted and acted upon it. They supported their argument by noting that many great ḥadīth scholars such as Mālik b. Anas, Ibn Ḥajar, Jalāl al-Dīn al-Suyūṭī (d. 1505/911), Ibn ʿAbd al-Barr (d. 463/1071), and even scholars celebrated by Salafis such as Ibn Qayyim believed in this concept.[25]

Some traditions were accepted by ḥadīth scholars if their meaning conformed with a verse or principle of law as long as its *isnād* did not contain a narrator who was a known liar. This attitude toward weak ḥadīth stems from a general trust in the scholarly class because if the scholars used a ḥadīth as evidence then it must be a legitimate proof-text.[26] Some scholars such as Muḥammad al-Sakhāwī (d. 902/1497) have gone so far as to state that if the Muslim community accepted a weak ḥadīth, it is not only to be acted upon, but it also reaches the level of *tawātur* and abrogates clear-cut evidence even if it be a Qurʾānic verse (*yansakh al-maqṭūʿ bihi*).[27] He does not give the ḥadīth this status due to the content of the ḥadīth, but its value lies in the community's collective agreement and application of its meaning.

Those who reject the use of weak ḥadīth find such a stance to be unreasonable and an example of uncritically following previous scholars. Albānī says that there is no way of verifying whether the scholars accepted such a ḥadīth due to a mistake, lack of information, or because they truly believed it to be authentic. The *isnād* is often the sole basis for determining the authenticity of ḥadīth. If there is a problem with the content of a ḥadīth, then such problem must have originated in the *isnād*. If the ḥadīth does not have a strong chain of narration it cannot be used as evidence or attributed to the Prophet. What is the purpose of the *isnād* system if the results of that system are going to be disregarded? What is the point of sifting through the

[25] M. Laknāwī, *Ajwiba*, 228–238. Ibn Qayyim explains that the deceased can hear those who are living when they perform *talqīn*. *Talqīn al-mayyit* is when the deceased is instructed about the answers to questions he will be asked in the grave upon burial. This act is based on a weak ḥadīth, but Ibn Qayyim explained that although the practice is based on a weak ḥadīth, it was still valid because the Muslim community has been practicing it for centuries. See Ibn Qayyim al-Jawziyya, *Kitāb al-Rūḥ* (Mecca: Dār ʿĀlam al-Fawāʾd, 2011), 8. Albānī was cynical about Ibn Qayyim being the actual author of *Kitāb al-Rūḥ*. He provides several reasons why the book is not likely to be the work of Ibn Qayyim. However, his rejection is primarily because the book contradicts his understanding of Ibn Qayyim's Salafi methodology. Albānī states: "And for these and other reasons, I severely doubt about authentically attributing *Kitāb al-Rūḥ* to Ibn Qayyim, or perhaps he wrote it in his early years of seeking knowledge." See Muḥammad al-Alūsī, *Al-Āyāt al-Bayyināt fī ʿAdam Samāʿ al-Amwāt ʿInd al-Ḥanafiyya al-Sādāt*, ed. Muḥammad Nāṣir al-Dīn al-Albānī (Riyadh: Maktabat al-Maʿārif, 2005), 60.

[26] For an explanation of the use of weak ḥadīth in law see J. Brown, *Ḥadīth*, 154–160.

[27] M. Laknāwī, *Ajwiba*, 232.

chain of narration if the ḥadīth is going to be accepted anyway because scholars used it or the general masses accepted it? Moreover, how could the meaning be authentically attributed to the Prophet and used as law if the *isnād* is incorrect? How and why do the actions of people authenticate a weak ḥadīth?

Traditionalists believe that historical reality needs to be taken into consideration when investigating a ḥadīth and not only the analysis of the *isnād*. In their view, this historical reality is given preference over following principles of the science of ḥadīth. At the same time, they insist that they are not disregarding the *isnād* system, but that they are rather taking other evidence into account. Traditionalists maintain that other evidence cannot be ignored because of a weak narrator who might be part of the *isnād*. The continuation of communal action on the ḥadīth is stronger evidence than the *isnād* itself.[28]

The legal implications of preference for authentic ḥadīth versus a weak narration bolstered by communal actions are perhaps best exemplified in the case of the number of units in *tarāwīḥ* prayer. The *tarāwīḥ* prayers are held during the nights of the month of Ramadan throughout the Muslim world. This prayer is often performed by congregations as either eleven or twenty units. While a significant number of Muslims perform eleven units, the majority perform twenty units of prayer; this includes in the holy mosques in Mecca and Medina. Albānī argued that the *tarāwīḥ* prayers cannot exceed eleven units because the Prophet's prayer was limited to eleven. His opinion is unique because he is the first scholar to consider it prohibited to pray more than eleven units, whereas other scholars have allowed it. Albānī argued that anything more than eight units of *tarāwīḥ* prayer is a reprehensible innovation (*bidʿa*). Traditionalists maintain that even if this practice was not established by an authentic text, consistent communal practice suffices as evidence to support it.[29] In other words, communal practice overrides the injunctions of a particular ḥadīth. Ismāʿīl al-Anṣārī had several heated debates with Albānī on this issue and maintained that even if one acknowledges that these ḥadīth are weak, communal action is sufficient to warrant the approval of the report. Among the arguments he made was that the *isnād* was designed to prevent foreign elements from entering the religion, not to "foreignize" parts of the religion that the ḥadīth scholars themselves acted on.[30] The continual action of the Muslim community was

[28] M. Laknāwī, *Ajwiba*, 237–238.
[29] I. Anṣārī, *Taṣḥīḥ*, 11–13.
[30] M. Laknāwī, *Ajwiba*, 237–238.

considered a verbal or communal *isnād*; it was an act that was passed down through action, but was not written down with a completely authentic chain.

Anṣārī contends that Islamic teachings do not need to always be based on an *isnād*. If a practice has been applied and accepted among the Muslims, then it is part and parcel of the religion, especially if it started during the early generations of Islam. As noted earlier, *ijmāʿ* or the actions of the majority of Muslims do not prevent Albānī from going against them. This does not mean that he rejects ijmāʿ, but that it is debatable whether there is consensus on the permissibility of praying more than eleven units. Albānī weakens all the narrations that describe the Companions as praying twenty units of *tarāwīḥ* prayers.

The crux of his argument is that the Prophet always performed the night prayer as eleven units, so it became an established Sunna (*Sunna muʾakkada*) regardless of whether it was in Ramadan or not. Since this established Sunna never exceeded eleven units it takes a similar ruling to the Sunna prayers before or after the daily compulsory prayers. These are performed in specific numbers and one is not allowed to increase or decrease the number of units. Therefore, it is necessary to follow the Prophet directly in acts of worship. Increasing the number of units in *tarāwīḥ* is similar to increasing the number of units in an obligatory prayer.[31] Traditionalists respond by arguing that Prophetic action on its own does not necessarily bring forth an obligation or mean that adding a number is prohibited.

Albānī also explains that even if it were permissible to increase the number of units in a prayer, it is better to pray eleven units exactly as the Prophet did.[32] What would it mean if the narrations that describe the Companions praying twenty units were authentic? Albānī explains that even if it were true that ʿUmar gathered the Companions to pray twenty units, he did not do it because he considered it permissible to pray as much as one wants. Rather he did so to make it easier for the people praying at the time, because the units were longer, and they would last until the morning. Since such a prayer does not exist today, this is not allowed.[33] Here Albānī interprets the narration because there is no clear evidence that describes all of the Companions praying in the mosque until the morning. Furthermore, Anṣārī highlights that there is an inconsistency in Albānī's position because he maintains the Prophet must be followed literally in acts of worship, but then explains that it was allowed in order to make it easy on people.

[31] N. Albānī, *Tarāwīḥ*, 32–33. [32] N. Albānī, *Tarāwīḥ*, 39. [33] N. Albānī, *Tarāwīḥ*, 61–62.

The reports concerning twenty units mostly refer to the actions of the Companions, not the Prophet. Many of the transmitters that Albānī weakened were *tābiʿīn* (Successors) who described the Companions praying twenty units. Traditionalists assume that if the Successors prayed twenty units it is very likely that they witnessed the Companions doing so. There are a few other narrations that describe the Prophet as praying thirteen units at night. Albānī accepts the authenticity of some of them, but states that the additional two units were not part of the night prayer, but the two Sunna units after the *ʿishāʾ* prayer.[34] These are two authentic texts that are in conflict; one that states eleven units, the other thirteen. However, the ḥadīth that states that the Prophet prayed thirteen units invalidates Albānī's argument that the Prophet only prayed eleven. Therefore, he interprets the ḥadīth that mentions thirteen units in order to consolidate the two, even though this interpretation is not based on textual evidence. This is not to discredit Albānī, but to illustrate that his conclusions, like those of his critics, are interpretations of the texts.

Anṣārī attempted to demonstrate how the narrations are authentic and have been accepted by most scholars. He argues that if a large number of scholars have accepted the narration it is sufficient to establish its validity, although he claims that the continuity of the act over the generations is sufficient evidence of its authenticity.[35] In other words, if an action has been accepted and performed continuously by the majority of Muslims since the time of the Prophet or the Companions, it is considered to be legitimate, even if no authentic ḥadīth exists supporting it. Albānī's methodology does not recognize continuous actions as an authoritative or reliable source, instead he only follows what is narrated in texts. If it does not have an *isnād* he does not consider it to be part of Islam.[36]

Otherwise, scholars and culture will play too large a role in deciding what "other evidence" might include. Hence, Albānī considers it safer to only use the *isnād* system to evaluate a ḥadīth. How can one really know the origin of

[34] N. Albānī, *Tarāwīḥ*, 16–18. [35] I. Anṣārī, *Taṣḥīḥ*, 11–13.

[36] Closely related to *tarāwīḥ* is the issue of *iʿtikāf*. On this issue Albānī also had a controversial and unique opinion. His rule that general expressions cannot be used if there is another text that specifies them also lead him to state that *iʿtikāf* is only allowed in Islam's three holy mosques. He does so because of a narration that states: "There is no *iʿtikāf* except in the three mosques." Since the verses about *iʿtikāf* mention the general term "mosque," this ḥadīth specifies which mosques are being referred to. See Muḥammad Nāṣir al-Dīn al-Albānī, *Qiyām Ramaḍān: Faḍluh wa-Kayfiyyat Adāʾih wa-Mashrūʿiyyat al-Jamāʿa fīh wa Maʿahu Baḥth Qayyim ʿan al-Iʿtikāf* (Amman: al-Maktaba al-Islāmiyya, 1997), 34 and N. Albānī, *S.A.S.*, 6: 667.

communal action, is it the Prophet or someone who misquoted him that initiated it? Since there is a stronger probability that the Prophet did not say it, then Albānī argues that it should not be acted upon.

Mamdūḥ attempts to demonstrate that a weak ḥadīth could be bolstered by the actions of the Muslim community by referring to the situation of the earliest Muslim generations. Not all Islamic teachings practiced in the time of the *salaf* were written down, rather some were passed down through communal actions. There were only a few Companions who recorded the Prophet's sayings. After the spread of Islam, there arose the need to compile the ḥadīth, but prior to this, people were emulating the actions of the Companions. Ḥadīth compilers then began collecting the evidence for the actions that were already being practiced in the community. It is for this reason that they did not only concern themselves with the sayings of the Prophet, but also with the sayings and fatwas of the Companions and Successors.[37] Mamdūḥ quotes al-Shāfiʿī who weakens the *isnād* of a particular ḥadīth, but then goes on to argue that it must be applied because it was passed down from the larger Muslim population to the next. He states: "This is the narration from one larger Muslim population to another. In some cases, this is stronger than one person narrating to another, and this is what we found the people of knowledge in agreement about."[38]

What Traditionalists consider to be a ḥadīth that was preserved through the actions of the Muslim community, Albānī considers a cultural interpolation. If such a proof-text does not exist, then that particular teaching cannot be part of the religion. If it is part of the religion, then God would have preserved it. The crux of the issue between the two groups concerns the role of the scholarly class in defining what constitutes authentic Islam. Traditionalists maintain that God would not allow the general Muslim community to continually practice something if it did not have a divine origin. On the other hand, Albānī only gives value to authentic proof-texts because an authentic text-based Islam is necessary in order to maintain a commitment to the *isnād* system and the texts of ḥadīth. Otherwise, there is a risk of non-Islamic teachings entering the tradition.

[37] M. Mamdūḥ, *Taʿrīf*, 1: 48–49.

[38] M. Mamdūḥ, *Taʿrīf*, 1: 187. Muḥammad b. Idrīs al-al-Shāʿfiʿī (d. 188/820), *Al-Risāla* (Lebanon: Dār al-Kutub al-ʿIlmiyya, 2005), 161.

DIVIDING THE ḤADĪTH CANON

The eighteenth and nineteenth centuries witnessed an increasing rise of intellectuals who were calling for reform. Many of these reformers were critical of weak ḥadīth for various reasons, but among the most important of them is that they introduced foreign elements into Islamic law. Rashīd Riḍā was a strong critic of the use of weak ḥadīth in scholarly works because they resulted in excessive Sufism and practices that are not based on authentic scripture.

Riḍā was involved in writing commentary on the Qurʾān and he found that the field of Qurʾānic exegesis was filled with extra-scriptural narrative supplements such as *isrāʾīliyyāt.* These narrations entered the Islamic corpus through Jewish and Christian converts to Islam. He argues that such narratives attribute inauthentic teachings to the Qurʾān and Sunna. Riḍā wrote an article in the *Manār* journal where he underlined how weak ḥadīth in Ghazālī's *Iḥyāʾ ʿUlūm al-Dīn* have been used to establish teachings that are not based on authentic scripture. Riḍā's article served as a turning point for Albānī during his formative years and inspired him to begin his study of ḥadīth and purging of Islamic law. To prevent people from following weak ḥadīth, Albānī tried to reexamine all the Sunan. This reexamination, as opposed to reliance on the findings of previous ḥadīth scholars, represents an assertion of independence from previous scholarship. Salafis consider Albānī to be one of the greatest ḥadīth scholars of his time and viewed him as capable enough to reexamine the ḥadīth corpus. This desire to reexamine the ḥadīth corpus stems from a rejection of *taqlīd*, a skeptical attitude toward previous scholarship, and placing the Sunna at the center of Islamic authorities and sources. While scholars have always debated, and criticized particular ḥadīth, no one prior to Albānī has ever republished the canonical works while removing their weak ḥadīth.

Albānī's project, which he called *Taqrīb al-Sunna Bayna Yaday al-Umma* (Bringing the Sunna Nearer to the Community), was, as the name suggests, an effort to make authentic ḥadīth more accessible to common Muslims. He therefore divided then republished the canonical ḥadīth works into authentic and weak. He arranged ḥadīth into *ṣaḥīḥ* and *ḥasan*, which are acceptable, and weak and fabricated ḥadīth that are not to be acted upon under any circumstances, and published them as two separate volumes. The objective of this project was to edit the major ḥadīth collections, establish the authenticity or weakness of the ḥadīth, and remove their *isnāds* to make it easier for the reader.[39] Accordingly, the authentic Sunna would become easily accessible to the Muslim community in a pure and purged form.[40]

This division was done to all four Sunan, but not the *Ṣaḥīḥayn*. Suhaib Hasan, who studied with Albānī at the University of Medina in the early 1960s, explained that dividing the Sunan into authentic and weak had never been done before. He says: "At the time, they used to say, 'the six authentic books' (*al-ṣiḥāḥ al-sitta*), whereas it should have been said 'the six books' (*al-kutub al-sitta*). But, Albānī was the first person to classify the ḥadīth in the four Sunan and other books."[41]

Albānī also notes that some people may not agree with his division of the Sunan and recommend that he simply indicate the grade of each ḥadīth instead while keeping the books intact. He acknowledges that this viewpoint has its validity because it incorporates keeping the books intact while at the same time making the Muslims aware of the grade of the ḥadīth.[42] However, Albānī defends his division of the Sunan by noting that it is more beneficial for the lay Muslims and even the scholars, because not all of them have the ability to remember the grade of each ḥadīth in a single book.[43] Albānī delineates himself as one of the only scholars who is truly capable of recognizing authenticity or weakness in ḥadīth. This provoked his Traditionalist critics because they thought it would sever the relationship Muslims might have had with these books. Why were Traditionalists critical of Albānī dividing the Sunan? What is the difference between the dividing of the Sunan and summarizing them? Abū Ghudda criticizes Albānī's project by saying:

> Indeed, some people in our time have continued to sever the four Sunan books and throw away parts of them that were compiled by their authors, the unparalleled imams, the trustees, protectors, champions, and callers to the Sunna. Generations after generations, and centuries after centuries have inherited these collections from them. So, he innovated (*fa ibtadaʿa*) at the end of times this evil innovation. He has made the early predecessors appear ignorant and has cut off the preservation of those great books.

[39] ʿAbd al-Aẓīm al-Mundhurī (d. 656/1258), *Mukhtaṣar Ṣaḥīḥ Muslim li-Abī l-Ḥusayn Muslim ibn al-Ḥajjāj al-Qushayrī al-Naysābūrī*, ed. Muḥammad Nāṣir al-Dīn al-Albānī (Damascus: Al-Maktab al-Islāmī, 1972), 1: 5–6.

[40] Muḥammad Nāṣir al-Dīn al-Albānī, *Ḍaʿīf al-Adab al-Mufrad li l-Imām al-Bukhārī* (Jubayl al-Sināʿīya: Maktabat al-Dalīl, 1998), 5. Hereafter *D.A.M.*

[41] Suhaib Hasan, Interview by author. [42] N. Albānī, *D.A.M.*, 6. [43] N. Albānī, *D.A.M.*, 6.

> Yet, he thinks and claims that he has produced a good thing, and how evil is what he concocted.[44]

Ḥasan al-Saqqāf, whose works are full of *ad hominem* attacks on Albānī, explains that the Sunan were not only collections of ḥadīth, but they served as primary sources in scholarly circles. They were studied, commented on, and passed down from one scholarly generation to the next. The division of these books was viewed as an attack on Traditionalist institutions and enforcing his own understanding and conclusions of the texts on laypeople. Scholars have always had different opinions of the ḥadīth in these compilations, but they never discarded all the weak ḥadīth and republished them as two separate books, one authentic and the other weak. In his attack on Albānī, Saqqāf points out that several of the ḥadīth Albānī places in the weak volumes are actually authenticated by him in other places.

By dividing the Sunan, removing their *isnāds*, and referencing to them in his other works, Saqqāf accused Albānī of trying to compel students to follow him. Albānī usually references his own books so those who read his edited version *Ṣaḥīḥ* of Tirmidhī, for example, will find a ḥadīth without an *isnād* that limits the reader to Albānī's grading of the ḥadīth.

Traditionalists perceive this as a threat to their tradition because it goes against the norm of referencing the original books that contain the *isnād*.[45] Essentially, Saqqāf is accusing Albānī of removing the earlier scholars and original compilers of the works from the picture and placing himself as the leading scholar in the field of ḥadīth. Saqqāf states:

> He has removed the sayings of the great ḥadīth scholars and only kept his sayings! For instance, in *Ṣaḥīḥ al-Tirmidhī* he removed Tirmidhī's comments on the ḥadīth and replaced them with his own blessed words! By doing this he is distancing the readers and students of knowledge, who are deluded by his words, from the original books.[46]

Albānī's revisionist project was attractive to common Muslim audiences and posed a threat to Traditionalists, otherwise they would not have spent so much time responding to him. Abū Ghudda, Saqqāf, and Mamdūḥ all accuse Albānī of trying to sideline earlier scholars and place himself at the forefront of ḥadīth scholarship. Yusrī Jabr, an Azhari scholar, notes that classical ḥadīth scholars used weak ḥadīth and they are considered to be among the

44 M. Laknāwī, *Ẓafar*, 186.

45 H. Saqqāf, *Tanāqaḍāt*, 1: 35. Mamdūḥ makes a similar argument. See M. Mamdūḥ, *Ta'rīf*, 1: 14–15.

46 H. Saqqāf, *Tanāqaḍāt*, 1: 34–35.

salaf. When Albānī rejects weak ḥadīth, he is going against the *salaf*.[47] For Traditionalists, it is the early scholars who are to be followed, and later scholars who should question their methodology if they arrive at different conclusions. Albānī's stance toward tradition, though, is a cynical one that reexamines everything in the light of what he sees as the true Sunna.

Because Albānī did not place any value in weak ḥadīth, he considered it futile to have weak or fabricated ḥadīth in these Sunan.[48] Traditionalists condemned his actions and reminded others of the sanctity of these books. Once Albānī's division of the Sunan was published it was too late for Traditionalists to do anything to remove the impact they would have on laypeople. Since common Muslims do not read scholarly books, they are not likely to be exposed to the Traditionalists' refutation of Albānī. However, they are likely to encounter Albānī's ḥadīth collections that challenge the judgments of earlier authorities, which in turn may cause them to look at tradition in a more skeptical manner. Traditionalists contend that by removing parts of the Sunan that were weak, Albani was also discarding the scholarship that revolved around it.

Albānī justified his division of the Sunan into weak and authentic ḥadīth by explaining that he was only following in the footsteps of previous scholars who compiled *Ṣaḥīḥ* collections such as Bukhārī, Muslim, and Abū Ḥātim ibn Ḥibbān (d. 354/965), as well as those who compiled *ḍaʿīf* or *mawḍūʿ* collections such as Ibn Jawzī and al-Shawkānī.[49] Albānī recognizes that his division of the Sunan may not be accepted by many, and he therefore justified it by demonstrating that it had precedent with previous ḥadīth scholars. Mamdūḥ, one of Albānī's most consistent critics, objects to this claim and notes that the scholars who compiled ḥadīth collections did not prevent people from acting on weak ḥadīth nor did they consider weak ḥadīth to be equivalent to fabricated ḥadīth. Many of the authors Albānī mentioned used weak ḥadīth in their works. For example, Bukhārī uses weak ḥadīth in his *Adab al-Mufrad* which Albānī also divided into two books, one containing its weak ḥadīth, the other its authentic.[50]

Albānī asks Muslims to only act on authentic ḥadīth in caution of acting upon something that is alien to Islam. Moreover, he believes that authentic texts are sufficient and that there is no need to refer to weak ḥadīth. Traditionalists argue that weak ḥadīth could be used if they do not add anything new to the religion and if their teachings were in accordance with

[47] Yusrī Jabr, "Laysa Kul Ḥaidth Muhmal Kamā Ibtadaʿahu al-Shaykh al-Albānī," www.youtube.com/watch?v=VtbshnqxJzo, last accessed April 13, 2018.

[48] N. Albānī, *S.J.S.*, 32.

[49] N. Albānī, *Ṣ.J.S.*, 33.

[50] M. Mamdūḥ, *Taʿrīf*, 1: 174–175.

authentic texts. However, Albānī's view is that there is no point in using weak ḥadīth because the existence of an authentic text serves the same purpose. It is important to note that Albānī was living in a time when most scholars allowed the use of weak ḥadīth and therefore rarely cited the authenticity of a ḥadīth they used. Albānī considered it his scholarly duty to distinguish between weak and authentic ḥadīth. By dividing the Sunan Albānī wanted to save Muslims from following the weak ḥadīth in these books, and instead he wanted them to follow the authentic ḥadīth he selects for them.

Albānī considered himself to be cleaning up Islamic tradition. By doing so, he rendered all tradition and Islamic scholarly history as being suspicious, which made it easier for his unconventional actions and opinions to be legitimized. In response to this, his critics spend much of their energy defending the scholarship and credibility of earlier scholars.

While his research may not have been superior to the works of classical ḥadīth scholars, Albānī succeeds in abstaining from directly rejecting scholarly tradition by suggesting that classical scholars are not concerned with a more complete version of ḥadīth texts. Rejecting the utility of weak ḥadīth means that the Sunan must be approached with caution and suspicion. The only trusted ḥadīth are those that are authentic, and since laypeople cannot distinguish between what is authentic or weak, Albānī provides them an authentic version of the Sunan. Traditionalists fear that Albānī will be perceived as the default ḥadīth scholar and the classical ḥadīth scholars as secondary.

Mamdūḥ published a six-volume response to Albānī's project of dividing the four Sunan into authentic and weak titled: *Al-Taʿrīf bi-Awhām man Qassama al-Sunan ilā Ṣaḥīḥ wa Ḍaʿīf* (*Making Known the Illusions of the One Who Divided the Sunan into Authentic and Weak*). This work has generated several responses from Albānī's students.[51] Mamdūḥ contended that Albānī was placing himself as the ultimate arbitrator of what is authentic and weak. He argues that scholars differed concerning the grading of ḥadīth, and Albānī was implying that his classification of the Sunan was the only correct one. Albānī did not only remove weak ḥadīth from the Sunan, but he did this to other books, even those that are not directly related to ḥadīth. By removing weak ḥadīth from classical books, Mamdūḥ accused Albānī of tampering with the books of the authors to conform to his own

[51] See, for example, T. ʿAwaḍ Allāh, *Radʿu al-Jānī* and ʿAbd al-Fattāḥ Surūr, *Iḥkām al-Ḥadīd ʿalā Maḥmūd Saʿīd: bi-Kashf Tajannī-hi ʿalā al-Imām al-Albānī wa l-Radd ʿalā Kitābi-hi: al-Taʿrīf bi-Awhām man Qassama al-Sunan ilā Ṣaḥīḥ wa Ḍaʿīf* (Riyadh: Aḍwāʾ al-Salaf, 2007).

views and then republishing them. Mamdūḥ perceived Albānī's project as an attempt to rewrite Islamic scholarly tradition. He rhetorically asks:

> Was Bukhārī unable to critique the ḥadīth of *Al-Adab al-Mufrad* as he did with the ḥadīth of the *Ṣaḥīḥ*? Was Ibn Qayyim incapable of choosing only what was authentic for the topic of his book *Al-Wābil al-Ṣayyib*? Or was either of them lacking in their zeal for the Sunna, what was authentic from it and acting upon it?[52]

Furthermore, Mamdūḥ argues that by dividing the Sunan, Albānī misses the point intended by the authors of those books. The authors of the Sunan did not blindly place ḥadīth in their compilations, instead they did so with the intent that they be acted upon.[53] The Sunan were intended to be *fiqh* manuals. They served to provide jurists with proof-texts that can support their legal arguments. The authors of the Sunan deliberately included weak ḥadīth in certain chapters of their compilations. By dividing the Sunan, Albānī changed the nature of the Sunan and it resulted in ḥadīth compilations that were vastly different from what the original authors intended. The nature and methodology of the two books are completely different.

Although it appears to be an overreaction by Albānī's critics, their concern is that his project will make people lose touch with classical sources. Mamdūḥ views Albānī as a threat because as time goes on and more authors follow Albānī's method of dividing the Sunan into authentic and weak, providing laypeople with only authentic ḥadīth, the Muslim community will lose trust in the classical sources. Several others have also followed in Albānī's footsteps, for example his student Salīm al-Hilālī divided the Muwaṭṭa'. Additionally, Jawād ʿAfānā, an engineer by training, followed Albānī's method of dividing ḥadīth books and published a controversial *Ṣaḥīḥ* of *Ṣaḥīḥ al-Bukhārī*.[54] ʿAwwāma notes that these works are a direct consequence of Albānī dividing the Sunan. He states that this has become a widespread problem in modern times. He complains that it has reached a point where a person like ʿAfānā who is not a scholar in any sense of the word, but rather an engineer, attacks *Ṣaḥīḥ al-Bukhārī*, the greatest book of the Sunna.[55]

From Albānī's perspective, it is not the relationship with the tradition that is important, but the relationship with God and the Prophet. Albānī lived in

[52] M. Mamdūḥ, *Taʿrīf*, 1: 31. [53] M. Mamdūḥ, *Taʿrīf*, 1: 23.

[54] Jawād ʿAfānā, *Ṣaḥīḥ Ṣaḥīḥ al-Bukhārī* (Beirut: Dār Jawād lil Nashr, 2003).

[55] Muḥammad ʿAwwāma, "ʿAwwāma's Statement on Albānī," www.youtube.com/watch?v=zus5-U3wTxM, last accessed December 1, 2019. Also see M. ʿAwwāma, *Ḥukm al-ʿAmal bil Ḥadīth al-Ḍaʿīf*, 154.

a time of strict, and sometimes uncritical, adherence to the *madhhabs*. Traditionalists were concerned about the relationship laypeople have with the scholarly tradition, while Albānī accentuated the relationship they have with texts. This difference stems from the fact that Traditionalists view the general Muslim community, and the scholarly community in particular, to be guided by God. Conversely, Albānī does not give any value to the scholarly class if they go against an authentic ḥadīth. Albānī did not trust Traditionalists because of their over-reverence for the scholarly tradition that he believed took away from their commitment to the Qurʾān and Sunna.

Another interesting point is that Traditionalists argue that Albānī empowered laypeople to interpret the religion by providing them with books that contain only authentic ḥadīth. If these works contained both weak and authentic ḥadīth, only those who were trained scholars would be equipped to deal with the texts and interpret them. In a way, Mamdūḥ's work is an attempt to keep interpretive authority in the hands of Traditionalists who were threatened by Albānī's methodology.

Mamdūḥ also criticizes Albānī's method by arguing that years of scholarly tradition will eventually be worthless. The "weak" ḥadīth discarded by Albānī have been commented on, interpreted, practiced, and studied by scholars for over a thousand years. By removing these ḥadīth, Albānī is not only discarding each ḥadīth itself, but the years of scholarly tradition revolving around all those ḥadīth.[56] Perhaps the biggest problem in Albānī's division of the Sunan and argument against weak ḥadīth, was the fact that Albānī believed in a category of ḥadīth called *ḥasan li-ghayri-hi*, which is a weak ḥadīth that is authentic due to external factors, such as it being strengthened by other weak ḥadīth.

By accepting the category *ḥasan li-ghayri-hi* Albānī is using a ḥadīth that has a possibility of being weak. The challenge that this presents is that such ḥadīth are in and of themselves *ḍaʿīf* but are strengthened by external factors. What this means then is that there *is* space for weak ḥadīths in Albānī's methodology. In essence, a *ḥasan li-ghayri-hi* ḥadīth is not weak, but rather it is on the border of *ḥasan* and *ḍaʿīf*. This puts into question the place of weak ḥadīth in Albānī's methodology, given his emphasis on the *ṣaḥīḥ/ḥasan* and downplaying the value of everything else. By using ḥadīth that have a possibility of being weak, but not terming them as such, Albānī was not much different from his detractors. In fact, Traditionalists like

[56] M. Mamdūḥ, *Taʿrīf*, 1: 30.

ʿAwwāma have argued that the rejection of weak ḥadīth is often only theoretical. Upon closer examination even those who theoretically reject the use of weak ḥadīth actually resort to using them in one way or another.[57]

There remains the distinction that Albānī would not use a single weak ḥadīth that cannot be strengthened by other narrations, whereas Traditionalists were open to using weak ḥadīth on their own. Albānī tended to sometimes portray things as black and white, and his critics attack him for oversimplifying Islamic sciences and the interpretation of Islamic texts. Had Albānī only accepted *ṣaḥīḥ* ḥadīth, it would have been understandable why he wants to avoid weak ḥadīth altogether. However, by accepting the *ḥasan li-ghayri-hi* category of ḥadīth, Albānī was venturing close to weak ḥadīth and there was a stronger possibility that he strengthens a ḥadīth that was actually weak. One might imagine that Albānī was very strict and cautious in his accepting of weak ḥadīth, but, as I illustrate in Chapter 7, many of the criticisms against him often accuse him of being too lenient.

[57] M. ʿAwwāma, *Ḥukm al-ʿAmal bil Ḥadīth al-Ḍaʿīf.*

7

Challenging Early Ḥadīth Scholarship

PURIST SALAFISM IS PRIMARILY A MOVEMENT THAT SEEKS TO understand Islam based on scripture and the earliest generations of Muslims, while eliminating all other sources of influence. This approach to Islamic jurisprudence sets purist Salafis apart from other Muslims who also follow scripture but include other sources in their legal theories. Consequently, a major concern of purist Salafis is to protect Islam from inauthentic influences. This is primarily done by focusing on ḥadīth studies and ensuring that creed, law, and moral teachings are all based on authentic scripture. In this regard, Albānī is recognized as the leading ḥadīth scholar in Salafi circles. He sought to revive authentic Islam and remove statements that were falsely attributed to the Prophet. What makes Albānī's ḥadīth verification controversial is that he does not consider the authentication or weakening of early scholars as binding, in the sense that one can disagree with the opinions of classical ḥadīth such as Bukhārī or Muslim. Albānī's method of determining the authenticity of a particular ḥadīth is largely based on the study of the *isnād*, using information found in biographical dictionaries, and finding corroborating narrations that might strengthen the authenticity of a ḥadīth. This chapter will examine Traditionalist response to Albānī's criticism of ḥadīth found in the *Ṣaḥīḥayn*, and Albānī's impact on the field of ḥadīth studies.

REEXAMINING THE COLLECTIONS OF BUKHĀRĪ AND MUSLIM

For Sunni Muslims, *Ṣaḥīḥ al-Bukhārī* and *Ṣaḥīḥ Muslim* are considered the most authentic books after the Qurʾān. These two books are held in high esteem and the authenticity of the ḥadīth they contain have generally been accepted. However, there have always been several scholars, although not the majority, who question the authenticity of some of the ḥadīth in these two books. In his attempt to purify the ḥadīth corpus, Albānī did not limit his reevaluation of ḥadīth in the four Sunan collection, but also extended it to all the ḥadīth in the *Ṣaḥīḥayn*. In response to Albānī's criticism of ḥadīth in the *Ṣaḥīḥayn*, Traditionalists argued that there was consensus regarding the authenticity of these two works, and Albānī was breaking with this *ijmāʿ*. Contrary to the Traditionalists' claim of consensus on the authenticity of these two works, there have always been scholars who criticized some of the ḥadīth in the *Ṣaḥīḥayn*. Traditionalists do not necessarily consider every single ḥadīth in the *Ṣaḥīḥayn* to be authentic, but besides a few ḥadīth that might not be completely authentic, there was a general agreement on their authenticity. Albānī argues that the Qurʾān is the only book that is completely authentic; he states:

> It is necessary that I put forward a statement of truth that I must express for the sake of scholarly integrity and to be free from blame. It is that a researcher who understands reality must acknowledge an academic truth that Imam al-Shāfiʿī, may God have mercy on him, expressed according to what was narrated of his saying: "God has forbidden that any book reach perfection except His book."[1]

The works of humans will never be perfect and are always subject to questioning. Being a ḥadīth scholar, Albānī certainly had great respect for the *Ṣaḥiḥayn* and often used them as measures of authenticity in polemics. He did not think that he was criticizing the *Ṣaḥīḥayn*, but was rather noting criticisms of earlier scholars.[2] Albānī correctly points out that he was not the first to criticize ḥadīth in Bukhārī and Muslim. The fact that previous scholars criticized the compilations of Bukhārī and Muslim cannot be denied. This includes esteemed ḥadīth scholars such as Ibn Ḥajar al-ʿAsqalānī, ʿAli b. ʿUmar al-Dāraquṭnī (d. 385/995), and Ibn Taymiyya, to name a few.[3] Although al-Dāraquṭnī criticized many ḥadīth in Bukhārī, Albānī notes that he found fewer than ten weak ḥadīth and sometimes it is only part of the ḥadīth that is inauthentic.[4]

When Albānī highlights the fact that he was not the first scholar to criticize some ḥadīth in Bukhārī, he does so as a defensive approach, not a

[1] Muḥammad Nāṣir al-Dīn al-Albānī, *Mukhtaṣar Ṣaḥīḥ al-Bukhārī* (Riyadh: Maktabat al-Maʿārif, 2002), 2: 5–6. Hereafter *M.S.B.*

[2] J. Brown, *Canonization*, 327.

[3] Ismāʿīl Ibn Kathīr, *Al-Bāʿith al-Ḥathīth Sharḥ Ikhtiṣār ʿUlūm al-Ḥadīth*, ed. Muḥammad Nāṣir al-Dīn al-Albānī (Riyadh: Maktabat al-Maʿārif, 1996), 125.

[4] Muḥammad Nāṣir al-Dīn al-Albānī, "Weak Ḥadīth in Bukhārī? Albānī Explains," www.youtube.com/watch?v=w46-M1XqsUQ, last accessed May 22, 2018.

methodological one.[5] Although he criticizes *taqlīd*, in this case he justifies his criticism of the *Ṣaḥīḥayn* by stating that he is following in the footsteps of others. In other words, he uses the same mode of argumentation that his critics have used against him; justifying his actions by noting that if Traditionalists accuse him of being disrespectful to tradition, they must also say the same of the scholars who he is following.

Moreover, it is important to note that although Albānī attempts to avoid performing *taqlīd* in *fiqh*, *taqlīd* in ḥadīth is inevitable. His method of authenticating ḥadīth is entirely based on the opinions of earlier scholars. For instance, when Bukhārī states that a certain narrator is weak, Albānī cannot perform *ijtihād* in this matter because of the time barrier between him and the narrator. It is not possible to completely reexamine the judgments made about ḥadīth narrators anew. However, Albānī only performs *taqlīd* when it concerns a judgment on a narrator's probity, but when it comes to the ruling on the ḥadīth he reexamines it himself and discards earlier judgments on the ḥadīth.

Because Traditionalists maintained that there is a consensus on the authenticity of the ḥadīth in the *Ṣaḥīḥayn*, they believed there was no point in reviewing the *isnād*s of these ḥadīth. Mamdūḥ states that the examination of the ḥadīth in the *Ṣaḥīḥayn* ended a long time ago. As a result, when scholars quote a ḥadīth from the *Ṣaḥīḥayn*, they do not comment on the *isnād* or the authenticity of the ḥadīth because it is understood to be authentic. Albānī goes against the claimed consensus and reexamines all ḥadīth anew. Traditionalists are concerned that Albānī's criticism of the *Ṣaḥīḥayn* will cause Muslims to doubt their general authenticity. The constant Traditionalist accusation against Albānī is that he is claiming to know better than the early ḥadīth scholars.[6] Mamdūḥ states:

> How can a man in the 15th century [Hijri], have the audacity to challenge what scholars of the great generations have authenticated while the scrolls have dried, and the pens have risen from ḥadīth of the *Ṣaḥīḥayn*? Otherwise, it would mean that the *umma* would have been misguided from the straight path in its agreement on the authenticity of the *Ṣaḥīḥ*.[7]

Albānī responds to this statement by arguing that no such *ijmāʿ* ever existed. He refers to Mamdūḥ as one who is a claimant of knowledge and accuses him of lying about there being a consensus on the *Ṣaḥīḥayn*'s authenticity. He explains that scholars have consistently criticized some of the ḥadīth in the *Ṣaḥīḥayn*. Regardless of whether or not these scholars were

[5] N. Albānī, *Sharḥ*, 37. [6] M. Mamdūḥ, *Tanbīh*, 3–7. [7] M. Mamdūḥ, *Tanbīh*, 7.

mistaken, the fact that they criticize some ḥadīth in the *Ṣaḥīḥayn* is an indication that there is no *ijmāʿ*.[8] Albānī states that besides the false assertion of consensus, the claim that Muslims will go astray because he criticizes some ḥadīth is exaggerated.[9] He gives a few examples of problematic ḥadīth in Bukhārī's *Ṣaḥīḥ*, and argues that lay Muslims have the right to know which ḥadīth are actual sayings of the Prophet and which ones are not. Albānī states:

> The *umma* should not be deceived by what some of the dissenters write against us, from among the ignorant *muqallid*s and *madhhab*ists who ramble incoherently about that which they do not know, and say that which they do not know, and purposely make themselves ignorant about what they do know. Examples of these individuals is the unjust Abū Ghudda from Aleppo, the junior Kawtharī, and that Egyptian loser Maḥmūd Saʿīd and those who are like them.[10]

Albānī characterizes his critics as ignorant *muqallid*s who are trying to fool people into believing that a consensus on the *Ṣaḥīḥayn* exists. Khalīl Mullā Khāṭir criticizes Albānī without mentioning his name; he states:

> If there comes an upstart at the end of times, and he is not of the people of this profession, and impudently challenges [the early scholars] and criticizes what he does not incline to or like. This person is disheveling himself and should not be given attention because before he criticizes these two honorable books, he actually criticizes the consensus of the *umma*.[11]

Traditionalists are again trying to refute Albānī by accusing him of thinking that he is greater than the early scholars. Mullā Khāṭir notes that Bukhārī and Muslim spent more than fifteen years compiling their works and reviewing the ḥadīth they contained. Afterwards, they presented their works to the great ḥadīth masters of their time, who further examined them and concluded that the ḥadīth they contain are of the highest level of authenticity. Since then, scholars have always relied on these books.[12] He ponders how to take seriously the critiques of someone who arises centuries later.[13]

Mamdūḥ also argues that Albānī's criticism of the ḥadīth in *Ṣaḥīḥayn* is actually a criticism of the scholars who accepted their authenticity.[14] Traditionalists do not want to open the door to a reexamination of authenticity of the *Ṣaḥīḥayn*. However, because Albānī is a purist Salafi he does not

[8] N. Albānī, *Ādāb*, 54–56. [9] N. Albānī, *Ādāb*, 62–63. [10] N. Albānī, *M.S.B.*, 2: 8.
[11] Khalīl Khāṭir, *Makānat al-Ṣaḥīḥayn* (Cairo: Al-Maṭbaʿa al-ʿArabiyya al-Ḥadītha, 1985), 127.
[12] K. Khāṭir, *Makānat*, 256. [13] K. Khāṭir, *Makānat*, 128. [14] M. Mamdūḥ, *Tanbīh*, 13.

have allegiance to any person or school other than the truth. His lack of loyalty to a particular school or tradition liberated him from the shackles of following people or institutions. Traditionalists want to end the discussion concerning the ḥadīth in the *Ṣaḥīḥayn*, but Albānī explains that knowledge is not stagnant and can always be corrected.[15] Albānī argues that he is not bound by the limitations of following anyone other than the Prophet and accuses his critics of accepting the alleged consensus simply because it was the scholarly culture to do so. His portrayal of them as blind adherents to scholarly tradition and culture further tarnished their image and enhanced his own. In a time when people felt autonomous and empowered to think for themselves and make their own judgments, Albānī's position might have been more attractive, even if it was not supported by a strong scholarly tradition.

Albānī believed that it was his duty as a scholar to acknowledge the weak ḥadīth in these two works. For Albānī, exempting the *Ṣaḥīḥayn* from critical review constitutes a betrayal of scholarly integrity. Embracing a canonical culture that sacrifices critical honesty for the security of scholarly institutions violates a Muslim scholar's responsibility.[16] Although it might be correct that part of the Traditionalists' defense of the canonical culture was for the security of their scholarly institution, Albānī's accusation leaves out the possibility that Traditionalists believed it based on critical honesty. In other words, it is likely that Traditionalists' opinion on the *Ṣaḥīḥayn* is based on research and not simply an attempt to protect scholarly institutions. They considered it necessary to respond to Albānī, not simply because he criticized some ḥadīth from the *Ṣaḥīḥayn*, but because he did so in a manner that also criticized thousands of scholars who they held in high esteem.

Albānī portrays his critics as nonacademics who are trying to conceal the fact that there are weak ḥadīth in the *Ṣaḥīḥayn* in order to protect their scholarly institutions. Traditionalists believe that God's guidance is embodied in the scholars of Islam and Albānī's claim to only have loyalty to authentic scripture is a shiny cover for his desire to establish himself as an authority.

Traditionalists accuse Albānī of trying to supersede Bukhārī and Muslim in ḥadīth expertise, something they consider impossible. It is not only due to their level of scholarship that later scholars cannot outdo them, but also because much of the material that was accessible to Bukhārī and Muslim, and earlier scholars, is no longer at our disposal.[17] Mullā Khāṭir argues that

[15] N. Albānī, *Ṣaḥīḥ al-Targhīb*, 1: 4. Also see N. Albānī, *S.A.D.*, 1: 44.

[16] J. Brown, *Canonization*, 332. [17] K. Khāṭir, *Makānat*, 488. J. Brown, *Canonization*, 330.

both Bukhārī and Muslim knew many transmissions of each ḥadīth, and chose to only include a few in their compilations. The rest remained in their memory and the ḥadīth scholars of their time were also aware of the other paths of transmission.[18] Albānī rightly questions how it is possible to really know that they had additional information on a particular ḥadīth if the chain is not available today? How can Traditionalists assume that the early ḥadīth scholars had extra sources if they did not cite them or provide an *isnād*?[19] This is what Albānī refers to when he states there is a blind following or over-reverence of scholars. In other words, Traditionalists would rather imagine that extra sources existed rather than state the scholar was incorrect. Mullā Khāṭir defends the tradition by accusing the likes of Albānī as trying to sell themselves as scholars who are so superb that they have outdone the greatest scholars of Islam. He states:

> Because of some who do not know true discipline: many have been led to display themselves as great scholars to the *umma*, and that it is they who are great scholars and not others. They think the *umma* did not produce anyone similar to them for hundreds of years. So, they exaggerated their abilities, made themselves lofty and criticized others in order to portray themselves as great scholars to the simpleminded, and make what the *umma* has agreed upon to appear as clear fabrication and misguidance.[20]

Traditionalists try to get others to see through Albānī's alleged pseudo-scholarship, but they are still challenged by his efforts to reform Islam, especially his expertise in the science of ḥadīth. Hence, in order to prevent people from falling for Albānī's alleged scholarly deception, Traditionalists must defend all of their stances according to Albānī's standards that are considered convincing to laypeople but shallow and superficial to Traditionalists. They are placed in a position where they must discard the complex scholarly methods found in Traditionalism and reframe them using what they consider to be a simplistic argumentative proof-text method used by Albānī. Traditionalists feared that they would now have to justify the authenticity of every single ḥadīth they quoted, even if it was in the *Ṣaḥīḥayn*.

The tension between Albānī and Abū Ghudda started in 1961 when Albānī published his third edition of *Sharḥ al-ʿAqīda al-Ṭaḥāwiyya* and he inserted the word "authentic" after mentioning ḥadīth from Bukhārī or Muslim. This implies that weak ḥadīth exist in these two works. According to Abū Ghudda, Albānī used to refer to him as a friend until he differed with him

[18] K. Khāṭir, *Makānat*, 475. [19] N. Albānī, *Sharḥ*, 29. [20] K. Khāṭir, *Makānat*, 488.

on the authentication of ḥadīth in the *Ṣaḥīḥayn*. After that, Albānī began calling Abū Ghudda names, to which Abū Ghudda writes: "Then woe to the one who corrects him, refutes him, or disagrees with him! These manners have become his characteristic and method in his refutations and introductions to his books!"[21] Abū Ghudda mentioned Albānī authenticating the ḥadīth in Bukhārī and Muslim to Albānī's then good friend and head of the publishing company Zuhayr al-Shāwīsh, who was surprised by this. It appears that al-Shāwīsh attempted to start a dialogue between Abū Ghudda and Albānī. Abū Ghudda explains:

> In the summer of 1389 [1969], I was in Beirut and went to visit Zuhayr in his home. I saw that the teacher (*al-ustādh*), shaykh Yūsuf al-Qaraḍāwī[22] was with him reviewing some issues, so I sat with him. After some time, shaykh Nāṣir al-Albānī came and sat down, and Zuhayr was with us in the room as well. Then, *al-ustādh* Yūsuf al-Qaraḍāwī began speaking with shaykh Nāṣir, saying very gently: Some of the brothers and teachers who love you pointed out an observation on your comments on "*Sharḥ al-ʿAqīda al-Ṭaḥāwiyya*" concerning the ḥadīth of Bukhārī and Muslim in the *Ṣaḥīḥayn*. Because in your commentary you authenticate the *Ṣaḥīḥayn* when [Abū Jaʿfar al-Ṭaḥāwī] says: "Bukhārī and Muslim have narrated in their *Ṣaḥīḥ* works, you then comment on the ḥadīth by saying: "authentic." They consider this to go against the method of ḥadīth scholars [in dealing] with the *Ṣaḥīḥayn*.
>
> Shaykh Nasir asked him, "Who says this?" The teacher, al-Qaraḍāwī said, "By God, I heard this criticism in Qatar from some teachers and I responded to it [by saying] that perhaps what motivated shaykh Nāṣir to do this is that he meant to show that these ḥadīth are not from the ḥadīth that have been criticized in the *Ṣaḥīḥayn*; because it is known that some of their ḥadīth were criticized for not meeting their conditions of high level of authenticity. So, perhaps shaykh Nāṣir meant that the mentioned ḥadīth is not from among the criticized ḥadīth. So, it is an authentic ḥadīth according to known conditions of Bukhārī and Muslim."
>
> Then, shaykh Nāṣir became very angry and his face got red, and he said "No, this is my way in commentary. By noting, after mentioning a ḥadīth from the *Ṣaḥīḥayn* that it is 'authentic' I intend to show its authenticity, not to negate it from being one of the ḥadīth that were criticized." So, I [Abū Ghudda] joined the conversation and said, "But this method is not correct. It causes doubt in the ḥadīth of the *Ṣaḥīḥayn* until their authenticity is

[21] A. Abū Ghudda, *Jawāb*, 15.

[22] Yūsuf al-Qaraḍāwī was a good friend of Abū Ghudda. When Abū Ghudda died, Qaraḍāwī gave the Friday sermon in Qatar about Abū Ghudda and also published an article about him in a newspaper. See M. Āl Rashīd, *Imdād*, 218.

> shown." So, his anger and discomfort increased and the gathering became very awkward. So, I became quiet in order that we do not enter into an atmosphere, the results of which would not be good.[23]

Traditionalists object to inserting the term "authentic" after mentioning that it was narrated in one of the *Ṣaḥīḥayn* because it causes people to doubt their authenticity. Mullā Khāṭir notes that it stems from "deception in the one who says it" and "a longing and advancement in the self to be above Bukhārī, Muslim, and their likes of the people of knowledge in ḥadīth."[24] Albānī explains that he inserts the term "authentic" before ḥadīth narrated in the *Ṣaḥīḥayn* for the sole purpose of making it easy for the reader to know the authenticity level of the ḥadīth in a very clear and straightforward manner.[25] Just as Albānī tries to discredit Traditionalists by assuming that they are blind defenders of tradition, they also attempt to discredit him by assuming he is trying to outdo great scholars.

Mamdūḥ states that Albānī's criticism of the *Ṣaḥīḥayn* opens a door that will be very difficult to close.[26] Mamdūḥ defends the *Ṣaḥīḥayn* because he wants to suppress discussion of mistakes that might be found in them. His argument assumes that proper criticism will not be recognized by the scholars. Mamdūḥ is not concerned about scholars being persuaded by Albānī's criticism of the *Ṣaḥīḥayn* but rather that laypeople are influenced by it and that unqualified people feel the right to also begin criticizing these texts. Albānī notes that his criticism is not outside the tradition, even if it is a minority opinion. While criticizing a ḥadīth in Bukhārī Albānī stated: "The aberration in this ḥadīth is one of tens of examples that demonstrate the ignorance of some of the impudent ones who are excessive for the *Ṣaḥīḥ* of Bukhārī and the *Ṣaḥīḥ* of Muslim with blind adherence and say with certainty that everything they contain is authentic!"[27] Albānī's "lack of decorum" played an important role in attracting criticism toward himself. He further legitimizes his position by placing himself between two extremes, blind followers who consider everything in the *Ṣaḥīḥayn* to be authentic, and those who follow their desires and reject ḥadīth in them because they do not conform with their intellectual inclinations.[28]

Albānī's criticism of certain ḥadīth in the *Ṣaḥīḥayn* should not give the impression that he does not revere them. Rather, he considers them to be the two most authentic books following the Qurʾān, and they are on a higher level than any other ḥadīth collection. He states that this does not mean that

23 A. Abū Ghudda, *Kalimāt*, 3. 24 K. Khāṭir, *Makānat*, 475. 25 N. Albānī, *Sharḥ*, 22.
26 M. Mamdūḥ, *Tanbīh*, 13. 27 N. Albānī, *S.A.S.*, 6: 93. 28 N. Albānī, *S.A.S.*, 6: 93.

every phrase or word in the two books is equal to what is in the Qurʾān, such that it is impossible to contain any mistake.[29] Mamdūḥ acknowledges that not every single word is free from criticism, but he limits it to what was criticized by earlier scholars. In other words, only previous criticisms by past scholars can be entertained, not new ones. His problem with Albānī is that he opens the door to anyone who wants to criticize any ḥadīth in the *Ṣaḥīḥayn* to do so, as long as they are following the "correct ḥadīth methodology," which he does not believe Albānī follows.[30] This not only threatens the *Ṣaḥīḥayn*, but the scholarship on which they are based as well.

Albānī correctly highlights that several Traditionalists have also weakened some ḥadīth in the *Ṣaḥīḥayn*, among them are the Ghumārī brothers and Muḥammad Zāhid al-Kawtharī. Albānī points out that Traditionalists like Mamdūḥ and Abū Ghudda attack him for criticizing some *isnāds* in the *Ṣaḥīḥayn*, but they turn a blind eye when their teachers do it. In his response to Abū Ghudda, Albānī explains that there is a long history of the Ḥanafī school criticizing ḥadīth from the *Ṣaḥīḥayn*.[31] Why did Abū Ghudda and Mamdūḥ not criticize their teachers? The answer to this lies in the fact that they were not actually concerned about the ḥadīth being criticized, but the threat Albānī posed to their Traditionalist institutions. Traditionalists were facing challenges and critiques on many different fronts. Secularists, Modernists, and Salafis all took issue with Traditionalist institutions.

Purist Salafism stood in stark contrast to Traditionalism and it posed the greatest threat to Traditionalist institutions because it was criticizing them from within the established scholarly tradition. Secularists and Modernists did not pose a great threat because these two groups were viewed as being influenced by the west. Previous criticisms of the *Ṣaḥīḥayn* were done at a time when Traditionalist institutions were strong. The compilations of Bukhārī and Muslim symbolized the way that Traditionalists have understood Islam and served as symbols of strength in Traditionalist institutions. These symbols are critical because they serve as the foundations of what the contested tradition is based on. Traditionalists believe that celebrated symbols such as the *Ṣaḥīḥayn* are too grand for someone like Albānī to approach. They considered him to lack the qualifications and credentials to criticize these ḥadīth and feared that it would open the door for other "unqualified" people to also criticize ḥadīth of the *Ṣaḥīḥayn*.

Traditionalists viewed Albānī's criticism of ḥadīth in the *Ṣaḥīḥayn* as a break with Traditionalism. It posed a threat to the value of their consensus,

[29] N. Albānī, *Sharḥ*, 22–23. [30] M. Mamdūḥ, *Tanbīh*, 24. [31] N. Albānī, *Sharḥ*, 42.

and in addition to having to defend the use of weak ḥadīth, they had to also defend two texts that they considered completely authentic. Even though other scholars did criticize ḥadīth in the *Ṣaḥīḥayn* in the past, they were relatively few. In the estimation of Traditionalists, those criticized reports fall outside the scope of *ijmāʿ* and do not impart certainty, though they may potentially be authentic and only impart *ẓann*. Hence, even if consensus did not exist, the majority are on the side of Traditionalists. Albānī fails to explain why the majority of scholars are mistaken on the issue. Mamdūḥ argues that if centuries of scholars have performed an experiment and came to the same results, their findings become a fact. However, if a later scholar performed the same experiment and came to a different conclusion, then one of their methodologies must be incorrect. What Mamdūḥ and Traditionalists do not take into consideration is that there always existed another group of scholars, even if they are few, who criticize this method and have come to opposite conclusions. For Traditionalists, the question became whether or not they can compete with Albānī's assurance of certainty and authenticity, which makes the purist Salafi appeal so powerful. They therefore tried to discredit him by criticizing his ḥadīth methodology.

TRADITIONALIST CRITICISMS OF ALBĀNĪ'S ḤADĪTH METHODOLOGY

To discredit Albānī's method of ḥadīth criticism Traditionalists tried to demonstrate that he differed with classical ḥadīth scholars. The debate surrounding Albānī's rejection of the Abū Zubayr narrations from Jābir in the *Ṣaḥīḥ* of Muslim highlights the critiques made against his ḥadīth methodology. The nature of the debate shifts from slogans to a more scholarly discussion. This is important because it illustrates that when the conversation moves beyond superficial slogans and accusations, the discussion becomes very technical. As a result, laypeople are unable to follow the discourse and might not even be interested. Hence, they are usually left to decide who to follow based on their trust of either Albānī or his critics. However, Albānī had two things on his side that might allow him a larger following: first is that his method and slogans are very simple and straightforward. Second, the methodology of Traditionalists is more complex, and is open to contested opinions that laypeople might find complex and inaccessible. While Albānī only weakened a few ḥadīth in the *Ṣaḥīḥ* of Bukhārī, he weakened many more in *Ṣaḥīḥ* Muslim.

He particularly weakens the ḥadīth that were narrated from Abū Zubayr through Jābir because Abū Zubayr used the term "from" (*ʿan*) when narrating from Jābir, instead of explicitly saying that he heard it (*sami'a*) from him. As a result, Albānī considered Abū Zubayr to be a *mudallis*, meaning one narrates a ḥadīth from someone he met, but did not necessarily hear the ḥadīth from him. *Tadlīs* occurs when a narrator transmits a ḥadīth despite not hearing it directly from the cited source. It is problematic because the person narrates it in a way that gives the impression that he heard it directly from his teacher. *Tadlīs* also occurs when a narrator does mention the name of his teacher or contemporary but uses a less-known name or nickname in order to not disclose the name of his teacher.

Therefore, Albānī regarded any ḥadīth in which Abū Zubayr narrates from Jābir to be weak. Albānī has two primary reasons for his weakening of the ḥadīth: first that some ḥadīth scholars considered Abū Zubayr to be a *mudallis*, and second because Abū Zubayr did not explicitly state whether or not he actually heard the ḥadīth from Jābir, but used the term "on the authority of" (*'an*) instead. Albānī notes that it is known in the science of ḥadīth that the narration of a *mudallis* was not relied upon unless he explicitly stated how he received it.[32] Albānī makes an exception to the narrations of Abū Zubayr from Jābir when the person narrating from Abū Zubayr is Layth b. Sa'd. Albānī states that Layth is reported to have said:

> I came to Abū Zubayr, and he gave me two books, and I was unhappy with them. Then I told myself: "If only I had revisited him and asked him if he heard this from Jābir?" So, I asked him. Then he said: "I heard some of it and was told some of it." I said: "Tell me what you heard of it." Then I said: "Tell me what you heard from him." So, he told me according to that which I have.[33]

Therefore, Albānī accepts all of the ḥadīth that contain Layth b. Sa'd from Abū Zubayr, from Jābir, because Layth explicitly noted that he only narrated what Abū Zubayr directly heard from Jābir. Albānī is consistent in his method and rejects all the ḥadīth from Abū Zubayr from Jābir unless they are narrated from Layth. Mamdūḥ notes that Abū Zubayr did not commit *tadlīs* because Abū Zubayr did not narrate to Layth, he only gave him some books as an *ijāza*, and *tadlīs* only occurs when he is narrating to him, not when he is handing him books. Mamdūḥ argues that Abū Zubayr handed his books over to Layth so he can read and copy them; if simply handing books to someone to read is considered *tadlīs*, then every ḥadīth scholar would be a

[32] N. Albānī, *S.A.D.*, 1: 161. Also see Kamaruddin Amin, "Nāṣiruddīn al-Albānī on Muslim's *Ṣaḥīḥ*: A Critical Study of His Method," *Islamic Law and Society*, 11, no. 2 (2004), 154.

[33] N. Albānī, *S.A.D.*, 1: 161.

mudallis.[34] Mamdūḥ also notes that Shuʿba b. al-Ḥajjāj (d. 160/776), who was one of the strictest scholars when it came to the issue of *tadlīs*, did not accuse Abū Zubayr of *tadlīs*. Shuʿba was known to not accept ḥadīth from his teachers who performed *tadlīs*, except what they heard. Mamdūḥ also quotes a narration where Shuʿba asks Abū Zubayr, who was standing next to the Kaʿba, to swear that he heard those ḥadīth from Jābir, and Abū Zubayr said three times: "By God I heard them from Jābir."[35] Interestingly, Shuʿba later criticized Abū Zubayr for other matters such as him not performing his prayers properly, or fabricating things about another Muslim, but he never accused him of being a *mudallis*.[36]

Several ḥadīth critics spoke highly of Abū Zubayr and make no mention of him performing *tadlīs*, among them are Bukhārī, Muslim, Ibn Ḥanbal, ʿAlī b. Al-Madīnī (d. 235/849), Yaḥyā b. Maʿīn (d. 233/847), al-Dāraquṭnī and others. It was only Abū ʿAbd al-Raḥmān al-Nasāʾī, the compiler of *Sunan al-Nasāʾī*, and later Ibn Ḥazm who accuse him of *tadlīs*; some later scholars followed them.[37] Mamdūḥ mentions these names in order to point out that classical ḥadīth scholars did not mention anything about Abū Zubayr being a *mudallis*, and therefore it is incorrect for anyone after them to accuse him of performing *tadlīs*. He then makes the amplified claim that a rejection of their opinion of Abū Zubayr's reliability is understood to be an undermining of their scholarship.

The difference between Albānī and Muslim is that Muslim did not use transmission terminology coined by the Successors as a definitive measure for determining a transmitter's reliability, but Muslim took other things into consideration. Albānī, on the other hand, used terminology as the decisive criterion for assessing the reliability of transmissions.[38] Therefore, he concluded that many ḥadīth that Muslim authenticated were weak because Muslim includes the *ʿan* transmissions in his book as well as ḥadīth where Abū Zubayr narrates from Jābir.

Kamaruddin Amin notes that while Albānī was consistent in applying his rejection of Abū Zubayr narrations, his method differed from that of Muslim.[39] Despite his consistency in the case of Abū Zubayr, Traditionalists maintain that he strayed from the traditional method because he did not follow the judgments of the early ḥadīth scholars. In the estimation of Traditionalists, the very fact that Muslim relied on Abū Zubayr is an attestation to his reliability as a ḥadīth narrator.

[34] M. Mamdūḥ, *Tanbīh*, 29–30. [35] M. Mamdūḥ, *Tanbīh*, 36. [36] M. Mamdūḥ, *Tanbīh*, 37.
[37] M. Mamdūḥ, *Tanbīh*, 39. [38] K. Amin, "Critical," 149. [39] K. Amin, "Critical," 151.

In the case of Abū Zubayr, Traditionalists try to discredit Albānī's scholarship based on his lack of research. They argue that Albānī does not weaken Abū Zubayr based on a comprehensive examination of his biography, but solely on the judgments of a few ḥadīth critics such as al-Dhahabī and Ibn Ḥazm.[40] Ḥadīth critics do not unanimously disparage Abū Zubayr; some of them consider him reliable. Mamdūḥ notes that in order to judge a ḥadīth, one must examine the entire history of a narrator and take into consideration what all of the major ḥadīth scholars said about him. The scholar must also take into consideration how the early ḥadīth scholars dealt with the narrator. This will result in a judgment being based on a comprehensive examination of what ḥadīth scholars said and how they treated a narrator.[41]

RELYING ON ABRIDGEMENTS

Because Albānī was a stern rejecter of weak ḥadīth one may have the impression that he was an overly cautious ḥadīth scholar. However, his critics accuse him of finding shortcuts to quickly determine the authenticity of ḥadīth. Amin's previous point that Albānī's judgments on narrators are not based on thorough research or analysis, but on the judgments of later ḥadīth critics, is echoed by Albānī's critics. Traditionalists, such as Mamdūḥ, attempt to discredit Albānī's scholarship not only because he lacks an *ijāza*, or traditional study, but also due to his relying on *mukhtaṣarāt* (abridged) works to judge narrators. Albānī himself has indicated in numerous places that he has relied on the authors of the *mukhtaṣar*s such as Ibn Ḥajar in judging ḥadīth narrators. He mentions this in the context of correcting a mistake he previously made in his *Silsilat al-Aḥādīth al-Ḍaʿīfa*. He explained that he mistakenly weakened a ḥadīth because Ibn Ḥajar stated that the narrator was weak and that no one considered the narrator to be reliable. However, it was brought to Albānī's attention that Ibn Ḥajar was mistaken and that other scholars considered the narrator to be reliable. Albānī excuses himself and acknowledges his mistake.[42] He highlights his willingness to correct his mistakes as evidence of his object and scholarly approach. He explains that the true researcher does not have a problem in changing his

[40] K. Amin, "Critical," 171. [41] M. Mamdūḥ, *Taʿrīf*, 1: 322.

[42] There are several occasions where Albānī acknowledges the mistakes he made in ḥadīth and corrects his position. However, one rarely, if ever, finds that he changes his *fiqh* opinions. This might be due to the fact that the science of ḥadīth is more factual and less interpretation takes place. These mistakes might include things such as confusing two narrators or their death dates. *Fiqh*, on the other hand is primarily interpretation and Albānī denied that he was interpreting.

opinion when new evidence is presented. He cites the example of al-Shāfiʿī who was known to have an old *madhhab* and a new *madhhab*.[43]

This outraged Traditionalists who were perplexed by how Albānī can compare his mistakes and lack of research to the *ijtihād* of al-Shāfiʿī. Mamdūḥ says that Albānī's ḥadīth judgments cannot be considered *ijtihād* because *ijtihād* necessitates that one who is qualified puts forth his utmost effort and has taken everything into consideration prior to making a judgment. Albānī's mistake is because he performs *taqlīd* of the most concise of handbooks, not after taking everything into consideration. Mamdūḥ states: "Where is the complete ability and effort put forth? Does the one who is fully qualified rely on the *Taqrīb*? Is looking into the *Taqrīb* considered looking into the *dalīl*?"[44] In other words, relying on abridgments is not considered a mistake in *ijtihād*, rather the mistake is a result of a lack of research. For Mamdūḥ, *ijtihād* is when the scholar makes a decision after exhausting all alternative options. He believes that Albānī relying on abridgments cannot be considered a form of *ijtihād*, but rather trying to find shortcuts. Saqqāf alleges that Albānī does not even rely on the *mukhtaṣar*s properly because he sometimes says that a narrator is not found in them, although the narrator is actually listed under his nickname (*kunya*).[45]

Additionally, Ṣalāḥ al-Dīn al-Idilbī argues that Albānī misunderstands the terminology in the abridgments. For example, when Ibn Ḥajar refers to a narrator as *ṣadūq* Albānī equates this with *thiqa*. When most of the narrators in the chain are *thiqa* and one is *ṣadūq*, Albānī generalizes it by saying the whole chain is full of *thiqa* narrators. Idilbī notes that by not differentiating between the different terminologies and levels of *ṣadūq*, and a *ṣadūq* and a *thiqa*, Albānī often authenticates ḥadīth that are actually weak.[46] Idilbī states:

> Some of those who studied with this conceded man say: "Ibn Ḥajar's referring to a narrator as *ṣadūq* means *thiqa*." If you ask him for a *dalīl* for that, he asks you for a *dalīl* against it!!! This is not accepted, because the evidence is on the claimant, but he does not know the difference between the claimant and defender because of his lack of attention to the science of *fiqh*.[47]

[43] N. Albānī, *S.A.D.*, 1: 5.

[44] M. Mamdūḥ, *Taʿrīf*, 1: 327. Mamdūḥ is referring to Ibn Ḥajar's *Taqrīb*, which is an abridged work mentioning only the very basic information on ḥadīth narrators.

[45] H. Saqqāf, *Tanāqaḍāt*, 1: 23.

[46] Ṣalāḥ al-Dīn Idilbī, *Kashf al-Maʿlūl Mimā Summiyya bi Silsilat al-Aḥādīth al-Ṣahīḥa* (Amman: Dār al-Fatḥ lil dirāsāt wa l-nashr, 2011), 8.

[47] S. Idilbī, *Kashf*, 8.

This further agitated Traditionalists, who see Albānī's efforts as a promotion of himself as a great ḥadīth scholar while simultaneously relying on abridgements. In this case, it is Traditionalists who accuse Albānī of performing *taqlīd*, not of a certain method or school of thought, but of an abridged work. Traditionalists maintain that one who took it upon himself to purify the religion is at the very least expected to do his research and not simply rely on abridgments. They point out his mistakes in order to attack his scholarship, make him appear as an amateur scholar, and delegitimize his criticisms against Traditionalism. After noting some of Albānī's alleged contradictions, Saqqāf addresses Albānī's admirers and followers and states:

> Let those merchant researchers and others from among those who rely on the books of this shaykh [Albānī] and quote from them reflect on all of these clear contradictions. They say: Albānī has authenticated it and Albānī has weakened it!! Have you commentators been deceived by his flashy advertisement?!! What is the explanation for these hundreds of contradictions? Why should we not rely on the great imams and genius *ḥuffāẓ* from whose books this Albanian himself quoted instead of relying on his contradicting books?!![48]

Albānī's reliance on abridgments to quickly make judgments on ḥadīth perhaps inspired a brand of "do it yourself" Islam. Whereas Traditionalists view Islamic sciences as complex and require years of study at the hands of scholars, Albānī's method characterizes Islamic sciences to be a more straightforward endeavor. His critics argued that his heavy reliance on simple biographical dictionaries and differing with earlier scholars on ḥadīth terminology was bound to yield many errors in judgment.

Traditionalists like Saqqāf and Mamdūḥ consider the reliance on *mukhtaṣars* and quick grading of ḥadīth to be grave mistakes, and the fact that Albānī often acknowledges his swiftness in grading a ḥadīth for publication reasons only makes it worse. Saqqāf makes a more personal and petty attack on Albānī, accusing him of being one who is only trying to make money. He questions how Albānī, who is so concerned with providing Muslims with what is authentic, scientific, and objective, quickly grades ḥadīth just to get the books published? Saqqāf condemns Albānī for this and concludes that Albānī did not really care for the science of ḥadīth, but for money. Saqqāf argues that Albānī publishing a second version with the reexamination of the ḥadīth once more is another indication that he is simply trying to sell more books for materialistic purposes.[49] He maintains that what is most

[48] H. Saqqāf, *Tanāqaḍāt*, 1: 19. [49] H. Saqqāf, *Tanāqaḍāt*, 1: 31.

detrimental is that Albānī relies on one or two books to grade narrators, and then divides the classical Sunan based on poor research. In other words, since his judgments on narrators must not be accepted because they are poorly researched, by extension his judgments on the authenticity of ḥadīth must also be rejected. Yet, because laypeople do not have the training to understand what he is doing, they may be deceived by him. Saqqāf explains that the damage is already done because "this has already happened."[50] It was Albānī's method to grade every single ḥadīth in each book he wrote or commented on. Because some of the books he wrote or commented on had hundreds and sometimes thousands of ḥadīth, he may have occasionally relied on abridgments. However, contrary to the critiques of his detractors, it is highly unlikely that this was his consistent practice.

EARLY VS. LATE ḤADĪTH SCHOLARSHIP

After noting that Bukhārī uses a ḥadīth that contains Abū Zubayr in one of his chapter titles, Mamdūḥ states: "It is as if these masters, Bukhārī the leader of this field, and other scholars did not pay attention to this defect that was noticed by Albānī, who is of the late modern era!!"[51] This pattern of argumentation and accusing Albānī of thinking he has outdone other scholars is consistent among his critics. Moreover, Mamdūḥ quotes a number of scholars, such as Nawawī, who argue that any *tadlīs* found in the *Ṣaḥīḥayn* is understood to have another completely connected chain. However, Bukhārī or Muslim chose to use the chain that contains *tadlīs* because the narrators meet their conditions, unlike the chain that is complete. Mamdūḥ also argues that it is also understood that Muslim knew from another source that the *mudallis* heard the ḥadīth directly.[52] This understanding stems from the assumption that earlier ḥadīth scholars had more information at their disposal than later scholars, and hence they have an upper hand in grading ḥadīth. Several Traditionalists follow Ibn al-Ṣalāḥ Abū ʿAmr ʿUthmān b. ʿAbd al-Raḥmān (d. 643/1245), who states: "The way to know the authentic and acceptable is to rely on what was compiled by the scholars of ḥadīth in their compilations which are reliable and known, and are protected (because of their

[50] H. Saqqāf, *Tanāqaḍāt*, 1: 201. [51] M. Mamdūḥ, *Tanbīh*, 45.
[52] M. Mamdūḥ, *Tanbīh*, 53–54.

being well known) from change and alteration."[53] For Ibn Ṣalāḥ, the purpose of *isnād* after the initial period of ḥadīth compilation was only for blessings.

In his classic introduction to the science of ḥadīth, Ibn Ṣalāḥ makes the argument that scholars can no longer grade the authenticity or weakness of ḥadīth; instead they must accept the judgments of earlier ḥadīth scholars. For many Traditionalists, the science of ḥadīth is really an attempt to understand the activity of ḥadīth criticism: the practical activity of the early generation of ḥadīth scholars such as Yaḥyā b. Maʿīn, ʿAlī b. al-Madīnī, Aḥmad b. Ḥanbal, Bukhārī, and Muslim. Both Salafis and Traditionalists consider such figures to be scholars who had unmatched insight and knowledge in the field of ḥadīth. Consequently, the science of ḥadīth was developed as an attempt to have a blind man's stick to guide those who do not have that kind of insight and experience, and this is essentially what Ibn Ṣalāḥ attempted to do in his classical *Muqaddima*. The judgments of the early ḥadīth scholars were developed by studying the narrations of each ḥadīth and all of its chains of transmission. This kind of experience, along with their scholarly achievements, led to a sense that allowed them to identify the level of reliability of a ḥadīth. This, according to Ibn Ṣalāḥ, no longer exists.

Ibn Ṣalāḥ and some Traditionalists maintain that the early ḥadīth scholars had a special sense in ḥadīth that they developed from long study and wide exposure in authenticating and weakening. Then, later scholars derived rules from their practices. Therefore, Ibn Ṣalāḥ argued that later scholars are naturally disadvantaged and cannot use these rules to judge those from whose practice these rules were derived. Not all ḥadīth scholars agreed with Ibn Ṣalāḥ, but some Traditionalists adopted a similar position. In theory, many of them agreed that one can question and reexamine ḥadīth. However, when it came to Albānī they often criticized him for reexamining the works of Bukhārī and Muslim.

Some Traditionalists argue that modern scholars, especially those who are untrained, do not have the abilities or the scholarly skills to authenticate or weaken ḥadīth. They argue that ascertaining the absence of hidden defects – one of the conditions of authenticity – is extremely difficult amongst later scholars.[54] For example, how would a later scholar know whether the

[53] Ibn al-Ṣalāḥ Abū ʿAmr ʿUthmān b. ʿAbd al-Raḥmān, *Muqaddimat Ibn Ṣalāḥ fī ʿUlūm al-Ḥadīth* (Beirut: Dar Al-Kotob Al-ʿIlmiyah, 2003), 25–26.

[54] See, for example, Aḥmad Khalīl, *Mustadrak al-Taʿlīl ʿalā Arwāʾ al-Ghalīl* (Saudi Arabia: Dār Ibn al-Jawzī, 2008).

narrators in a chain were reading from their books or reciting the ḥadīth from memory, both of which affect the status of a ḥadīth? How can a later scholar judge a ḥadīth in the same way as earlier scholars? They argue that later scholars are disadvantaged because they could only reexamine written statements. Early scholars had the advantage of meeting the narrators and graded not only their memory, but their probity as well. It could be argued that neither of these conditions will ever be completely known to later scholars as they were to earlier ones, especially the condition of probity.

If we assume that this is the method ḥadīth scholars used to judge the scholarly accuracy of narrators, there is the likely possibility that not everything was written down. Therefore, early ḥadīth scholars might have been aware of different chains that make a narrator stronger or weaker; later scholars might not have all of this information. As a result, modern scholars are limited and can only rely on the judgment of the early ḥadīth critics. It may be accurate that earlier scholars had certain advantages, but does this necessitate that later scholars are completely unable to contribute to the authentication of ḥadīth, especially when they use the same evidence used by early scholars? How does one discern between an earlier scholar making a mistake and his having evidence unknown to later scholars? Furthermore, what is the proper method of determining which scholars are considered early, and others late?

In judging the probity of a narrator, the only thing modern scholars can do is rely on sources written by early ḥadīth scholars and this puts them at a disadvantage. Since later scholars rely on, and generally accept, the judgments of early ḥadīth scholars on narrators, by extension some Traditionalists argue that one should also accept their judgments on ḥadīth. They maintain that early ḥadīth scholars would give their judgments on narrators after grading their ḥadīths first. One cannot accept the former and leave the latter without falling into a contradiction. In a sense, Traditionalists insist on a form of *taqlīd*, or trust, in the grading of the earlier scholars. On the other hand, Albānī does his best to review everything he could in order to make decisions himself.

The modern ḥadīth scholar Ḥamza al-Malībārī states that the difference between early and late scholars is not in time, but in methodology. He states that the methodology of "later scholars" allows authenticating and weakening based on a cursory examination of the *isnād* and the grades of the narrators. Additionally, they strengthen a ḥadīth by finding other ḥadīth that serve as corroborations and attestations, without looking into whether the ḥadīth really do corroborate. As long as there is no liar or narrator who is abandoned in the chain, the methodology of "later scholars" will find this ḥadīth acceptable. According to Malībārī this method was developed after the time of narrators of ḥadīth. The method of "early scholars" depends on the judgments of the earlier generations, regardless of what might be suggested by the superficial aspect of the *isnād*. In other words, Malībārī would consider modern ḥadīth scholars to be going against the methodology of the "early scholars" if they only use the *isnād* and disregard the judgments of Muslim and other scholars of the time.[55] He quotes Ibn Ḥajar who says:

> Whenever we find a ḥadīth that an early scholar, from among the scholars who are relied on, has judged to be weak, then following him takes precedence, just as we would follow him in the authentication of a ḥadīth if he authenticates it. Al-Shāfiʿī, despite his great scholarship defers to the scholars of ḥadīth in his books when he says: "And there is a ḥadīth about the topic which has not been verified by the scholars of ḥadīth."[56]

By asserting himself as a ḥadīth scholar of the highest caliber, Traditionalists accuse Albānī of causing people to doubt the findings of centuries of institutional scholarship. Albānī not only criticized modern Traditionalists but attacked their scholarly institutions. By doing so, Traditionalists claim that he has caused many people to turn away from the great scholars of Islam and follow him instead. Ṣalāḥ al-Dīn al-Idilbī summarizes the effect Albānī had on many in the Muslim world and why this outraged Traditionalists. Idilbī states:

> One of the researchers has put in great effort in this regard [the science of ḥadīth] after looking expansively at the books of narrators, but he is deficient in the understanding of this science. So, he authenticated, weakened, commented, and compiled hadith, and it gives the impression that he belongs among the scholars of this science. Even to the degree that some of them turned away from the peerless scholars' words and confined themselves to this researcher's words, so they have exchanged that which is better for that which is lower.[57]

Saqqāf says that when laypeople begin to question the works of scholars like Bukhārī and Muslim, they will logically also begin to argue, deny, and ultimately reject them. Saqqāf ends the first volume of his *Tanāquḍāt* by

[55] Ḥumza al-Malībārī, *Al-Muwāzana Bayn al-Mutaqaddimīn wa l-Mutaʾkhirīn fī Taṣḥīḥ al-Aḥādīth wa Taʿlīli-hā* (Beirut: Dār Ibn Ḥazm, 2001), 17–18.

[56] Ibn Ḥajar al-ʿAsqalānī, *Al-Nukat ʿalā kitāb Ibn Ṣalāḥ* (Medina: Islamic University of Medina, 1984), 2: 711; H. Malībārī, *Muwāzana*, 18.

[57] S. Idilbī, *Kashf*, 7.

demanding Albānī clarify his mistakes and publicly recant his opinions so that laypeople not be deceived by him. He states:

> You must publish, clean, and constrict your books, then publicize this to the Muslims and say: "This is what I had and thought was correct." It is not permitted for you under any circumstances to claim that your opponents are misguided and describe them as the enemies of the Sunna and *tawḥīd*, as it has been confirmed by you. And you must not make people think that they must follow your teachings.[58]

Saqqāf recognizes that laypeople will most likely not read the scholarly arguments made against Albānī, and for that reason he asks him to recognize his mistakes and publicly recant them. In order to tarnish Albānī's reputation, Traditionalists attempt to show how he actually goes against the early scholars in whose footsteps he claims to follow.

Although Albānī approaches Islamic scholarly disciplines with a sense of skepticism because they were passed down through Traditionalist institutions, at the same time he depends on and draws from this tradition. Even though he does not trust the Traditionalist institution and accuses them of being blind followers, by putting his faith in the science of ḥadīth criticism, he is implicitly putting his faith in the institution of Traditionalists.

ALBĀNĪ'S IMPACT ON MODERN ḤADĪTH STUDIES

Despite the many attempts to discredit his scholarship, Albānī had a significant impact on the study of ḥadīth in the modern era. His scholarly career began with a petition for Traditionalists to abandon the *madhhab*s and follow Islam as it is preserved in scripture. However, his insistence that nobody has the right to quote a ḥadīth without evaluating it had the greatest impact. Historical sensibility balks at the idea of one person changing the course of history. However, Albānī's impact on the field of ḥadīth studies in the modern era makes it challenging to deny the fact that he played a major role in changing the field of ḥadīth studies in the last few decades.[59] Albānī was extremely efficient in grading ḥadīth, which led to a level of productivity unforeseen in modern history. Most of the controversy surrounding Albānī was not about his ḥadīth scholarship, but rather his legal rulings. His ḥadīth methodology is not much different than other Sunni ḥadīth scholars. He

[58] H. Saqqāf, *Tanāqaḍāt*, 1: 201.

[59] Ghassan Abdul-Jabbar, "The Classical Tradition," in *The Wiley Blackwell Concise Companion to the Hadith*, ed. Daniel Brown (Hoboken, NJ: John Wiley & Sons, 2019), 35–36.

often complained about how many scholars and writers did not cite ḥadīth or note their level of authenticity.

When we consider Albānī's contribution to ḥadīth studies compared to other works in the nineteenth and twentieth centuries, we find that Albānī started a trend of grading and citing ḥadīth that had not been done regularly before. Many authors would comment and explain a ḥadīth at great length while it was considered as fabricated. Outside of the canonical ḥadīth books, not all ḥadīth were graded. Furthermore, Albānī often discovered ḥadīth from neglected sources of rare manuscripts. When Albānī encountered ḥadīth outside of the canonical ḥadīth corpus, such as in *Tarīkh Ibn ʿAsākir*, he was sometimes the only scholar to offer grading of the ḥadīth.

How did these books exist for centuries without anyone grading their ḥadīth? Prior to the introduction of the printing press in the Muslim world, these books were primarily read by scholars. These scholars did not see the need to stamp or grade every ḥadīth since the only people with access to these texts were those who had already passed a high entry barrier and could do the grading themselves.

In order to revive the importance of ḥadīth authenticity Albānī tried to adhere to the method of ḥadīth verification as found in classical works on the science of ḥadīth. In one of his earliest articles, Albānī explains how one can verify the level of authenticity of a particular ḥadīth. He states:

> The student is to examine the *isnād* and its individual narrators, and then pronounce a judgment on its authenticity or weakness using the rules and principles of the science of ḥadīth without blindly following a particular imam in his authenticating or weakening. This is something rare in these times and unfortunately there are only a few people who practice it.[60]

Albānī argues that if all scholars make this effort, the Sunna will be pure. His practice of reexamining the authenticity of every ḥadīth had an impact in several ways. He inspired university students to follow his practice, although Traditionalists thought that the reexamination of ḥadīth is beyond Albānī's reach, let alone ordinary university students. Additionally, prior to Albānī, it was not the habit of Traditionalists to mention the grade of a ḥadīth in their books unless it was fabricated. However, after Albānī we find that many authors, even his critics, started citing and grading each ḥadīth. They perhaps did this because Albānī initiated a scholarly trend of demanding ḥadīth be both cited and graded in all books.

[60] Muḥammad Nāṣir al-Dīn al-Albānī, *Wujūb al-Tafaqquh fī l-Ḥadīth*, www.alalbany.net/4935, last accessed July 1, 2014.

Suhaib Hasan explained that in the 1960s, people used to follow the rulings of scholars like Bukhārī, Muslim, and others on ḥadīth. For a modern person to present his rulings on the four Sunan and other books was a major problem for many scholars. He said: "They used to say the knowledge of ḥadīth was cooked, eaten and digested. There was no room, and no one thought that a man will come and give rulings on ḥadīth."[61] Essentially, Albānī started cooking all over again. Suhaib Hasan continues:

> Albānī was unique in that he used to give rulings about ḥadīth and classified them into *ṣaḥīḥ* and *ḍaʿīf*. This is something that was not practiced by any other *muḥaddith* of the time, so his rulings sometimes differed with the previous scholars, like the four traditionalists Tirmidhī, Ibn Māja, Abū Dāwūd, and Nasāʾī, and those who came after them like Ibn Ḥajar. His uniqueness was that he was giving rulings on ḥadīth and going against scholars who were known to be masters in ḥadīth attracted criticism.[62]

Albānī's challenge of Traditionalists pressured them to go back to the basics and explain and defend their entire methodology. Furthermore, Albānī would encourage his students and common Muslims to question other scholars about the authenticity of ḥadīth they used. Albānī was holding scholars accountable by their congregations and audiences by empowering individuals to question the authenticity of ḥadīth. This, in turn, led many scholars to use only authentic ḥadīth or justify their use of a weak ḥadīth in their sermons and lessons. Even Muḥammad al-Ghazālī, a Modernist, felt the need to justify why he went against Albānī's grading of ḥadīth. Ghazālī published a book on the life of the Prophet and invited Albānī to include his comments on the authenticity of the ḥadīth. Ghazālī cautions the readers that they will notice some instances where Albānī grades certain ḥadīth as weak, but Ghazālī still uses them. He justifies this by noting that although the *isnād* may have some issues, the meaning is in conformity with the Qurʾān.

Ghazālī states that Albānī may not believe the ḥadīth to be authentic because of its *isnād*, but if it is in conformity with a Qurʾānic verse or an authentic ḥadīth it should be accepted. Hence, there is no harm in narrating such a ḥadīth since it is not adding anything new to the religion. He states that a weak ḥadīth could be acted upon as long as it is in conformity with the general principles of the religion. Ghazālī goes further than others and even rejects an authentic ḥadīth if he perceives its meaning to contradict the

[61] Suhaib Hasan, Interview by author. [62] Suhaib Hasan, Interview by author.

Qur'ān.[63] This is problematic because it replaces the *isnād* with the perception of individuals concerning what conforms to the meaning of the Qur'ān. It also does away with the works of earlier ḥadīth scholars and leaves it up to the modern jurist to decide a ḥadīth authenticity. Interestingly, although Ghazālī's approach is the complete opposite of Albānī's, they were both accused of disregarding the works of earlier scholars and placing themselves as the final authorities on ḥadīth authenticity.[64] Ghazālī goes on to say that he is not the first to follow this methodology, but the majority of scholars dealt with weak ḥadīth in this manner. Ghazālī requested Albānī's assistance but then chose to not follow it because he viewed the role of ḥadīth scholars to be limited to the isnād. On the other hand, legal scholars decide on the applicability of the ḥadīth.

This was not only an issue of *madhhab*s, but more an issue of hermeneutics. Albānī preferred textual conformity, while his critics preferred historical realism. One might wonder why Traditionalists, and even Modernists, felt the need to justify why they went against Albānī's grading of particular ḥadīth? This was perhaps because Albānī was one of the few scholars who concerned himself with the reexamination of ḥadīth. He garnered the reputation of being the greatest ḥadīth scholar of the twentieth century. Although they believed themselves to be refuting Albānī, Traditionalists also submitted to his mode of arguing. This is not to say that they changed their methodology, but Albānī forced them to start proving to the laity that their positions were based on authentic proof-texts.

Therefore, Albānī must be credited with sparking a renewed interest in the study of the authenticity of ḥadīth. For purist Salafis, Albānī plays the role of a *mujaddid.* Traditionalists did not accept him as such and hence had to defeat him at his own game of authenticating and weakening of ḥadīth. Because some Traditionalists did not challenge the judgments of the earlier scholars, there was never a reexamination of ḥadīth. Albānī's reexamination of ḥadīth forced his critics, who generally were not interested in such a thing, to also review the ḥadīth, even if it was only to refute him. Albānī revived the practice of *taṣḥīḥ* and *taḍ'īf,* which was not always practiced by Traditionalists. This should not be misunderstood to mean that there were no ḥadīth scholars until Albānī's arrival, but that the ḥadīth scholars did not

[63] Muḥammad al-Ghazālī, *Fiqh al-Sīra* (Cairo: Dār al-Shurūq, 2000), 11–17.

[64] For instance, Salmān al-'Awda criticized Ghazālī for rejecting the ḥadīth that notes a woman's bloodmoney is half of a man. 'Awda's reasoning is that many earlier scholars have authenticated this ḥadīth and accused Ghazālī of contradicting these leading scholars. See Salmān al-'Awda, *Fī Ḥiwār Hādī' ma' Muḥammad al-Ghazālī* (Buraydah: n.p., 1989), 66–67.

challenge the judgments of the early ḥadīth scholars in the same manner as Albānī. Albānī promoted the study of *isnād*s by insisting that anyone who quotes a ḥadīth provide its level of authenticity. Whether supporters or detractors, everyone had to hit the books and that is why many scholars appreciate him for reviving interest in the authentication of ḥadīth. Certainly, this led to some shallow scholarship, but in refuting it, people came face to face with the actual works of the ḥadīth scholars instead of just repeating their previous findings.

Conclusion

THIS BOOK TRACED THE ORIGINS AND MANIFESTATION OF THE tensions between purist Salafis and Traditionalists. Frustrated with the religious, social, and political circumstances of the twentieth century, purist Salafis attempted to purge Islamic tradition in order to secure a pure version of Islam. The fall of the Ottoman Empire played a major role in shifting the religious paradigm that was present in the Muslim world. Traditionalists losing the support of the state and their monopoly over education provided other groups, such as Salafis, the opportunity to rise and challenge Traditionalist institutions. When Traditionalists lost the support of the state, they were uncertain of what would unfold and what their role in society would become. This uncertainty led many of them to rigidly adhere to Traditionalism because it was the only system they knew and trusted. This resulted in a culture of strict *madhhab*ism where some Traditionalists adhered to the *madhhab*s in an uncompromising and uncritical manner. Furthermore, Traditionalists garnered the reputation of being outdated and unable to provide solutions to the swift changes that were taking place in the Muslim world. Leading Salafis emerged from this environment and they criticized the *madhhab*s as a source of division in the Muslim community.

The shift in educational practices also played a role in facilitating the prevalence of Salafi critiques of Traditionalism. The change in the nature of Islamic education was crucial to the emergence of purist Salafis as authorities because prior to that scholars who bypassed the system might not have been given much consideration. Moreover, the rise of the printing press and the accessibility of books allowed intellectual Muslims to access knowledge without teachers and propagate their ideas directly to the public. Purist Salafism inspired a critical approach toward scholarly tradition and contributed to the creation of new religious scholars who mostly find their audience through print, cassettes, television, and now the internet. This expanded the number of people who can participate in religious dialogue and rendered irrelevant and unworkable the traditional mechanisms for regulating access to scholarly status. The autodidactic method of many purist Salafis, along with their sometimes callous interactions with other Muslims, led them to be regarded as iconoclasts who lacked scholarly etiquette. Their purist approach toward Islam led them to clash with all those who disagreed with their particular understanding of Islam. Purist Salafism found its appeal in simplicity and heavy textual reference. The arguments of Traditionalists were not simplistic and often involved much scholarly discourse; this naturally meant that they lost the appealing element of simplicity.

I also examined the role of tradition from the perspectives of purist Salafis and Traditionalists in order to highlight the repercussions of this intra-religious contact. Purist Salafis and Traditionalists both held scripture to be the most authoritative reference; however, Traditionalists believed that the understanding of scripture was best found in the *madhhab*s and scholarly tradition. Purist Salafis based authority upon neither school of law nor teacher, but rather based it solely in scripture. Of all Salafis, Albānī was the most vocal anti-*madhhab*ist scholar. He advanced his own scripture-based understanding of Islam by removing himself from the interpretative process and presenting his understandings as the direct teachings of the Qurʾān and Sunna.

Albānī's differences with Traditionalists stem from his belief that his understanding of scripture is the absolute truth. The crux of the purist Salafi argument against Traditionalists is their reluctance to reevaluate the positions of the legal schools in light of authentic scripture, especially ḥadīth. Purist Salafis like Albānī launched their polemic against Traditionalists by discrediting their legal methodology and accusing them of favoring the judgments of the *madhab*s over the authentic Sunna. Traditionalists responded by attempting to discredit Salafis by highlighting their self-learning and accusing them of trying to overshadow the classical scholars of Islam, most of whom belonged to such institutions.

The straightforward proof-text approach of Salafism inspired nonscholars to consistently demand scriptural evidence from scholars. The appeal of Salafism was in removing the human element from the interpretive process. While Traditionalists consider this to be unscholarly, the anti-hierarchical and individually empowering hermeneutics of Salafism correlate well with many Muslims in the modern world.

Unlike Traditionalists, Albānī did not have a school of law, or a teacher, in which he found authority. Hence, he ultimately outdid those who found their authority in a *madhhab* by claiming that his authority was not in any school of law or scholar, but in the words of God and the Prophet. In order to establish himself as a scholar who has absolute truth on his side, he needed to present himself as a scholar who persevered in the path of the truth, almost like an Ibn Ḥanbal-type figure. Certainly, by arguing that he is following the Qurʾān and Sunna and others were not, he was bound to clash with other scholars because he believed his understanding to be the final word. His critics believe that there is a large "fictional element" when Albānī implies that no one has understood Islam correctly except the Prophet, early Muslims, and himself.[1]

In the estimation of purist Salafis, teachings are not correct simply because they are traditional or part of a scholarly heritage. Conversely, Traditionalists assume that the tradition is guided by God, and following of any another path will destroy the religion. However, in Islamic history, there were scholars and schools who did not follow the four *madhhab*s, yet the religion was not destroyed. Albānī assumes that foreign elements enter Islam only by the scholarly class accepting weak ḥadīth but does not take into account other avenues such as lay individuals who have spiritual experiences that are not supported by a ḥadīth.

In an attempt to address the problems presented by modernity, Albānī and his critics have resorted to solutions where texts became the main source of legitimacy. Albānī considered any form of moral thought or legal judgment that was not entirely based on scripture as a form of self-legislation or heretical innovation in the religion. He approached much of Islamic history and scholarship with the understanding that they have been contaminated by foreign elements. Traditionalists and purist Salafis created systems they believed to be self-sufficient and incapable of engaging with others except from a dominating position. Both these groups were not overly concerned with politics, but instead viewed each other as the primary enemy that is out to destroy the religion. Traditionalists and purist Salafis believe that God will ultimately preserve the religion, and that it will never be destroyed or go off the straight path. They present each other as a threat to the stability of true Islam. Although they both rightfully try to correct what they perceive as incorrect, they tend to exaggerate the threat presented by the other side.

For Albānī, the *madhhab*s contaminated Islam with opinions that conflicted with "pure" Islam and he took it upon himself to clean it up. His deconstruction of the Traditionalist methodology in *fiqh* and ḥadīth was

[1] See Nuh Ha Mim Keller, "Who or What Is a Salafi and Is Their Approach Valid?," Masʿud Ahmed Khan's Home Page, www.masud.co.uk/ISLAM/nuh/salafi.htm, last accessed June 17, 2017.

done in an attempt to construct his own ḥadīth-based *fiqh*. Albānī essentially partakes in the same things he criticizes Traditionalists for, such as *taqlīd* and forming his own *madhhab*. The difference is that he presents it under the guise of *ittibāʿ* and the following of the Qurʾān and Sunna. Despite the point that Albānī recreated the wheel by forming his own *madhhab*, he singlehandedly revived a new interest in the authentication of ḥadīth. Although this might have resulted in shallow scholarship from both sides in comparison to earlier works, Albānī forced his critics to rethink their own methodologies, even if they did so only to refute him. Additionally, Albānī's demand for the use of authentic ḥadīth created a sense awareness among Muslims concerning the ḥadīth they used.

Ultimately, what Albānī and strict Traditionalists have in common is a conviction that they are the only possessors of the absolute truth. Purist Salafism and strict Traditionalism ultimately balance each other at a communal level. Perhaps this balancing of each other caused a more scriptural-based form of Traditionalism to emerge. It would certainly make an interesting study to examine whether Albānī's scripturally based challenge to Traditionalism caused Traditionalists to become more textual or proof-text oriented. Prior to Albānī scholars rarely indicated the grade of a ḥadīth in their works, but today citing the source and grade of ḥadīth in works appears to be a general trend among Traditionalists. This book will hopefully serve as a springboard for future research on Salafism and Traditionalism. Finally, it is important to note that although part of their differences might stem from a struggle for scholarly authority, it is not intended, nor is it correct to interpret all their differences as going back to sectarian image or scholarly jurisdiction. Doing so takes away from the existence of actual scholarly substance to their differences highlighted in this book. At the core of their differences was their conflicting perspectives on the place of tradition in Islam.

Bibliography

ʿAbd al-Ḥamīd, ʿAlī. *Maʿa Shaykhi-nā Nāṣir al-Sunna wa l-Dīn Muḥammad Nāṣir al-Dīn al-Albānī Mujaddid al-Qarn, wa Muḥaddith al-ʿAṣr fī Shuhūr Ḥayāti-hi al-Akhīra* (Ra's al-Khayma: Maktabat Dār al-Ḥadith, n.d.).

Abdul-Jabbar, Ghassan. "The Classical Tradition," in *The Wiley Blackwell Concise Companion to the Hadith*, ed. Daniel Brown (Hoboken, NJ: John Wiley & Sons, 2019), 15–38.

ʿĀbidīn, Muḥammad Amīn b. (d. 1252/1836). *Ḥāshiyat Ibn ʿĀbidīn: Radd al-Muḥtār ʿalā al-Durr al-Mukhtār* (Damascus: Dār al-Thaqāfah wa l-Turāth, 2000).

Abū Dāwūd, Sulaymān b. al-Ashʿath al-Sijistānī (d. 275/889). *Sunan Abī Dāwūd* (Damascus: Dār al-Risāla al-ʿĀlamīya, 2009).

Abū Ghudda, ʿAbd al-Fattāḥ (d. 1997). *Al-Isnād Min al-Dīn* (Aleppo: Maktabat al-Maṭbūʿāt al-Islāmiyya, 1996).

Jawāb al-Ḥāfiẓ Abī Muḥammad ʿAbd al-ʿAẓīm al-Mundhirī al-Miṣrī ʿAn Asʾilah fī l-Jarḥ wa l-Taʿdīl: wa-Yalīh Umarāʾ al-Muʾminīn fī al-Ḥadīth wa-Kalimāt fī Kashf abāṭīl wa iftirāʾāt (Aleppo: Maktab al-Maṭbūʿāt al-Islāmīyah, 1990).

Kalimāt fī Kashf Abāṭīl wa Iftirāʿāt (Aleppo: Maktabat al-Maṭbūʿāt al-Islāmiyya, 1990).

Khuṭbat al-Ḥāja Laysat Sunna fī Mustahal al-Kutub wa l-Muʾallafāt (Beirut: Dār al-Bashāʾir al-Islāmiyya, 2008).

Lecture in Turkey, lecture from www.youtube.com/watch?v=dobft16fNe8, last accessed December 20, 2016.

Namādhij Min Rasāʾil al-Aʾimmat al-Salaf wa Adabi-him al-ʿilmī (Beirut: Dār al-Bashāʾir al-Islāmiyya, 1996).

Abū Rayya, Maḥmūd (d. 1970). *Aḍwāʾ ʿalā al-Sunna al-Muḥammadiyya* (Cairo: Dār al-Maʿārif, 1980).

Abu Rumman, Mohammad, and Abu Hanieh, Hassan. *Conservative Salafism: A Strategy for the "Islamization of Society" and an Ambiguous Relationship with the State* (Amman: Friedrich-Ebert-Stiftung, 2010).

ʿAfānā, Jawād. *Ṣaḥīḥ Ṣaḥīḥ al-Bukhārī* (Beirut: Dār al-Jawād lil Nashr, 2003).

Afsaruddin, Asma, and Brown, Jonathan. "How Islamic Is Isis, Really?," Here & Now, Boston NPR News Station (Boston, MA: WBUR, November 19, 2015).

Åkesson, Joyce. *Arabic Morphology and Phonology: Based on the Marāḥ al-arwāḥ by Aḥmad b. ʿAlī b. Masʿud* (Leiden: Brill, 2001).

Āl Rashīd, Muḥammad b. ʿAbd Allāh. *Imdād al-Fattāḥ bi-Asānīd wa-Marwīyāt al-Shaykh ʿAbd al-Fattāḥ: wa-huwa Thabat al-ʿAllāma al-Muḥaddith al-Faqīh al-Uṣūlī al-Adīb al-Musnid Faḍīlat al-Shaykh ʿAbd al-Fattāḥ Abū Ghudda* (Riyadh: Maktabat al-Imām al-Shāfiʿī, 1999).

Albānī (al-), Muḥammad Nāṣir al-Dīn (d. 1999). *Ādāb al-Zafāf fī l-Sunna al-Muṭahhara* (Amman: Al-Maktaba al-Islāmiyya, 1988).

"Aḥwāl al-Ijtihād waʾl-Ittibāʾ waʾl-Taqlīd," lecture from www.islamweb.net, last accessed January 24, 2012.

"Al-ʿAmal bi l-Ḥadīth al-Ḍaʿīfa," lecture from www.youtube.com/watch?v=VZHWdFx5L4M&feature=youtu.be, last accessed April 13, 2018.

Al-ʿAqīda al-Ṭaḥāwiyya Sharḥ wa Taʿlīq (n.p.: n.d.).

Aṣl Ṣifat Ṣalāt al-Nabī Min al-Takbīr ilā al-Taslīm Kaʾanaka Tarā-hā (Riyadh: Maktabat al-Maʿārif, 2006).

Ḍaʿīf al-Adab al-Mufrad li l-Imām al-Bukhārī (Jubayl al-Sināʿīya: Maktabat al-Dalīl, 1998).

Difāʿ ʿan al-Ḥadīth al-Nabawwī wa l-Sīra fī l-Radd ʿalā Jahālāt al-Būṭī fī kitābi-hi Fiqh al-Sīra (Damascus: Manshūrāt Muʾassasat wa Muhtabat al-Khāfiqīr, 1977).

"Al-Farq Bayna al-Ijtihād wa al-Taqlīd," lecture from www.youtube.com/watch?v=IS2Xhr7ZBfY, last accessed February 28, 2018.

"Fī l-Masʾala Qawlān," lecture from www.islamway.com, last accessed January 10, 2012.

Ghāyat al-Marām fī Takhrīj Aḥādīth al-Ḥalāl wa l-Ḥarām (Beirut: al-Maktab al-Islāmī, 1980).

Al-Ḥadīth Ḥujja Binafsi-hi fī l-ʿAqāʾid wa l-Aḥkām (Riyadh: Maktabat al-Maʿārif, 2005).

Ḥajjat al-Nabī (Beirut: Al-Maktab al-Islāmī, 1985).

"Ittibāʾ Sayyid al-Umma Ṣallā Allāhu ʿalay-hi wa sallam 1," lecture from www.ar.islamway.net/lesson/47201/, last accessed November 9, 2011.

Jilbāb al-Marʾa al-Muslima fī l-Kitāb wa l-Sunna (Riyadh: Dār al-Salām, 2002).

"Kalimat ḥaq wa Inṣāf fī Muʾalifāt Sayyid Quṭb Raḥimahu Allāh," lecture from www.islamway.com, last accessed December 25, 2011.

Kashf al-Niqāb ʿAmmā fī Kalimāt Abī Ghudda min al-Abāṭīl wa l-Iftirāʾāt (Damascus: n.p., 1978).

Kayfa Yajibu ʿAlay-nā an Nufassir al-Qurʾān (Amman: Al-Maktaba al-Islāmiyya, 2000).

Khuṭbat al-Ḥāja (Beirut: Al-Maktab al-Islāmī, 1979).

"Mā Ḥukm Taqlīd Madhhab Muʿayyan?," lecture from www.youtube.com/watch?v=pPuzToEXunQ, last accessed January 14, 2016.

"Masāʾil wa Ajwibatuhā," *Al-Aṣāla*, 2, no. 10 (1994).

Mukhtaṣar Ṣaḥīḥ al-Bukhārī (Riyadh: Maktabat al-Maʿārif, 2002).

Qiyām Ramaḍān: Faḍluh wa-Kayfiyyat Adāʾih wa-Mashrūʿiyyat al-Jamāʿa fīh wa Maʿahu Baḥth Qayyim ʿan al-Iʿtikāf (Amman: al-Maktaba al-Islāmiyya, 1997).

"Refutation of Yusuf al Qaradawi," lecture from www.youtube.com/watch?v=Lg4R5YBCdfI, last accessed November 1, 2018.

Ṣaḥīḥ al-Jāmiʿ al-Ṣaghīr wa Ziyādati-hi (Beirut: Al-Maktab al-Islāmī, 1988).
Ṣaḥīḥ al-Targhīb wa l-Tarhīb (Riyadh: Maktabat al-Maʿārif, 2000).
"Al-Salafiyya wa l-Madhāhib," lecture from www.ar.islamway.com/lesson/17857, last accessed November 9, 2016.
Ṣalāt al-Tarāwīḥ (Beirut: Al-Maktab al-Islāmī, 1985).
Sharḥ al-ʿAqīda al-Ṭaḥāwiyya (Beirut: Al-Maktab al-Islāmī, 1984).
"Shubah Ḥawl al-Salafiyya," lecture from www.alalbany.net/?p=4075, last accessed October 14, 2013.
Ṣifat Ṣalāt al-Nabī (Riyadh: Maktabat al-Maʿārif, 1996).
Silsilat al-aḤādīth al-Ḍaʿīfa wa l-Mawḍūʿa wa Atharu-hā al-Sayyiʾ fī l-Umma (Riyadh: Maktbat al-Maʿārif, 1992).
Silsilat al-Aḥādīth al-Ṣaḥīḥa (Riyadh: Maktabat al-Maʿārif, 1995).
"Silsilat al-Hudā wa l-Nūr tape 331," lecture from www.alalbany.net/catplay.php?catsmktba=1269, last accessed December 7, 2016.
"Sīrat al-Imām al-Albānī 1," lecture from www.alalbany.net/?p=4654, last accessed May 28, 2018.
Taḥdhīr al-Sājid min Itikhādh al-Qubūr Masājid (Riyadh: Maktabat al-Maʿārif, 2001).
Taḥrīm ālāt al-Ṭarb (Serbia: Maktabat al-Dalīl, 1997).
Tamām al-Minna fī Taʿlīq ʿalā Fiqh al-Sunna (Riyadh: Dār al-Rāya, 1998).
"Ṭāmāt wa Munkirāt al-Jahūl al-Albānī al-Wahhābī Muddaʿī al-Salafiyya Raḥima-hu Allāh," www.youtube.com/watch?v=yRpKoWWUECU&feature=player_embedded#!, last accessed December 12, 2011.
"Al-Taqlīd wa l-Ittibāʾ," lecture from www.alalbany.net, last accessed April 5, 2012.
"Tarjamat al-Shaykh al-Albānī-Nashʾat al-Shaykh fī Dimashq," lecture from www.islamway.com, last accessed May 30, 2011.
Al-Taṣfiya wa l-Tarbiya wa Ḥājat al-Muslimīn Ilay-hā (Riyadh: Maktabat al-Maʿārif, 2007).
Al-Tawassul Anwāʿu-hu wa Aḥkāmu-hu (Riyadh: Maktabat al-Maʿārif, 2001).
"Weak Ḥadīth in Bukhārī? Albānī Explains," www.youtube.com/watch?v=w46-M1XqsUQ, last accessed May 22, 2018.
"Wujūb al-Tafaqquh fī l-Ḥadīth," lecture from www.alalbany.net/4935, last accessed July 1, 2014.
ʿAlī, Muḥammad Ibrāhīm. *Muḥammad Nāṣir al-Dīn al-Albānī, 1332–1420 H / 1914–1999 Muḥaddith al-ʿAṣr wa-Nāṣir al-Sunna* (Damascus: Dār al-Qalam, 2001).
Alūsī (al-), Muḥammad (d. 1317/1899). *Al-Āyāt al-Bayyināt fī ʿAdam Samāʿ al-Amwāt ʿInd al-Ḥanafiyya al-Sādāt*, ed. Muḥammad Nāṣir al-Dīn al-Albānī (Riyadh: Maktabat al-Maʿārif, 2005).
Amin, Kamaruddin, "Nāṣiruddīn al-Albānī on Muslim's *Ṣaḥīḥ*: A Critical Study of His Method," *Islamic Law and Society*, 11, no. 2 (2004), 149–176.
Amīn, ʿUthmān. *Rāʾid al-Fikr al-Misrī: al-Imām Muḥammad ʿAbduh* (Cairo: Maktabat al-Anjlū al-Miṣrīyah, 1965).
Anani, Khalil, and Maszlee, Malik. "Pious Way to Politics: The Rise of Political Salafism in Post-Mubarak Egypt," *Digest of Middle East Studies*, 22, no. 1 (2013), 57–73.
Anderson, Jerome N. D., and Coulson, Norman J. "Islamic Law in Contemporary Cultural Change," *Saeculum*, 18 (1967), 13–92.

Anderson, W. Jon. “The Internet and Islam’s New Interpreters,” in *New Media in the Muslim World*, ed. Dale F. Eickelman and Jon W. Anderson (Bloomington: Indiana University Press, 1999), 45–60.

Anjum, Ovamir. “Salafis and Democracy: Doctrine and Context,” *The Muslim World*, 106, no. 3 (2016), 448–473.

Anṣārī (al-), Ismāʿīl (d. 1997). *Ibāḥat al-Taḥallī bi l-Dhahab al-Muḥallaq wa l-Radd ʿalā al-Albānī fī Taḥrīmi-hi* (Riyadh: Maktabat al-Imam al-Shāfiʿī, 1988).

Al-Intiṣār li Shaykh al-Islām Muḥammad ibn ʿAbd al-Wahhāb bi l-Radd ʿalā Mujānabat al-Albānī li l-Ṣawāb (n.p.: n.d.).

Taṣḥīḥ Ṣalāt al-Tarāwīḥ ʿIshrīn Rakʿa wa l-Radd ʿalā al-Albānī fī Taḍʿīfi-hi (Riyadh: Maktabat al-Imam al-Shāfiʿī, 1988).

Ansari, I. Zafar. “The Authenticity of Traditions: A Critique of Joseph Schacht’s Argument,” *E Silentio. Hamdard Islamicus*, 7, no. 2 (1984), 51–61.

Asad, Talal. *The Idea of an Anthropology of Islam* (Washington, DC: Center for Contemporary Arab Studies, Georgetown University, 1986).

Aslan, Reza. *No God but God* (New York: Random House, 2011).

ʿAsqalānī (al-), Ibn Ḥajar (d. 852/1448). *Al-Nukat ʿalā kitāb Ibn Ṣalāḥ* (Medina: Islamic University of Medina, 1984).

Taqrīb al-Tahdhīb (Amman: Bayt al-Afkār al-Dawlīya, 2005).

ʿAwaḍ Allāh, Ṭāriq Ibn. *Radʿu al-Jānī al-Muʿtadī ʿalā al-Albānī* (Abū Dhabi: Maktabat al-Tarbiyaa al-Islāmiyya, 2009).

ʿAwda, ʿAṭiyya. *Ṣafaḥāt Bayḍāʾ min Ḥayāt al-Imām Muḥammad Nāṣir al-Dīn al-Albānī* (Al-Sanaʿa: Maktaba al-Islāmiyya, 2001).

ʿAwda, Salmān, *Fī Ḥiwār Hādīʾ maʿ Muḥammad al-Ghazālī* (Buraydah: n.p., 1989).

ʿAwwāma, Muḥammad. *Adab al-Ikhtilāf fī Masāʾil al-ʿIlm wa l-Dīn* (Beirut: Dār al-Bashāʾir al-Islāmiyya, 1997).

Athar al-Ḥadīth al-Sharīf fī Ikhitlāf al-Aʾiʾmma al-Fuqahāʾ Raḍī Allāhu ʿan-hum (Beirut: Dār al-Bashāʾir al-Islāmiyya, 1997).

“ʿAwwāma’s Statement on Albānī,” www.youtube.com/watch?v=zus5-U3wTxM, last accessed December 1, 2019.

“Ḥadīth al-Dhikrayāt maʿ al-Shaykh Muḥammad ʿAwwāma,” www.youtube.com/watch?v=6cgbKunEEQY, last accessed February 27, 2014.

Ḥukm al-ʿAmal bil Ḥadīth al-Ḍaʿīf Bayna al-Nadhariyya wa l-Taṭbīq, wa l-Daʿwā (Jedda: Dār al-Minhāj lil Nashr wal Tawzīʿ, 2017).

Aʿẓamī (al-), Ḥabīb al-Raḥmān (d. 1992). *Al-Albānī: Shudhūdhu-hu wa Akhṭāʾu-hu* (Kuwait: Maktabat Dār al-ʿUrūbah, 1984).

Azami (al-), M. Mustafa. *The History of the Qurʾanic Text from Revelation to Compilation: A Comparative Study with the Old and New Testaments* (Leicester: UK Islamic Academy, 2003).

On Schacht’s Origins of Muhammadan Jurisprudence (Cambridge: Islamic Texts Society, 1996).

Studies in Hadith Methodology and Literature (Indianapolis, IN: Islamic Teaching Center, 1977).

Ben Cheneb, Moh. “al-Ḳudūrī,” in *Encyclopaedia of Islam, First Edition (1913–1936)*, ed. M. Th. Houtsma, T. W. Arnold, R. Basset, and R. Hartmann, https://referenceworks.brillonline.com/browse/encyclopaedia-of-islam-1, last accessed June 2, 2020.

Berkey, Jonathan. *Popular Preaching and Religious Authority in the Medieval Islamic Near East* (Seattle: University of Washington Press, 2001).

The Transmission of Knowledge in Medieval Cairo: A Social History of Islamic Education (Princeton, NJ: Princeton University Press, 1992).

Blanchard, M. Christopher. *The Islamic Traditions of Wahhabism and Salafiyya* (Washington, DC: Congressional Research Service, Library of Congress, 2007).

Bonnefoy, Laurent. *Salafism in Yemen: Transnationalism and Religious Identity* (New York: Columbia University Press, 2011).

Brown, Daniel. *Rethinking Tradition in Modern Islamic Thought* (Cambridge: Cambridge University Press, 1996).

Brown, Jonathan. *The Canonization of al-Bukhārī and Muslim* (Leiden: Brill, 2007).

"Even If It's Not True It's True: Using Unreliable Ḥadīths in Sunni Islam," *Islamic Law and Society*, 18, no. 1 (2011), 1–52.

Hadith Muhammad's Legacy in the Medieval and Modern World (Oxford: Oneworld Publications, 2009).

"Is Islam Easy to Understand or Not?: Salafis, the Democratization of Interpretation and the Need for the Ulema," *Journal of Islamic Studies*, 26, no. 2 (2014), 117–144.

Misquoting Muhammad: The Challenge and Choices of Interpreting the Prophet's Legacy (London: Oneworld, 2014).

"The Rules of Matn Criticism: There Are No Rules," *Islamic Law and Society*, 19 (2012), 356–396.

"The Salafi Transformation from Quietism to Parliamentary Giant: Salafism in Egypt and the Nour Party of Alexandria," an unpublished paper based on a talk delivered at a conference, Islam in the New Middle East, March 29–30, 2012, University of Michigan-Ann Arbor.

Bukhārī (al-), Muḥammad b. Ismāʿīl (d. 256/870). *Kitāb al-Tarīkh al-Kabīr* (Beirut: Dār al-Kutub al-ʿIlmiyya, 1986).

Ṣaḥīḥ al-Bukhārī (Beirut: Dār Ibn Kathīr, 2004).

Bunt, Gary. *Islam in the Digital Age: E-Jihad, Online Fatwas and Cyber Islamic Environments* (London: Pluto Press, 2003).

Virtually Islamic: Computer-Mediated Communication and Cyber Islamic Environments (Cardiff: University of Wales Press, 2000).

Būṭī (al-), Ramadan Muḥammad (d. 2013). *Fiqh al-Sīra al-Nabawiyya maʿ Mawjiz li-Tārīkh al-Khilāfa al-Rāshida* (Beirut: Dār al-Fikr al-Maʿāṣir, 1991).

Al-Lā Madhhabiyya Akhṭar Bidʿa Tuhaddid al-Sharīʿa al-Islāmiyya (Damascus: Dār al-Farābī, 2005).

"Mubarāt Yafūtuhā ʿalā Nafsihī fī Hajr al-Ḥadīth al-Ḍaʿīf fī Faḍāʾil al-Aʿmāl," www.youtube.com/watch?v=MlZJ2SerzCo, last accessed April 10, 2018.

Al-Salafiyya Marḥala Zamaniyya Mubāraka lā Madhhab Islāmī (Damascus: Dār al-Fikr, 1988).

Calder, Norman. "Al-Nawawī's Typology of *Muftīs* and Its Significance for a General Theory of Islamic Law," *Islamic Law and Society*, 3, no. 2 (1996), 137–164.

Campbell, Heidi. "Who's Got the Power? Religious Authority and the Internet," *Journal of Computer-Mediated Communication*, 12, no. 3 (2007), 1043–1062.

Cardinal, C. Monique. "Islamic Legal Theory Curriculum: Are the Classics Taught Today?," *Islamic Law and Society*, 1, no. 2 (2005), 224–272.

Christmann, Andreas. "Islamic Scholar and Religious Leader: A Portrait of Shaykh Muḥammad Saʾīd Ramaḍān al-Būti," *Islam and Christian–Muslim Relations*, 9, no. 2 (1998), 149–169.

Commins, David. *Islamic Reform Politics and Social Change in Late Ottoman Syria* (New York: Oxford University Press, 1990).

The Wahhabi Mission and Saudi Arabia (London: I. B. Tauris, 2006).

Coulson, N. J. *A History of Islamic Law* (Edinburgh: Edinburgh University Press, 1964).

Cuno, Kenneth. *Modernizing Marriage: Family, Ideology, and Law in Nineteenth- and Early Twentieth-Century Egypt* (Syracuse, NY: Syracuse University Press, 2015).

Dāraquṭnī (al-), ʿAlī b. ʿUmar (d. 385/995). *Sunan al-Dāraquṭnī* (Beirut: Dār al-Maʿrifa, 2001).

DeLong-Bas, Natana. *Wahhabi Islam from Revival and Reform to Global Jihad* (New York: Oxford University Press, 2004).

DeLorenzo, Yusuf. *Imam Bukhari's Book of Muslim Morals and Manners* (Alexandria, VA: Al-Saadawi Publications, 1997).

Dover, Cedric. "The Black Knight," *Phylon*, 1, no. 4 (1954), 41–57.

Dutton, Yasin. "ʿAmal v Ḥadīth in Islamic Law: The Case of Sadl al-Yadayn (Holding One's Hands by One's Sides) When Doing the Prayer," *Islamic Law and Society*, 3, no. 1 (1996), 13–40.

Echchaibi, Nabil. "From Audiotapes to Videoblogs: The Delocalization of Authority in Islam," *Nations and Nationalism*, 17 (2009), 1–20.

Eickelman, Dale. "The Art of Memory: Islamic Education and Its Social Reproduction," *Comparative Studies in Society and History*, 20, no. 4 (1978), 485–516.

"Mass Higher Education and the Religious Imagination in Contemporary Arab Societies," *American Ethnologist*, 19, no. 4 (1992), 643–655.

El-Rouayheb, Khaled. "Sunni Muslim Scholars on the Status of Logic, 1500–1800," *Islamic Law and Society*, 11, no. 2 (2004), 213–232.

Emon, Anver. "To Most Likely Know the Law: Objectivity, Authority, and Interpretation in Islamic Law," *Hebraic Political Studies*, 4, no. 4 (2009), 415–440.

Encyclopedia of Islam. New edition: Vol. i, Leiden: E. J. Brill; Paris: Maisonneuve, M. Besson, 1960; Vols. ii–xii, Suppl., Leiden: E. J. Brill; Paris: Maisonneuve & Larose, 1965–2007.

Fadel, Mohammad. "Islamic Law and Constitution-Making: The Authoritarian Temptation and the Arab Spring," *Osgoode Hall Law Journal*, 53, no. 2 (2016), 472–507.

"*Istafti qalbaka wa in aftaka al-nas wa aftuka*: The Ethical Obligations of the Muqallid between Autonomy and Trust," in *Islamic Law in Theory: Studies on Jurisprudence in Honor of Bernard Weiss*, ed. A. Kevin Reinhart and Robert Gleave (Leiden: Brill, 2014), 105–126.

"The Social Logic of Taqlīd and the Rise of the Mukhataṣar," *Islamic Law and Society*, 3, no. 2 (1996), 193–233.

Farouki, Suha, and Nafi, Basheer. *Islamic Thought in the Twentieth Century* (London: I. B. Tauris, 2004).

Farquhar, Michael. *Circuits of Faith: Migration, Education, and the Wahhabi Mission* (Stanford, CA: Stanford University Press, 2016).

Feldman, Noah. *The Fall and Rise of the Islamic State* (Princeton, NJ: Princeton University Press, 2012).

Garden, Kenneth. "Al-Ghazālī's Contested Revival: Iḥyā' 'Ulūm al-Dīn and Its Critics in Khorasan and the Maghrib" (Ph.D. Dissertation, University of Chicago, 2005).

Gauvain, Richard. *Salafi Ritual Purity: In the Presence of God* (London: Routledge, 2013).

Ghazālī (al-), Abū Ḥāmid (d. 505/1111). *Iḥyā' 'Ulūm al-Dīn* (Beirut: Dār al-Ma'rifa, 1982).

Ghazālī (al-), Muḥammad (d. 1996). *Fiqh al-Sīra* (Cairo: Dār al-Shurūq, 2000).

Ghumārī (al-), 'Abd Allāh (d. 1993). *Al-Radd 'alā al-Albānī* (Beirut: Dār al-Janān, 1991).

Ghumārī (al-), Aḥmad (d. 1960). *Al-Jawāb al-Mufīd li l-Sā'il al-Mustafīd*, ed. Abū al-Faḍl Badr al-'Imrānī (Beirut: Dār al-Kutub al-'Ilmiyya, 2002).

Gibb, H. A. R. *Mohammedanism*, 2nd ed. (New York: Oxford University Press, 1962).

Goldziher, Ignaz (d. 1921). *Introduction to Islamic Theology and Law*, trans. Andras Homari and Ruth Homari (Princeton, NJ: Princeton University Press, 1981).

Graham, William. "Traditionalism in Islam: As Essay in Interpretation," *Journal of Interdisciplinary History*, 23, no. 3 (1993), 495–522.

Griffel, Frank. "What Do We Mean by 'Salafī'? Connecting Muḥammad 'Abduh with Egypt's Nūr Party in Islam's Contemporary Intellectual History," *Die Welt des Islams*, 55 (2015), 186–220.

Haddad, Gabriel F. *Al-Albani: A Concise Guide to the Chief Innovator of Our Time*, http://sunnah.org/history/Innovators/al_albani.htm, last accessed June 17, 2020.

Albani & His Friends: A Concise Guide to the Salafi Movement (Birmingham, UK: AQSA Publications, 2004).

Haddad, Yvonne. "Muhammad Abduh: Pioneer of Islamic Reform," in *Pioneers of Islamic Revival*, ed. Ali Rahnema (London: Zed Books, 1994), 30–63.

Haenni, Patrick, and Tammam, Husam. "Egypt's Air-Conditioned Islam," *Le Monde Diplomatique*, September 2003, https://mondediplo.com/2003/09/03egyptislam, last accessed May 20, 2020.

Ḥāfiẓ, Muḥammad, and Abāẓa, Nizār. *Tarīkh 'Ulamā' Dimashq fī l-Qarn al-Rābi' 'Ashar Hijrī* (Damascus: Dār al-Fikr, 1986).

Haj, Samira. *Reconfiguring Islamic Tradition: Reform, Rationality, and Modernity* (Stanford, CA: Stanford University Press, 2009).

Halim, Fachrizal. "Reformulating the *Madhhab* in Cyberspace: Legal Authority, Doctrines, and *Ijtihād* among Contemporary Shāf'i'ī 'Ulamā'," *Islamic Law and Society*, 22, no. 4 (2015), 413–435.

Hallaq, Wael. *Authority, Continuity and Change in Islamic Law* (Cambridge: Cambridge University Press, 2005).

An Introduction to Islamic Law (Cambridge: Cambridge University Press, 2009).

"On the Origins of the Controversy about the Existence of Mujtahids and the Gate of Ijtihad," *Studia Islamica*, 69 (1986), 129–141.

The Origins and Evolution of Islamic Law (Cambridge: Cambridge University Press, 2005).

"Takhrīj and the Construction of Juristic Authority," in *Studies in Islamic Legal Theory*, ed. Bernard Weiss (Boston: Brill, 2002), 317–355.

"Was the Gate of Ijtihad Closed?," *International Journal of Middle East Studies*, 16 (1984), 3–41.

Hamdeh, Emad. "The Formative Years of an Iconoclastic Salafi Scholar," *The Muslim World*, 106, no. 3 (2016), 411–432.

"Qur'ān and Sunna or the Madhhabs?: A Salafi Polemic against Islamic Legal Tradition," *Islamic Law and Society*, 24, no. 3 (June 2017), 211–253.

"The Role of the 'Ulamā' in the Thoughts of 'Abd al-Fattāḥ Abū Ghudda," *The Muslim World*, 107, no. 3 (2017), 359–374.

Ḥasan, Karīma. "Al-Bābī al-Ḥalabī Akthar min 130 Sana fī Nashr 'Ulūm al-Dīn," *Al-Maṣrī al-Yawm*, September 2, 2009. http://today.almasryalyoum.com/ article2 .aspx? ArticleID=224645&IssueID=1517, accessed August 22, 2014.

Hasan, Suhaib. Interview by author. Phone interview. London, August 26, 2013.

Hāshimī, Muḥammad 'Alī. *Al-Shaykh 'Abd al-Fattāḥ Abū Ghudda Kamā 'Araftuh* (Beirut: Dār al-Bashaī'r al-Islāmīya, 2004).

Hassan, Mona. *Longing for the Lost Caliphate: A Transregional History* (Princeton, NJ: Princeton University Press, 2017).

Ḥaydar, 'Alī (d. 1935). *Durrar al-Ḥukkām Sharḥ Majallat al-Aḥkām* (Riyadh: Dār 'Ālam al-Kutub, 2003).

Haykel, Bernard. "On the Nature of Salafi Thought and Action," in *Global Salafism*, ed. Roel Meijer (New York: Columbia University Press, 2009), 33–57.

Revival and Reform in Islam: The Legacy of Muhammad al-Shawkani (Cambridge: Cambridge University Press, 2003).

Heath, Peter. "A Critical Review of Modern Scholarship on 'Sīrat 'Antar ibn Shaddad' and the Popular Sīra," *Journal of Arabic Literature*, 15 (1984), 19–44.

Heck, Paul. "The Epistemological Problem of Writing in Islamic Civilization: al-Ḫaṭīb al-Baġdādī's (d. 463/1071) 'Taqyid al-'ilm'," *Studia Islamica*, no. 94 (2002), 85–114.

Hegghammer, Thomas. "Jihadi-Salafis or Revolutionaries?," in *Global Salafism*, ed. Roel Meijer (New York: Columbia University Press, 2009), 244–266.

Hegghammer, Thomas, and Lacroix, Stéphane. *The Meccan Rebellion: The Story of Juhayman al-'Utaybi Revisited* (Bristol: Amal Press, 2011).

"Rejectionist Islamism in Saudi Arabia: The Story of Juhayman al-'Utaybi Revisited," *International Journal of Middle East Studies*, 39, no. 1 (2007), 103–122.

Hilālī (al-), Salīm, and 'Abd al-Ḥamīd, 'Alī Ḥasan. *Al-Radd al-'Ilmī 'alā Ḥabīb al-Raḥmān al-A'ẓamī al-Mudda'ī bi Ana-hu Arshad Salafī fī Raddi-hi 'alā al-Albānī wa Bayān Iftirā'u-hu 'alya-hi* (Amman: Al-Maktaba al-Islāmiyya, 1983).

Hirschkind, Charles. *The Ethical Soundscape: Cassette Sermons and Islamic Counterpublics* (New York: Columbia University Press, 2009).

"Media and the Qur'ān," in *The Encyclopedia of the Quran*, ed. Jane McAuliffe (Leiden: Brill, 2003), 341–349.

Hitou, Muḥammad Ḥasan. *Al-Mutafayhiqūn* (Syria; Dār al-Farābī, 2009).

Ḥuwaynī (al-), Abū Isḥāq. *Tanbīh al-Hājid ilā mā Qaqa'a min al-Nadhar fī Kutub al-Amjād: Iṭilī'āt al-Juz' al-Rābi' min Kitāb: al-Thamar al-Dānī fī l-Dhab 'an al-Albānī* (Cairo: Maktabat al-Taw'īyah al-Islāmīyah, 1998).

Ibn 'Abd al-Barr, Yūsuf (d. 463/1071). *Jāmi' Bayān al-'Ilm wa Faḍlihi wa mā Yanbaghī fī Riwāyatihi wa Ḥamlihi* (Cairo: Dār al-Kutub al-Ḥadītha, 1975).

Ibn 'Ābidīn, Muḥammad Amīn (d. 1258/1842). *Radd al-Muḥtār 'alā al-Durra al-Mukhtār Sharḥ Tanwīr al-Abṣār* (Riyadh: Dār 'Ālim al-Kutub, 2003).

Ibn Adam, Muhammad. "Learning from a Teacher & the Importance of Isnad," *Daruliftaa*, September 3, 2004, www.daruliftaa.com/node/5795?txt_QuestionID, last accessed September 15, 2015.

Ibn ʿAsākir, ʿAlī (d. 571/1175). *Tārīkh Madīnat Dimashq: wa-Dhikr Faḍlihā wa-Tasmīyat man Ḥallahā min al-Amāthil aw Ijtāza bi-Nawāḥīhā min Wāridīhā wa-Ahlihā* (Damascus: Maṭbūʿāt al-Majmaʿ al-ʿIlmī al-ʿArabī, 1951).

Ibn Ḥasan, Mashhūr, and Aḥmad al-Shakūkānī. *Qamūs al-Bidaʿ Mustakhraj min Kutub al-Imām al-ʿAlāma Muḥammad Nāṣir al-Dīn al-Albānī* (Doha: Dār al-Imām Bukhārī, 2007).

Ibn Ḥazm, ʿAlī (d. 456/1064). *Al-Faṣl fi-l-Milal wa-l-Ahwāʾ wa-l-Niḥal* (Beirut: Dār al-Jīl, 1996).

Al-Iḥkām fī Uṣūl al-Aḥkām (Cairo: Dār al-Ḥadith, 2005).

Ibn Jamāʿa, Muḥammad (d. 733/1333). *Tadhkirat al-Sāmiʿ wa-l-Mutakallim fī Adab al-ʿĀlim wa-l-Mutaʿalim* (Beirut: Dār al-Bashāʾir al-Islāmiyya, 2012).

Ibn al-Jawzī, ʿAbd al-Raḥmān (d. 597/1201). *Kitāb al-Quṣṣāṣ wa-l-Mudhakkirīn* (Beirut: Dār al-Mahriq, 1971).

Ibn Kathīr, Ismāʿīl (d. 774/1373). *Al-Bāʿith al-Ḥathīth Sharḥ Ikhtiṣār ʿUlūm al-Ḥadīth*, ed. Muḥammad Nāṣir al-Dīn al-Albānī (Riyadh: Maktabat al-Maʿārif, 1996).

Ṭabaqāt al-Shāfiʿiyya (Beirut: Dār al-Madār al-Islāmī, 2002).

Ibn Māja, Muḥammad b. Yazīd (d. 273/886). *Sunan Ibn Māja* (Damascus: Dār al-Risāla al-ʿālamiyā, 2009).

Ibn Malak, ʿAbd al-Laṭīf (d. 801/1398). *Mabāriq al-Azhār Sharḥ Mashāriq al-Anwār fī al-Jamʿ Bayna al-Ṣaḥīḥayn lil-Ṣaghānī* (Beirut: Dār al-Jīl, 1995).

Ibn Masʿūd, Aḥmad b. ʿAlī. *Marāḥ al-Arwāḥ fī l-Ṣarf* (Qom: Iʿtimād, 1994).

Ibn Qayyim, al-Jawziyya (d. 751/1350). *Iʿlām al-Muwwaqiʿīn* (Jeddah: Dār Ibn al-Jawzī, 2002).

Kitāb al-Rūḥ (Mecca: Dār ʿĀlam al-Fawāʾd, 2011).

Masʾalat al-Samāʿ (Riyadh: Dār al-ʿĀṣima, 1988).

Ibn Rajab, Abū al-Faraj Abd al-Raḥmān (d. 795/1393). *Majmūʿ Rasāʾil Ibn Rajab al-Ḥanbalī* (Cairo: Al-Fārūq al-Ḥadītha li-l-Ṭibāʿa wa-l-Nashr, 2001).

Ibn al-Ṣalāḥ, Abū ʿAmr ʿUthmān b. ʿAbd al-Raḥmān (d. 643/1245). *Muqaddimat Ibn Ṣalāḥ fī ʿUlūm al-Ḥadīth* (Beirut: Dar Al-Kotob Al-ʿIlmiyah, 2003).

Ibn Taymiyyah, Taqī al-Dīn (d. 728/1328). *Al-Kalim al-Ṭayyib*, ed. Muḥammad Nāṣir al-Dīn al-Albānī (Riyadh: Maktabat al-Maʿārif, 2001).

Naqd Marātib al-Ijmāʿ (Beirut: Dār al-Fikr, 1988).

Rafʾ al-Malām ʾan al-Aʾimma al-Aʾlām (Beirut: Dār Al-Kotob al-ʿIlmiyya, 2003).

Ibrahim, Ahmed Fekry. "Legal Pluralism in Sunni Islamic Law: The Causes and Functions of Juristic Disagreement," in *Routledge Handbook of Islamic Law*, ed. Khaled Abou El Fadl, Ahmad Atif Ahmad, and Said Fares Hassan (New York: Routledge, 2019), 208–220.

"Rethinking the Taqlīd-Ijtihād Dichotomy: A Conceptual Historical Approach," *Journal of American Oriental Society*, 136, no. 2 (2016), 285–305.

Idilbī, Ṣalāḥ al-Dīn. *Kashf al-Maʿlūl Mimā Summiyya bi Silsilat al-Aḥādīth al-Ṣaḥīḥa* (Amman: Dār al-Fatḥ lil dirāsāt wa l-nashr, 2011).

Inge, Anabel. *The Making of a Salafi Muslim Woman: Paths to Conversion* (Oxford: Oxford University Press, 2016).

Ingram, Brannon. *Revival from Below: The Deoband Movement and Global Islam* (Oakland: University of California Press, 2018).

ʿIrāqī, Zayn al-Dīn (d. 806/1404). *Al-Mughnī ʿan Ḥaml al-Asfār fī l-Asfār fī Takhrīj mā fī l-Iḥyāʾ min al-Akhbār* (Riyadh: Maktabat Dār Ṭabarrīya, 1995).

ʿItr, Nūr al-Dīn, *Sharḥ al-Nukhba: Nuzhat al-Naẓar fī Tawḍīḥ Nukhbat al-Fikar fī Muṣṭalaḥ Ahl al-ʿAthar* (Karachi: Al-Bushra Publishers, 2011).

Jabr, Yusrī. "Laysa Kul Ḥaidth Muhmal Kamā Ibtadaʿahu al-Shaykh al-Albānī," www.youtube.com/watch?v=VtbshnqxJzo, last accessed April 13, 2018.

Jackson, Sherman. *Ijtihād* and *taqlīd*: Between the Islamic Legal Tradition and Autonomous Western Reason," in *Routledge Handbook of Islamic Law*, ed. Khaled Abou El Fadl, Ahmad Atif Ahmad, and Said Fares Hassan (New York: Routledge, 2019), 255–272.

Islamic Law and the State: The Constitutional Jurisprudence of Shihāb al-Dīn al-Qarāfī (Leiden: E. J. Brill, 1996).

Islam and the Problem of Black Suffering (Oxford: Oxford University Press, 2009).

Janson, Marloes. "Roaming about for God's Sake: The Upsurge of the Tablīgh Jamāʿat in the Gambia," *Journal of Religion in Africa*, 35, no. 4 (2005), 450–481.

Jifrī, Ḥabīb ʿAlī. "Dealing with Weak Ḥadīth Methodology of Traditional Sunni Scholars," www.youtube.com/watch?v=MNL14f9MVQg, last accessed April 10, 2018.

Jumʿa, ʿAlī. "Liman Yasʾal: Hal Naʿmal bi-l-Ḥadīth al-Ḍaʿīf," www.youtube.com/watch?v=yGW9-9To8nU, last accessed January 7, 2020.

"Al-Shaykh ʿAlī Jumʿa Yaruddu ʿalā Bidʿat al-Shaykh al-Albānī," www.youtube.com/watch?v=D9oxpuOvsz8, last accessed April 10, 2018.

"Wallāhu Aʿlam: Al-Dactor ʿAlī Jumʿa Yataḥaddath ʿan Adawāt al-Albānī fī Taḍʿīf al-Aḥādīth," www.youtube.com/watch?v=yhiYnXx2B9Q, last accessed April 11, 2018.

Juwaynī (-al), Abū al-Maʿālī (d. 478/1085). *Kitāb al-Ijtihād min Kitāb al-Talkhīṣ*, ed. ʿAbd al-Ḥamīd Abū Zunayr (Damascus: Dar al-Qalam, 1987).

Kadi, Waddad. "Education in Islam-Myths and Truths," *Comparative Education Review*, 50, no. 3 (2006), 311–324.

Kazmi, Yedullah. "The Notion of Murrabī in Islam: An Islamic Critique of Trends in Contemporary Education," *Islamic Studies*, 38, no. 2 (1999), 209–233.

Keller, Nuh Ha Mim. "Who or What Is a Salafi and Is Their Approach Valid?" Masʿud Ahmed Khan's Home Page. www.masud.co.uk/ISLAM/nuh/salafi.htm, last accessed June 17, 2017.

Khalīl, Aḥmad. *Mustadrak al-Taʿlīl ʿalā Arwāʾ al-Ghalīl* (Saudi Arabia: Dār Ibn al-Jawzī, 2008).

Al-Khaṭīb al-Baghdādī, Abū Bakr Aḥmad b. ʿAlī. (d. 463/1071). *Al-Jāmiʿ li Akhlāq al-Rāwī wa Ādāb al-Sāmiʿ* (Al-Dammām: Dār Ibn al-Jawzī, 2011).

Khāṭir, M. Khalīl. *Makānat al-Ṣaḥīḥayn* (Cairo: Al-Maṭbaʿa al-ʿArabiyya al-Ḥadītha, 1985).

Khārūf, Yūnus. "Al-Samāʿāt wa-l-iIāzāt fī-l-Makhṭūṭāt al-ʿArabīya," *Risālat al-Maktaba* (Jordanian), 10 (1975).

Khujnadī (al-) Maʿṣūmī, Muḥammad Sulṭān (d. 1960). *Hal al-Muslim Mulzam bi-ittibāʿ Madhhab Muʿayyan Min al-Madhāhib al-Arbaʿa?*, ed. Salīm Hilālī (Amman: Al-Maktaba al-Islāmīya, 1984).

Kruk, Remke. "Warrior Women in Arabic Popular Romance: Qannāṣa bint Muzāḥim and other Valiant Ladies. Part One," *Journal of Arabic Literature*, 24, no. 3 (1993), 213–230.

Lacroix, Stéphane. *Awakening Islam: The Politics of Religious Dissent in Contemporary Saudi Arabia* (Cambridge, MA: Harvard University Press, 2011).

"Between Revolution and Apoliticism: Nasir al-Din al-Albani and His Impact on the Shaping of Contemporary Salafism," in *Global Salafism*, ed. Roel Meijer (New York: Columbia University Press, 2009), 58–80.

Laher, Suheil. "Re-forming the Knot: ʿAbdullāh al-Ghumārī's Iconoclastic Sunnī Neo-Traditionalism," *Journal of College of Sharia and Islamic Studies*, 36, no. 1 (2018), 201–216.

Laknāwī, Muḥammad ʿAbd al-Ḥayy (d. 1304/1886). *Al-Ajwiba al-Fāḍila li l-Asʾila al-ʿAshra al-Kāmila*, ed. ʿAbd al-Fattāḥ Abū Ghudda (Cairo: Dār al-Salām, 2009).

Al-Fawāʾid al-Bahīyya fī Tarājum al-Ḥanafīyya (Beirut: Dār al-Maʿrifa, 1975).

Al-Rafʿ wa l-Takmīl fī l-Jarḥ wa l-Taʿdīl, ed. ʿAbd al-Fattāḥ Abū Ghudda (Beirut: Maktab al-Maṭbūʿāt al-Islāmiyya, 2004).

Ẓafar al-Amānī bi Sharḥ Mukhtaṣar al-Sayyid al-Sharīf al-Jurjānī fī Muṣṭalaḥ al-Ḥadīth, ed. ʿAbd al-Fattāḥ Abū Ghudda (Aleppo: Maktab al-Maṭbūʿāt al-Islāmiyya, 1995).

Larsson, Göran. *Muslims and the New Media: Historical and Contemporary Debates* (Burlington, VT: Ashgate, 2011).

Lauzière, Henri. "The Construction of *Salafiyya*: Reconsidering Salafism from Perspective of Conceptual History," *International Journal of Middle East Studies*, 42, no. 3 (2010), 369–389.

The Making of Salafism: Islamic Reform in the Twentieth Century (New York: Columbia University Press, 2015).

"What We Mean Versus What They Mean by 'Salafi': A Reply to Frank Griffel," *Die Welt des Islams*, 56, no. 1 (2016), 89–96.

Lav, Daniel. *Radical Islam and the Revival of Medieval Theology* (New York: Cambridge University Press, 2012).

Loya, Arieh. "The Detribalization of Arabic Poetry," *International Journal of Middle East Studies*, 5, no. 2 (1974), 202–215.

Lucas, Scott. *Constructive Critics, Hadith Literature, and the Articulation of Sunni Islam: The Legacy of Ibn Saʿd, Ibn Maʿīn, and Ibn Ḥanbal* (Boston: Brill, 2004).

MacIntyre, Alasdair, *Whose Justice? Which Rationality?* (Notre Dame, IN: University of Notre Dame Press, 1989).

Madawi, Al-Rasheed, *Contesting the Saudi State: Islamic Voices from a New Generation* (Cambridge: Cambridge University Press, 2006).

Makdisi, George (d. 2002). "Institutionalized Learning as a Self-Image of Islam," in *Islam's Understanding of Itself*, ed. Speros Vryonis, Jr. (Los Angeles: University of California Press, 1983), 73–85.

The Rise of Colleges: Institutions of Learning in Islam and the West (Edinburgh: Edinburgh University Press, 1981).

Malībārī (al-), Ḥumza. *Al-Muwāzana Bayn al-Mutaqaddimīn wa l-Mutaʾkhirīn fī Taṣḥīḥ al-Aḥādīth wa Taʿlīli-hā* (Beirut: Dār Ibn Ḥazm, 2001).

Mamdūḥ, Maḥmūd. *Al-Shadhā al-Fawwā Min Akhbār al-Shaykh ʿAbd al-Fattāḥ Abū Ghudda, 1337–1418 H* (Cairo: Dār al-Baṣāʾir, 2009).

Tanbīh al-Muslim ilā Taʿaddī al-Albānī ʿalā Ṣaḥīḥ Muslim (Cairo: Maktabat al-Mujallad al-ʿArabī, 2011).

Al-Taʿrīf bi-Awhām man Qassama al-Sunan ilā Ṣaḥīḥ wa Ḍaʿīf (Dubai: Dār al-Buḥūth li al-Dirāsāt al-Islāmiyya wa Iḥyāʾ al-Turāth, 2000).

Wuṣūl al-Tahānī bi Ithbāt Sunniyyat al-Subḥa wa l-Radd ʿalā al-Albānī (Cairo: Dār al-Imām al-Tirmidhī, 1994).

Mandaville, Peter. *Islam and Politics*, 2nd ed. (New York: Routledge, 2014).

"Reimagining Islam in Diaspora: The Politics of Mediated Community," *International Communication Gazette*, 63, no. 2–3 (2001), 168–186.

Masud, K. Muhammad. *Travellers in Faith: Studies of the Tablīghī Jamāʿat as a Transnational Islamic Movement for Faith Renewal* (Leiden: Brill, 2000).

Mathiesen, Kasper. "Anglo-American 'Traditional Islam' and Its Discourse of Orthodoxy," *Journal of Arabic and Islamic Studies*, 13 (2013), 191–219.

Meijer, Roel. *Global Salafism: Islam's New Religious Movement* (New York: Columbia University Press, 2009).

Metcalf, D. Barbara. *Islamic Revival in British India: Deoband, 1860–1900* (New Delhi: Oxford University Press, 2002).

"Living Hadith in the *Tablighi Jamaʿat*," *The Journal of Asian Studies*, 52, no. 3 (1993), 584–608.

"Travelers' Tales in the *Tablighi Jamaʿat*," *Annals of the American Academy of Political and Social Science*, 588 (2003), 136–148.

Miller, William. *The Ottoman Empire and Its Successors, 1801–1927* (New York: Frank Cass, 1966).

Mitchell, Timothy. *Colonising Egypt* (Berkeley: University of California Press, 1991).

Moosa, Ebrahim. *What Is a Madrasa?* (Chapel Hill: University of North Carolina Press, 2015).

Moubayed, Sami. *Steel & Silk: Men and Women Who Shaped Syria 1900–2000* (Seattle, WA: Cune, 2006).

Munajjid, Ṣalāḥ al-Dīn. "Ijāzāt al-Samāʿ fī-l-Makhṭūṭāt al-Qadīma," *Majallat Maʿhad al-Makhṭūṭāt al-ʿArabīya/Revue de l'institut des manuscrits arabes* (Cairo), 1 (1955), 232–251.

Mundhurī, ʿAbd al-Aẓīm (d. 656/1258). *Mukhtaṣar Ṣaḥīḥ Muslim li-Abī l-Ḥusayn Muslim ibn al-Ḥajjāj al-Qushayrī al-Naysābūrī*, ed. Muḥammad Nāṣir al-Dīn al-Albānī (Beirut: Al-Maktab al-Islāmī, 1987).

Murad, Abdul Hakim. "The Salafi Fallacy," lecture from www.youtube.com/watch?v=1MRXs5fqlXQ, last accessed May 7, 2013.

Muslim, b. al-Ḥajjāj (d. 261/875). *Ṣaḥīḥ Muslim* (Riyadh: Dār Ṭayba, 2006).

Mustafa, Abdul-Rahman. *On Taqlid Ibn al Qayyim's Critique of Authority in Islamic Law* (Oxford: Oxford University Press, 2013).

Motzki, Harald. "Dating Muslim Traditions: A Survey," *Arabica*, 52, no. 2 (2005), 204–253.

Nafi, Basheer. "The Rise of Islamic Reformist Thought and Its Challenge to Traditional Islam," in *Islamic Thought in the Twentieth Century*, ed. Suha Farouki and Basheer Nafi (London: I. B. Tauris, 2004), 28–60.

"Ṭāhir Ibn ʿĀshūr: The Career and Thought of a Modern Reformist ʿālim, with Special Reference to His Work of Tafsīr," *Journal of Qurʾanic Studies*, 7, no. 1 (2005), 1–32.

Nasr, Seyyed Hossein. "Oral Transmission and the Book in Islamic Education: The Spoken and the Written Word," *Journal of Islamic Studies*, 3, no. 1 (1992), 1–14.

Nawawī, Muḥyī al-Dīn (d. 676/1277). *Kitāb al-Majmūʾ Sharḥ al-Muhadhdhab liʾl-Shīrāzī* (Beirut: Dār Iḥyāʾ al-Turāth al-ʿArabī, 2001).

Nichols, Tom, "The Death of Expertise," *The Federalist*, January 17, 2014. http://thefederalist.com/2014/01/17/the-death-of-expertise/#disqus_thread, last accessed August 21, 2015.

The Death of Expertise (New York: Oxford University Press, 2017).

Nuʿmānī (al-), A. Muḥammad (d. 1999). *Makānat al-Imām abī Ḥanīfa fī l-Ḥadīth*, ed. ʿAbd al-Fattāḥ Abū Ghudda (Beirut: Maktabat al- Maṭbūʿāt al-Islāmiyya, 2007).

Olidort, Jacob. *The Politics of "Quietist" Salafism* (Washington, DC: The Brookings Institution, 2015).

Paul, Annie Murphy. "Are College Lectures Unfair?," *The New York Times*, September 12, 2015. Gray Matter Science and Society sec., www.nytimes.com/2015/09/13/opinion/sunday/are-college-lectures-unfair.html, last accessed September 15, 2015.

Philips, Bilal, "Reply to Critics," article from www.bilalphilips.com, last accessed August 28, 2012.

Pierret, Thomas. *Religion and State in Syria: The Sunni Ulama from Coup to Revolution* (Cambridge: Cambridge University Press, 2013).

Peters, Rudolph. "*Idjtihād* and *Taqlīd* in the 18th and 19th Century Islam," *Die Welt des Islams*, 20, no. 3/4 (1980), 131–145.

"Religious Attitudes towards Modernization in the Ottoman Empire: A Nineteenth Century Pious Text on Steamships, Factories and the Telegraph," *Die Welt des Islams*, 1, no. 4 (1986), 76–105.

Poljarevic, Emin. "Islamic Tradition and Meanings of Modernity," *International Journal for History, Culture, and Modernity*, 3, no. 1 (2015), 29–57.

"The Power of Selective Affinities in Contemporary Salafism," *The Muslim World*, 106, no. 3 (2016), 474–500.

Qadhi, Yasir. Interview with Yasir Qadhi, "Salafi Muslims: Following the Ancestors of Islam," *Interfaith Voices* (February 21, 2013).

"Reformation or Reconstruction: Dr. Ḥatim al-ʿAwnī's Critiques of Modern Wahhabī Thought," presentation of an unpublished paper at the American Academy of Religion, November 21, 2016.

"On Salafi Islam," http://muslimmatters.org/2014/04/22/on-salafi-islam-dr-yasir-qadhi, last accessed June 26, 2014.

Qaraḍāwī, Yūsuf. *Approaching the Sunnah: Comprehension and Controversy* (London; Washington, DC: The International Institute of Islamic Thought, 2006).

Qārī (al-), Mullā ʿAlī (d. 1014/1605). *Mirqāt al-Mafātīḥ: Sharḥ Mishkāt al-Maṣābīḥ* (Beirut: Dār al-Fikr, 1992).

Qudūrī, Abū al-Ḥasan (d. 428/1037). *Mukhtaṣar al-Qudūrī* (Beirut: Dār al-Kutub al-ʿIlmiyya, 1997).

Qureshi, Jawad. "Zuhayr al-Shāwīsh (1925–2013) and al-Maktab al-Islami: Print, Hadith Verification, and Authenticated Islam," presentation of an unpublished paper at the American Academy of Religion, November 21, 2016.

Rabbani, Faraz. "Al-Albani, Salafis, Prayer Beads, and the Question of Innovation in Matters of Religion," fatwa from www.qa.sunnipath.com, last accessed July 1, 2011.

Rahman, Fazlur (d. 1988). "Islamic Modernism: Its Scope, Method and Alternatives," *International Journal of Middle East Studies*, 1, no. 4 (1970), 317–333.

Reynolds, Dwight Fletcher, and Brustad, Kristen. *Interpreting the Self: Autobiography in the Arabic Literary Tradition* (Berkeley: University of California Press, 2001).

Robinson, Francis. "Technology and Religious Change: Islam and the Impact of Print," *Modern Asian Studies*, 27, no. 1 (1993), 229–251.

Sakhāwī, Muḥammad (d. 902/1497). *Al-Qawl al-Badī' fī al-Ṣalāt 'alā al-Ḥabīb al-Shafī'* (Medina: Al-Maktaba al-'Ilmiyya, 1963).

Salīm, 'Amr 'Abd al-Mun'im. *Barā'at al-Dhimmah bi-Nuṣrat al-Sunna: al-Difā' al-Sanī 'an al-Albānī wa l-Jawāb 'an Shubah Ṣāḥib al-Ta'rīf* (Tanta: Dār al-Ḍiyā', 2001).

Al-Fatāwā al-Manhajiyya li-Faḍīlat al-Shaykh Muḥammad Nāṣir al-Dīn al-Albānī (Cairo: Dār al-Ḍiyā', 2008).

Al-Manhaj al-Salafī 'ind al-Shaykh Nāṣir al-Dīn al-Albānī (Tanta: Dār al-Ḍiyā', n.d.).

Sāmarrā'ī, Qāsim. "Al-Ijāzāt wa-Taṭawwuruhā al-Ta'rīkhīya," *'Ālam al-Kutub*, 2 (1981).

Ṣan'ānī (al-), Muḥammad (d. 1182/1768). *Raf' al-Astār li Ibṭāl Adillat al-Qā'ilīna bi Fanā' al-Nār*, ed. Muḥammad Nāṣir al-Dīn al-Albānī (Beirut: Al-Maktab al-Islāmī, 1984).

Saqqāf, Ḥasan. *Iḥtijāj al-Khā'ib bi-'Ibārat man Idda'ā al-Ijmā' Fahuwa Kādhib* (Amman: Maktabat al-Imām al-Nawawī, 1990).

Majmū' Rasā'il al-Saqqāf (Amman: Dār al-Rāzī, 2000).

Qāmūs Shatā'im al-Albānī (Amman: Dār al-Imām al-Nawawī, 1993).

Tanāqaḍāt al-Albānī al-Wāḍiḥāt (n.p., 2007).

Schacht, Joseph (d. 1969). *An Introduction to Islamic Law* (New York: Oxford University Press, 1964).

The Origins of Muhammadan Jurisprudence, 4th ed. (New York: Oxford University Press, 1964).

Scholz, Jan, Selge, Are, Stille, Max, and Zimmermann, Johannes, "Listening Communities? Some Remarks on the Construction of Religious Authority in Islamic Podcasts," *Die Welt des Islams*, 48, no. 3–4 (2008), 457–509.

Schulze, Reinhard. "The Birth of Tradition and Modernity in the 18th and 19th Century Islamic Culture – The Case of Printing," *Culture and History*, 16 (1997), 29–72.

Shāfi'ī (al-), Muḥammad b. Idrīs (d. 188/820). *Al-Risāla* (Lebanon: Dār al-Kutub al-'Ilmiyya, 2005).

Shākir, Aḥmad (d. 1958). *Taṣḥīḥ al-Kutub wa Ṣun' al-Fahāris wa Kayfīyat Ḍabṭ al-Kitāb wa Sabq al-Muslimīn al-Afranj fī Dhālik*, ed. 'Abd al-Fattāḥ Abū Ghudda (Cairo: Maktabat al-Sunna, 1994).

Shamrānī (al-), 'Abd Allāh. *Thabat Mu'alifāt al-Muḥadith al-Kabīr al-Imam Muḥammad Nāṣir al-Dīn al-Albānī*, www.dorar.net, last accessed June 17, 2020.

Shāṭibī (al-), Abū Isḥāq (d. 790/1388). *Al-Muwāfaqat*. Vol. 1. (Al-Khubar: Dār Ibn 'Affān, 1997).

Shaybānī, Muḥammad. *Ḥayāt al-Albānī wa-Āthāru-hu wa Thanā' al-'Ulamā' 'alay-hi* (Cairo: Maktabat al-Sarrāwī, 1986).

Shoshan, Boaz. "High Culture and Popular Culture in Medieval Islam," *Studia Islamica*, no. 73 (1991), 67–107.

"On Popular Literature in Medieval Cairo," *Poetics Today*, 14, no. 2 (1993), 349–365.

Shurunbūlālī, Ḥasan b. 'Ammār (d. 1069/1659). *Marāqī al-Falāḥ Sharḥ Nūr al-Īḍāḥ wa Najāt al-Arwāḥ* (Damascus: Dār al-Nu'mān li l-'Ulūm, 1990).

Sibā'ī (al-), Muṣṭafā (d. 1964). *Al-Sunna wa Makānatuhā fī al-Tashrī' al-Islāmī* (Beirut: Al-Maktab al-Islāmī/Cairo: Darussalam, 2006).

Silvers, Laury. "The Teaching Relationship in Early Sufism: A Reassessment of Fritz Meier's Definition of the Shaykh al-Tarbiya and the Shaykh al-Taʿlīm," *The Muslim World*, 93, no. 1 (2003), 69–97.

Sisler, Vit. "The Internet and the Construction of Islamic Knowledge in Europe," *Masaryk University Journal of Law and Technology*, 1, no. 2 (2007), 205–217.

Skovgaard-Petersen, Jakob. "New Media in the Muslim World," *Oxford Encyclopedia of Islam and Politics*, ed. Emad El-Din Shahin (Oxford and New York: Oxford University Press, 2014), 183–188.

Stewart, Devin. "The Doctorate of Islamic Law in Mamluk Egypt and Syria," in *Law and Education in Medieval Islam*, ed. Joseph Lowry, Devin Stewart, and Shawkat Toorawa (Cambridge: E. J. W. Gibb Memorial Trust, 2004), 45–90.

Surūr, ʿAbd al-Fattāḥ. *Iḥkām al-ḥadīd ʿalā Maḥmūd Saʿīd: bi-Kashf Tajannī-hi ʿalā al-Imām al-Albānī wa l-Radd ʿalā Kitābi-hi: al-Taʿrīf bi-Awhām man Qassama al-Sunan ilā Ṣaḥīḥ wa Ḍaʿīf* (Riyadh: Aḍwāʾ al-Salaf, 2007).

Syamsuddin, Sahiron. "Abū Ḥanīfah's Use of the Solitary Ḥadīth as a Source of Islamic Law," *Islamic Studies*, 40, no. 2 (2001), 257–272.

Ṭaybī (al-), ʿUkāshah. *Fatāwā al-Shaykh al-Albānī wa Muqāranatu-hā bi Fatāwā al-ʿUlamāʾ* (Cairo: Maktabat al-Turāth al-Islāmī, 1994).

Tirmidhī (al-), Muḥammad b. ʿĪsā (d. 279/892). *Al-Jāmiʿ al-Kabīr Sunan al-Tirmidhī* (Riyadh: Maktabat al-Maʿārif, 1996).

Vickers, Miranda. *The Albanians: A Modern History* (London: I. B. Tauris, 1995).

Vogel, E. Frank. *Islamic Law and Legal Systems: Studies of Saudi Arabia* (Leiden: Brill, 2000).

Voll, John. *Islam: Continuity and Change in the Modern World* (Syracuse, NY: Syracuse University Press, 1994).

Wādiʿī, Muqbil. *Ijābat al-Sāʾil ʿalā Aham al-Māsāʾil* (Cairo: Dār al-Ḥaramayn, 1999).

Response to question on his leaning toward Ibn Ḥazm's teachings, www.muqbel.net/fatwa.php?fatwa_id=4463, last accessed May 1, 2020.

Tarjamat Abī ʿAbd al-Raḥmān Muqbil b. Hādī al-Wādiʿī (Sanaʿa: Maktabat al-Athariyya, 1999).

Wagemakers, Joas. *A Quietist Jihadi: The Ideology and Influence of Abu Muhammad al-Maqdisi* (Cambridge: Cambridge University Press, 2012).

"Salafism's Historical Continuity: The Reception of 'Modernist' Salafis by 'Purist' Salafis in Jordan," *Journal of Islamic Studies*, 30, no. 2 (2019), 205–231.

Waines, David. "Islam," in *Religion in the Modern World: Traditions and Transformations*, ed. Linda Woodhead (New York: Routledge, 2002), 210–234.

Ware, Rudolph. *The Walking Quran: Islamic Education, Embodied Knowledge, and History in West Africa* (Chapel Hill: University of North Carolina Press, 2014).

Warren, David, "Debating the Renewal of Islamic Jurisprudence (Tajdīd al-Fiqh): Yusuf al-Qaradawi, His Interlocutors, and the Articulation, Transmission and Reconstruction of the Fiqh Tradition in the Qatar-Context" (Ph.D. Dissertation, The University of Manchester, 2015).

Weismann, Itzchak. "The Politics of Popular Religion: Sufis, Salafis, and Muslim Brothers in 20th Century Hamah," *International Journal of Middle East Studies*, 37, no. 1 (2005), 39–58.

"Sufi Brotherhoods in Syria and Israel: A Contemporary Overview," *History of Religions*, 43, no. 4 (2004), 303–318.

A Taste of Modernity: Sufism, Salafiyya, and Arabism in Late Ottoman Damascus (Leiden: E. J. Brill, 2009).

Weiss, G. Bernard. "Interpretation in Islamic Law: The Theory of *Ijtihād*," *The American Journal of Comparative Law*, 26, no. 2 (1978), 199–212.

"The Primacy of Revelation in Classical Islamic Legal Theory As Expounded by Sayf al-Dīn al-Āmidī," *Studia Islamica*, 59 (1984), 79–109.

The Spirit of Islamic Law (Athens: University of Georgia Press, 2006).

Wiktorowicz, Quintan. "Anatomy of the Salafi Movement," *Studies in Conflict & Terrorism*, 29, no. 3 (2006), 207–239.

The Management of Islamic Activism: Salafis, the Muslim Brotherhood, and the State Power in Jordan (Albany, NY: SUNY Press, 2000).

Witkam, J. Jan. "The Human Element between Text and Reader: The Ijāza in Arabic Manuscripts," in *Education and Learning in the Early Islamic World*, ed. Claude Gilliot (Burlington, VA: Ashgate, 2012), 149–162.

Yusuf, Hamza. "The Crisis of ISIS: A Prophetic Prediction," www.youtube.com/watch?v=hJo4B-yaxfk, last accessed May 28, 2019.

"The Four Schools (Madhabs) or Albānī," www.youtube.com/watch?v=FUigJfAcKgE, last accessed February 28, 2018.

Zaman, Q. Muhammad. "The ʿUlamāʾ: Scholarly Tradition and New Public Commentary," in *The New Cambridge History of Islam, Vol. 6*, ed. Robert W. Hefner (Cambridge: Cambridge University Press, 2010), 335–354.

Zarnūjī, Burhān al-Islām. *Taʿlīm al-Mutaʿallim Ṭarīq al-Taʿallum* (Beirut: Al-Maktab al-Islāmī, 1981).

Zisser, Eyal. "Syria, the Baʿth Regime and the Islamic Movement: Stepping on a New Path?" *The Muslim World*, 95, no. 1 (2005), 43–65.

Zuhayrī, Samīr. *Fatḥ al-Bārī fī l-Dabb ʿan al-Albānī wa l-Rad ʿalā Ismāʿīl al-Anṣārī* (Taqaba: Dār al-Hijra, 1990).

Zysow, Aron. *The Economy of Certainty: An Introduction to the Typology of Islamic Legal Theory* (Atlanta, GA: Lockwood Press, 2013).

Index

CPSIA information can be obtained
at www.ICGtesting.com
Printed in the USA
LVHW030938120222
710984LV00001B/119

9 781108 485357